The Social Psychology of Prejudice

THE SOCIAL PSYCHOLOGY OF PREJUDICE

A Systematic Theoretical Review
and Propositional Inventory of
the American Social Psychological
Study of Prejudice

HOWARD J. EHRLICH

A WILEY-INTERSCIENCE PUBLICATION

JOHN WILEY & SONS, New York ● London ● Sydney ● Toronto

Library of Congress Cataloging in Publication Data
Ehrlich, Howard J.
   The social psychology of prejudice.

   "A Wiley-Interscience publication."
   Bibliography: p.
   1. Prejudices and antipathies.   2. Social
interaction.   I. Title.   [DNLM: 1. Prejudice.
2. Psychology, Social.   BF 575.P9 E33s   1973]

BF575.P9E36   301.45   72-10058
ISBN 0-471-23415-X

Printed in the United States of America

10-9 8 7 6 5 4 3 2 1

42284

To Carol

Who taught me how to love

PREFACE

Two types of theory are required to explain the state of ethnic group relations in a society. One must be a theory of intergroup behavior, sociological in orientation and using for its evidence materials that are
primarily historical. The other theory is social psychological. Its concern is primarily cognitive factors and the relations of these factors with
the interpersonal behavior of individuals. This book is concerned almost
exclusively with social psychological issues.

This book probably will provoke almost everyone across the spectrum
of social science theories and across the spectrum of the political ideolo-
gies—which most social scientists like to pretend they don't have. I
certainly hope so.

To accomplish this review and achieve the synthesis of this book, I
read almost every piece of research on prejudice that has been published
in English. For every item of the approximately 600 items in the Reference section, I think I read about eight other articles that were so inept
methodologically or so unbelievably devoid of content that I relegated
them to what turned out to be my biggest file category, "Read—of no
value." I will make no further comments about the state of social science.

I started this book attempting to summarize what we truly know
about ethnic prejudice. I wound up by presenting not only a new paradigm for its study but, if I am correct, a new paradigm for a great deal
of social psychological inquiry. My colleagues in psychology will probably find this work too sociological, and my colleagues in sociology will

probably find this too psychological. I hope that this too is so, and that this work contributes to the inevitable breakdown of most of the artificial distinctions that social scientists maintain as a part of the political divisions of Academia.

If my scientific colleagues are disturbed, so too will be my sisters and brothers in the movements of liberation.

I do not believe that ethnic prejudice is the exclusive property of a capitalistic economy, although I do think that the institutions of this society provide an incredibly viable medium for its growth. Nor do I believe that the elimination of social structures that perpetuate institutionalized racism and sexism is either possible or strategic if we remain ignorant of how attitudes are formed, developed, and organized. Almost two years ago, in a set of "notes from a radical social scientist," I wrote the following:

> I have another friend who is also concerned about my work. I am writing a book on prejudice, a book which he acknowledges as relevant. But he is disturbed that the principles of attitude theory I have formulated can and will be used to support racism and the political ideologies I oppose. He is, of course, correct. Just the same I continue my work.
>
> I believe that racism, poverty, and human exploitation persist in this society because they are a part of its political economy. Only a radical transformation of our systems of political and economic organization will do away with these pathologies. As long as power remains with those who control the political economy, then any new knowledge—even any social reform—can be, and probably will be, coopted. To some extent, then, virtually all art and all scholarship may be viewed as counter-revolutionary.
>
> There is no direct way that a theory of attitudes will topple political and economic structures. I continue my work, however, because I know that such structures will not be toppled until enough people come to believe in the forms of social justice that will make this political economy untenable. I think that the study of human prejudice and the structure of attitudes can be applied powerfully to that end; and I hope, not only to make that application myself, but also to recruit and train people to do so.

Still some of my friends argue that although my scholarship and research will be clearly needed in postrevolutionary society, it will do nothing now to speed the revolution. With this I disagree—but the full development of that argument will probably be my next book. For now I will only say that I think that the new American revolution has already begun and that radical scientists can contribute in part through research and scholarship that will assist in the development of new social forms.

It is my faith that this book makes such a contribution, and that future historians will write about ethnic prejudice and ethnic conflicts as a pathological manifestation of postliterate, prehuman civilization.

HOWARD J. EHRLICH

Baltimore, Maryland
August, 1972

CONTENTS

The Social Psychology
of Prejudice

Chapter One

THE COMPONENTS
OF PREJUDICE

The study of prejudice and intergroup relations in American social psychology has been beguiled throughout its history by the extremes of emotional involvement and professional detachment of its scientist-participants, by the unrealistic and unwitting demands for action of professional community workers who fail to comprehend the necessary gap between social science and social engineering, by truly weird theories which distort and obscure the realities of the subject they purport to explain, and by impoverished research which—in the manner of the alchemists of an earlier age—has sought simple and sovereign explanations. But four decades of sincere and intense study—these chronic difficulties notwithstanding—have yielded a body of empirical generalizations of overwhelming consequence. Old mythologies have been dispelled, and compelling hypotheses have been laid to rest. Nevertheless, the theorist concerned with a systematic, empirically grounded statement of the nature of prejudice would have to pick and choose his supporting evidence with a calculated insensitivity to the methodology and research operations that produce the data.

The systematic theorist confronts two primary methodological dilemmas. The first is choosing between conflicting findings derived from different research operations and techniques. This standard scientific dilemma gets resolved by two means: by choosing those data most consistent with the theorist's perspective and by his judgment of the relative quality of the procedures and evidence being examined. The second dilemma is judging the validity of consistent and replicated findings derived from single research techniques or procedures that are known to be systematically biased. For example, we know that on forced response questionnaire formats people tend to systematically overstate their degree of acceptance of prejudiced statements (Ehrlich, 1964; Ehrlich and Rinehart, 1965). Similarly, we know that, under certain circumstances, the ethnicity of the interviewer or tester can result in the systematic understatement of a respondent's ethnic attitudes (Hyman et al., 1954; Pettigrew, 1964; Robinson and Rohde, 1946; Rosenthal, 1966; Summers and Hammonds, 1966). We do not know yet how to correct for such measurement errors, but we cannot escape making assessments of research quality, study by study.

Judgments of research quality sometimes led me to ignore massive bodies of research. The prime example was that research involving the California Ethnocentrism scale. The E-scale is an omnibus instrument that measures an unbalanced mix of cognitive, conative, and affective components toward an unsystematic collection of seven ethnic targets. The instrument as such cannot provide any sound or systematic evidence on the specific operating characteristics of stereotypes, behavioral intentions, or affect. As a crude index of prejudice, the E-scale can be helpful only for limited purposes.

Having resolved the methodological problems through some balance of conventional and idiosyncratic criteria, the theorist now confronts the problem of conceptual strategy, perhaps the most difficult problem of all. Although my own strategy decisions will be apparent in the pages to follow, the problem may be clarified if four of these strategy decisions are now made explicit. First, I have chosen to write a social psychology of prejudice. This means, quite simply, that the *person* is my unit of analysis and that I will examine primarily the properties of attitudes and the determinants of interpersonal behavior. This examination will not provide full understanding or explanation of the structure or dynamics of minority group relations in a society—no single domain of social science analysis could do so. The study of minority group relations is necessarily multidisciplinary; and the social psychologist who thinks, for example, that he or she can explain Negro-white relations in American society independent of an historical and sociological comprehension of this society is naive if not inept.

Second, I have chosen to examine a set of topics and problems which I regard as crucial both for the development of social psychology and for an understanding of prejudice. My strategy, then, is to always operate at the most general level of social psychological analysis. For this reason, the explication of the basic conceptual units of analysis is emphasized. Third, since I feel we are not yet ready for the development of a hierarchical, deductive theory, this book is in the form of a propositional inventory of our present knowledge. A propositional inventory, appropriately conducted, can provide the most systematic statement possible short of a formal theory. This inventory is, of course, a prototheory.

Finally, I have chosen to go beyond the data in many formulations. Through attempts at explication, revision, and summary, I have developed new ideas, new hypotheses, new directions for research. Although the same tone is used for all propositions, I shall try to signal the degree of confirmation that accompanies each statement. For me, the measure of this book will be the degree to which it can stimulate the systematic accumulation—replication and extension—of that body of materials that comprises a social psychology of prejudice.

THE CONCEPT OF PREJUDICE

In the specialized language systems that characterize sociology and social psychology, the concept of prejudice has no consensual meaning. In its most common usage, prejudice is defined as "an unfavorable ethnic attitude" (*Dictionary of the Social Sciences*, 1964; *Handbook of Social Psychology*, 1954). This core definition, however, is frequently qualified. Consider this panorama of selected, current definitions:

ACKERMAN AND JAHODA (1950): *A pattern of hostility in interpersonal relations which is directed against an entire group, or against its individual members; it fulfills a specific irrational function for its bearer.*

ALLPORT (1954): *Ethnic prejudice is an antipathy based upon a faulty and inflexible generalization.*

COOPER AND McGAUGH (1963): *Prejudices are social attitudes which are developed before, in lieu of, or despite objective evidence.*

KLINEBERG (1954): *A feeling or response to persons or things which is prior to, and therefore not based upon, actual experience. It may be either positive or negative, and it may be directed to any one of a large variety of objects.*

KRECH, CRUTCHFIELD, AND BALLACHEY (1962): *An unfavorable attitude toward an object which tends to be highly stereotyped, emotionally charged, and not easily changed by contrary information.*

MARDEN AND MEYER (1962): *An attitude unfavorable to or disparaging of a whole group and all the individual members of it.*

McDONAGH AND RICHARDS (1953): *Preconceived judgments toward persons, beliefs, or objects.*

NEWCOMB, CONVERSE, AND TURNER (1965): *An unfavorable attitude . . . a predisposition to think, feel, and act in ways that are "against" or "away from" rather than "for" or "toward" other persons, especially as members of groups.*

ROSE (1965): *An attitude that considers selected categories of people in terms of stereotypes, usually for some purpose (conscious or unconscious) believed to be of advantage to the person who has the prejudice: Usually used to refer to a negative attitude toward a racial, religious, or nationality group.*

SECORD AND BACKMAN (1964): *An attitude that predisposes a person to think, feel, and act in favorable or unfavorable ways toward a group or its individual members.*

SHERIF AND SHERIF (1956): *The negative attitudes of group members derived from their established norms, toward another group and its members.*

SIMPSON AND YINGER (1965); *an emotional, rigid attitude . . . toward a group of people.*

VANDER ZANDEN (1966): *A system of negative conceptions, feelings, and action-orientations regarding the members of a particular group.*

WESTIE (1964): *Prejudice [is] . . . a facet of the normative system of culture. Prejudice is built into the culture in the form of normative precepts . . . which define the ways in which members of the group ought to behave in relation to the members of selected outgroups.*

YOUNG AND MACK (1962): *Culturally predetermined, biased attitude toward or conception of a person or group.*

These qualifications share two interwoven biases. First, they derogate their subject. Prejudiced persons are viewed as having adopted preconceived societal norms of disparagement and hostility toward selected others. They generalize incorrectly, are rigid, are emotional, are irrational. Second, these derogations are couched in the terms of the discipline. In his sociological treatment, the prejudiced person is an uncritical conformist; in his social psychological treatment he is cognitively defective; and in his psychiatric treatment, he is irrational. This may be a caricature of the bias that does exist, but the point must be emphasized. The social fact of ethnic prejudice is a matter of moral and political concern and scientists share in the values and attitudes of their society.

On a substantive level, there are two conceptual pivots in the definitions displayed. One is the problem of defining an attitude, and the other is the issue of the attitude object. (The other differences among the definitions are concerned with origins and maintaining mechanisms of prejudice. These matters are definitionally irrelevant; they will be considered as issues in their appropriate context.)

Attitude is defined in this book in a traditional manner. *An attitude is an interrelated set of propositions about an object or class of objects which are organized around cognitive, behavioral, and affective dimensions.*

The set of propositions that comprise an attitude represents a body of fundamental beliefs about the attitude object. These fundamental beliefs are analogous to the axioms and theorems of a formalized theory. An attitude *is* an individual's theory of an object.

The identification of the cognitive dimensions of beliefs is a matter of moderate agreement among social psychologists. There are four dimensions, however, which are emphasized in this study of prejudice: salience, intensity, direction, and centrality.

All beliefs have a truth value. For example, the proposition that "Jews are tradition-loving" is a statement of belief. When a person asserts that belief, he is implicitly asserting that he believes that statement to be true or probably true. In everyday conversation we take it for granted that people "believe" what they say, that is, they believe what they say to be true. It is only under special circumstances that we ask people to declare the truth value of their assertions. (Under such circumstances our inquiry borders on insult since people who do not know the truth value of their assertions are conventionally defined as unreliable or untrustworthy. Thus we have such queries as "Do you really mean that?" or "Do you know what you are saying?") A *salient* belief, then, may be defined as a presumably true statement about an object or class of objects.

Propositions about objects are frequently qualified. Not only is the statement "Jews are tradition-loving" presumably true, but being unqualified it may be correctly read "All Jews are tradition-loving." The presumed truth value of a statement is not altered by limiting its scope. The person who asserts that "All Jews are tradition-loving" may be just as convinced of its truth value as the person who asserts that "Some Jews are tradition-loving." However, the cogency of a statement is altered by limiting its scope. Therefore, salience is treated in this book as a variable characteristic of beliefs. The degree of salience of a belief, then, may be defined as the degree to which a presumably true statement may be thought to characterize an object or class of objects. The statement "All Jews are tradition-loving" is a more salient belief than "Some Jews are tradition-loving." Similarly, the statement "Eighty percent of the Jews are tradition-loving" is more salient than "Seventy percent of the Jews are tradition-loving."

All beliefs are accepted or rejected at some level of *intensity*. Intensity may be defined as the degree of acceptance-agreement or rejection-disagreement with a belief statement. All of the beliefs that an individual has about an object or class of objects may be organized along an intensity dimension. (Any proposition that registers zero on an individual's intensity scale is not a belief for that individual.)

The *direction* of a belief is its position on an evaluative continuum: good-bad, favorable-unfavorable, desirable-undesirable. All beliefs that an individual has about an object or class of objects can be organized along an evaluative continuum. On this scale, unlike the intensity scale, there is a neutral register. Some beliefs are nonevaluative.

The fourth cognitive dimension that is frequently cited by attitude theorists has received relatively little systematic study. This is the dimension of *centrality*, defined as the degree of importance of a belief to a person. An individual's set of beliefs about an object or class of objects can be organized along a dimension of centrality-peripherality. (If central beliefs come close to representing the basic beliefs of the attitude, they should be highly resistant to change. If they are changed, then the entire set of propositions that comprises the attitude probably requires reorganization.)

Finally, an individual's attitude toward an object or class of objects is *cognitively articulated* to the extent that it is composed of a set of highly differentiated beliefs which are quite salient, strongly evaluated, and intensely and centrally endorsed. There are, of course, other cognitive dimensions of attitudes which appear in the theoretical literature. These have received little confirmation in research and even less attention in the study of prejudice. Among these other dimensions are time, ambivalence, prominence; overtness; embeddedness, flexibility; and consciousness. General discussions of attitude theory and the meaning of these and similar dimensions can be found in Rokeach (1968) and Scott (1968).

The discussion thus far has focused exclusively on the way in which people hold beliefs about objects. An examination of the structural characteristics and manifest content of beliefs is not relevant to the problem of defining prejudice and therefore is reserved for a later section.

The second major analytic dimension of an attitude is behavioral. The direct manifestation of this dimension has probably been the most popularly discussed subject in the prejudice literature. All beliefs have a behaviorally associative or dissociative component. Some beliefs that comprise an attitude assert a direct relation between the person and the belief-objects; other beliefs do so indirectly, by implication. The proposition, "I would be willing to marry a Negro," is not only a belief-statement, but it is also a direct statement of a behavioral intention. In contrast, the proposition, "Negroes are musical," is a belief-statement that only indirectly points to a behavioral intention.

Although the content of intentions to behave toward an object differs clearly from other beliefs about objects, the structure of the dimensions is the same. This becomes apparent if these dimensions are described in their most general form:

1. Salience: the degree to which an intention encompasses a class of objects.
2. Intensity: the position of an intention on an intensity scale.
3. Direction: the position of an intention on an evaluative scale.
4. Centrality: the importance of a behavior to a person.

The belief, "I would be willing to vote for any qualified candidate for public office," is restricted only by a person's conception of proper qualification. Assuming that the only qualifications are those related to fulfilling the obligations of the office, let us now consider the belief, "I would be willing to vote for any qualified Negro candidate for public office." The salience of that intention would be the extent to which the qualifications remained unchanged. Put more generally, the salience of a behavioral intention is the degree to which it includes the entire class of eligible objects. The other cognitive dimensions—the number of different behaviors and the degree of acceptance-rejection, desirability-undesirability, and centrality-peripherality—require no further illustration.

The affective dimension of attitudes is not well understood, nor has it been clearly incorporated into attitude theories. Although some theorists would regard what is termed "direction" in this book as an affective response (Fishbein, 1965; Rosenberg, 1965), the basic affective component is here considered one that identifies the valence between a person and an object or class or objects. Affect represents the set of feelings experienced by a person about, or directed toward an attitude object. Affect is marked at one pole by love-liking-attraction, and at the other by hate-disliking-repulsion. The direction of a belief may not be related to its affective valence. People may like objects which they evaluate as bad or undesirable, and they may dislike objects which they know to be good or desirable.

Not only is affect manifested toward objects, affect is also displayed in a person's reaction toward beliefs or systems of beliefs. The defining characteristics of the valence between a person and beliefs are elusive. Certainly at the negative pole we can identify some beliefs as personally repulsive, disgusting, forbidding, dreadful, and so on. At the positive pole, there are beliefs which are clearly attractive, pleasant, fascinating, and inviting. Considering these three dimensions, an attitude may be termed *well developed* to the degree that it is cognitively articulated and the affective valence and behavioral orientations are mutually consistent. To the degree that an attitude is not well developed—to the degree that there is inconsistency among its three dimensions—the attitude is unstable (cf. Rosenberg, 1965).

The second problem in the definition of prejudice is that of specifying the object of prejudice. An attitude object has no boundary. A person may have an attitude about an idea, an event, a situation, a physical object, himself, another person, or a category of persons. The question that has to be raised is one of both conceptual and research strategy. Given our interest in the study of prejudice and our presystematic conceptions of what this study should entail, how is the object of study defined?

The question is difficult to answer, first, because the differences that exist between the perception of people and the perception of things (physical objects and events) are unclear. If as social psychologists we restrict our focus to social perception, we run the risk of studying a biased class of phenomena and possibly failing to comprehend the more general principles we seek. For now, we shall accept that risk and limit the study of prejudice to social objects.

The question is difficult to answer, second, because in limiting study to social objects, one must then consider: What objects? The standard reply has been "ethnic groups." Ethnic groups, in their broadest construction, subsume all groups distinguishable on the basis of national origin, citizenship, race, and religion. But is this adequate? The study of prejudice is, quite correctly, the study of attitudes toward a *class* of people. The dynamics of interpersonal attitudes and interpersonal behavior are sufficiently different from the dynamics of intergroup attitudes and behavior that attitudes toward individuals may be excluded from the domain of prejudice study. This, too, is a conceptual strategy of some risk.

Attitudes toward the physically disabled, the mentally retarded, the adolescent, the atheist, physicians, scientists, or policemen are in no fundamental way different from attitudes toward ethnic groups. If this empirical assertion is true, and from the limited evidence presented in subsequent chapters it does appear to be true, then there is no justification for excluding these groupings. Therefore, the focus of prejudice study should embrace any category or categorization of people. Prejudice can then be defined as an attitude toward any group of people.

PREJUDICE AND BEHAVIOR [1]

Studies on the relation of prejudice and behavior have almost consistently resulted in a summary statement of the form that prejudice is a poor predictor of discrimination (Bray, 1950; Brookover and Holland, 1952; DeFleur and Westie, 1958; Fishman, 1961; Killian, 1953; Kutner et al., 1952; LaPiere, 1935, 1936; Linn, 1965; Lohman and Reitzes, 1952; Malof and Lott, 1962; Minard, 1952; Nettler and Golding, 1946; Saenger and Gilbert, 1950).

It is clear that many social scientists concerned with the study of prejudice and intergroup behavior have taken the prevailing interpretations of the evidence of attitude-behavior inconsistency as a premise toward the conclusion that attitude theory has proven inadequate. In his presidential address to the Society for the Study of Social Problems, Deutscher (1966, p. 247) asserts that "no matter what one's theoretical orientation may be, he has no reason to expect to find congruence between attitudes and actions and every reason to expect to find discrepancies between them." DeFleur and Westie (1963, p. 28), for another example, declare a *necessary* inconsistency between verbal scale scores and other overt actions, pointing to "social constraints" or situational norms as the crucial determinants of behavior. Consistency between attitudes and behavior occurs, they argue, "if the normative processes of the groups within which they [people] are interacting are consistent."

The arguments that may be adduced to invalidate these interpretations of inconsistency need not be tied to a specific theory of attitudes. In almost all current theories, attitudes are construed as having a componential structure. Not all of the components of an attitude imply behavior. It follows from this that without a direct assessment of the "action potential" of an attitude component, the researcher's inference about the subject's behavior, or intentions, may be phenomenologically naive. This possibility is illustrated in a study by Kay (1947), who demonstrated that 36% of a sample of presumably anti-Jewish items, drawn from the Levinson-Sanford scale of anti-semitism, were judged by naive subjects as friendly or directionally unclear. Predictions of anti-Jewish behavior from these items would probably have displayed high error.

To adopt the argument that not all attitude components imply behavior it is not necessary to endorse a multidimensional strategy of attitude theory construction. The argument, from the standpoint of a unidimensional theory, simply becomes: Not all attitudes imply behavior. Whatever the other outcomes of these theoretical strategies, they agree in their fundamental statements concerning the relation of attitudes and behavior. Fishbein (1966, p. 213), a leading unidimensional theorist, states his position clearly:

Because attitude is a hypothetical variable abstracted from the *totality* of an individual's beliefs, behavioral intentions, and actions, toward a given object . . . any given belief, behavioral intention, or behavior, therefore, may be uncorrelated or even negatively correlated with his attitude. Thus, rather than viewing specific beliefs or classes of beliefs and specific behavioral intentions or types of behavioral intentions as part of attitude, these phenomena must be studied as variables in their own right, that, like attitudes, may or may not function as determinants of a specific behavior.

Different scaling models and measurement procedures differentially assess the behaviorally directive components of attitudes. The current major scaling models focus primarily on two attitude components, usually direction and intensity; only the procedure of summated ratings considers both dimensions simultaneously. When an attitude scale is focused on a single component and when that component has a low action potential, successful prediction should be highly unlikely. Tittle and Hill (1967) provide some confirming evidence. Aside from formal scaling, the two major procedures for measuring prejudice—the stereotype checklist and the so-

cial distance questionnaire—similarly tap only a single attitude component. The checklist assesses only the salience of a stereotype, and that
usually in a categorical manner, whereas social distance measures provide
solely a report of behavioral intentions, usually abstracted from situational
reference. Only where these components entail a high directiveness for
behavior should a high congruence with behavior be expected.

It may be argued further that the determination of the structure of an
attitude at any point in time requires the determination of the interrelations of the components that constitute the attitude. An attitude was defined as well developed if all of its components achieve some balance and
that balanced state persists over time. If this conceptualization is adequate,
it follows that reliable predictions of behavior can occur only from well-
formed attitudes, or, in the absence of a well-formed attitude, only when
the predicted behavior is close in time to the attitude measurement. Even
then it may be the case that the measurement process per se can change
the state of a poorly balanced attitude.

Not only does a single attitude comprise several components, but a single attitude object may implicate many attitudes. Predictions of behavior
which do not account for all (or at least the major) attitudes evoked by
an object probably are wrong. In a variation on this argument, Rokeach
(1967, p. 530) has contended that at least two attitudes are required to
make a correct prediction of behavior:

> Especially important for the major thesis of this paper is that an attitude
> may be focused either on an object or on a situation. In the first instance we
> have in mind an attitude-object, which may be concrete or abstract, involving
> a person, a group, an institution, or an issue. In the second instance the atti-
> tude is focused on a specific situation, an event, or an activity. To say that a
> person has an enduring attitude toward a given object is to say that this atti-
> tude will, when activated, somehow determine his behavior toward the atti-
> tude-object across situations; conversely, to say that a person has an enduring
> attitude toward a given situation is to say that this attitude will, when acti-
> vated, determine his behavior toward the situation, across attitude-objects.

The reported inconsistency between attitude and behavior may be a
partial result of our naivete at phenomenological analysis, that is, our inability to ascertain the intentional meaning of an actor's verbal and nonverbal acts. Without denying the crudities of phenomenological analysis
in contemporary social psychology, the fundamental problem may be that
our presumed observations of inconsistencies derive from our failure to
specify the criteria for judging a consistent or inconsistent response.
Campbell (1961, p. 160) provides a graphic illustration of the problem of
assessing consistency:

On an arithmetic test of four items, the child who gets only two items correct is not necessarily regarded as less consistent than the child who gets all right or all wrong. If he gets the two easiest right and the two hardest wrong, he is equally consistent. On intelligence we today think in terms of a continuum, and can conceive of consistent mediocrity. . . . we can regard honesty as something people have in degree, rather than as all-or-none trait. A person of intermediate degree can be just as consistent as a person of extreme position, and his attitude can be determined from his behavior just as well. . . . For intelligence and honesty, we have achieved dimensionality in our thinking. For more emotion-laden topics, such as standing up for civil rights, we have not. If a university president protects a pacifist professor but fires an atheist, we call him inconsistent. If he protects a pacifist and an atheist, but fires a Communist, we accuse him of backing down under pressure. Conceptually, we have the notion of a total nondefendant of professors' rights and a total defender of professors' rights, and lack any concept of genuine mediocrity which would *in consistency* produce defense in a situation of low threshold and firing in another situation with a higher threshold value.

The assessment of consistency is initially contingent on the conditions of adequate measurement and the stability of an attitude. Assuming these conditions, it is then necessary to enumerate the set of obligatory and optional behaviors that comprise the attitude domain. Presumably this is a highly limited set of behaviors, or at least the obligatory behaviors form a highly limited subset. The number of observations required for a sample of this set or subset of behaviors doubtlessly will be fixed by the degree to which these behaviors are scalar. The extent to which an individual's verbal and nonverbal behaviors may achieve some level of consistency will then depend upon quasi-logical (probably social psychological) criteria of contradiction. Such criteria, implicit in everyday behavior, have yet to be made explicit.

The search for a strategy to relate prejudice and behavior is best pursued through the identification of the social and psychological conditions that intervene between attitudes and behavior. Only those variables most directly related to attitude theory and intergroup behavior are discussed here.

Clarity

For consistency to occur there has to be a clear way for an attitude to be expressed in behavior. For some attitudes and for some behaviors, the relationship may not be clear. This indeterminacy may appear under a number of conditions, the importance of which we shall probably have to ferret out through intensive descriptive research. Williams (1964, p. 329), in discussing the characteristics of behavior in unclear interracial situations, provides a prospectus for research:

The unfamiliar situation is, by definition, initially one of uncertainty, which is another way of saying that it induces some degree of insecurity. Past experience does not suffice as a guide, and old norms may not lead to the usual results. New situations are likely, therefore, to instigate heightened alertness—including a generalized vigilance toward cues that may indicate what action will lead to what consequences. Under the circumstances of uncertainty and sharpened attentiveness, the individual who first acts with an appearance of decisiveness and confidence is likely to have marked influence. It can and does often happen that the people in leadership positions are themselves confused; for them the situation is not even structured enough to suggest where to turn for clarification. We saw that, in consequence, action on the part of any other participant became disproportionately important in determining their definitions. Confused participants sought indices of how others defined the situation. Since the crucial question in many of these situations was whether or not membership in a particular racial category (Negro) precluded membership in other groups or categories, the first action to be taken by a white was often interpreted by all as an index of acceptance or rejection.

Expressibility

Some attitudes may be clearly expressible only in verbal behavior. Extremely radical, highly unconventional, or strongly antisocial attitudes may in fact have their primary expression in verbal behaviors or in fantasy. Some attitudes may have their expressions in sublimated behaviors. Attitudes about matters which a person defines, or which are socially defined, as highly intimate may also have their primary expression in verbal and fantasy behavior. Other expressions may be deliberately concealed from observation.

Disclosure

Related to expressibility is the willingness of a person to disclose his attitude. Under many circumstances, however, the failure to disclose one's attitude may be neither an attitude-consistent nor an attitude-inconsistent act. In the case of attitudes toward oneself, their disclosure or concealment has indicated such a regular pattern of occurrence that the conditions of disclosure could represent an important class of variables for more general consideration.

The research stimulated by Jourard (1964) has confirmed that people vary in their characteristic level of disclosure of self-attitudes. It has also been established, particularly from the work of Altman and Haythorn (1965), that these individual differences are responsive to controlled situational variation both for the number of self-attitudinal statements disclosed and their depth of intimacy. Following from this, Worthy, Gary, and Kahn (1969) and Ehrlich and Graeven (1971) have demonstrated that most people, regardless of their characteristic levels of self-disclosure, reciprocate the intimacy levels of the disclosures made by another person.

This limited research suggests that reciprocity in the verbal and nonverbal expressions of attitudes may be a standard interpersonal tactic as well as a more generalized norm of interpersonal behavior. Thus it may be hypothesized that attitudes expressible in interpersonal situations may not be disclosed either because others do not express their attitudes or because the actor fails to perceive them. Further, the "principle of categorical congruity" (to be introduced in Chapter 3) suggests an obverse to the disclosure hypothesis: Attitudes expressible in interpersonal situations may not be disclosed when the actor perceives his attitudes as contrary to the attitudes of others in the situation. These disclosure hypotheses will no doubt have to be qualified by considerations of the duration of the situation, among other situational properties.

Perspective and the Definition of the Act

The indeterminate status of the attitude-behavior relation may also be a consequence of perspective. An act consistent from the standpoint of the actor may appear to the observer to be inconsistent. This becomes particularly problematic when an actor deliberately chooses not to act, or when the outcome of an act is contrary to what the actor intended.

Perhaps the most confounding problem of the matter of intent as related to the outcome of an act is the social definition of an act. Regardless of the actor's intent, the scientist as an observer and the actor as an observer of himself both must cope with the prevailing social definition. Where the disparity between a personal and social construction of an act is very great, it seems likely that over time an actor may come to question or even redefine his own behavior. The presumed seriousness of this problem has led some social scientists to take the position that a motivational theory must necessarily be a theory of rationalization of behavior (Mills, 1940, pp. 906–907):

The aspect of motive which this conception grasps is its intrinsically social character. A satisfactory or adequate motive is one that satisfied the questioners of an act or program, whether it be the other's or the actor's. As a word, a motive tends to be one which is to the actor and to the other members of a situation an unquestioned answer to questions concerning social and lingual conduct. A stable motive is an ultimate in justificatory conversation. The words which in a type situation will fulfill this function are circumscribed by the vocabulary of motives acceptable for such situations. Motives are accepted justifications for present, future, or past programs or acts.

As a theory of motivation the conspectus of Mills is seriously defective. Nevertheless, the systematic study of vocabularies of motives should lead to a more sophisticated understanding of intentional behavior and self-report. This uniquely sociological perspective furthermore points to three parameters of self-report requiring serious consideration: the strength of prevailing definitions of social acts, the disparity between personal and social definitions of social acts, and the time between an act and the actor's report of his intent, or vice-versa.

The fact that people sometimes confuse a label with the object itself adds subtly to the problem of assessing the relationship of attitudes and behavior. Some people's response to a scale item, a form of label, may represent precisely the way in which they construe the item, and very imprecisely the way in which they view the object. In this case, the attitude may actually have the label—not the object itself—as its object.

In one of the more dramatic tests of the effects of labeling on attitude-consistent behavior, Dillehay, Bruvold, and Siegel (1969) conducted a study dealing with community drinking water as the attitude object. (The study was done in communities where the drinking water had a high mineral content.) Measures of a person's attitude toward the water were obtained first, then subjects were given labeled and unlabeled samples of water to taste and evaluate. Attitude scores were found to correlate with the evaluations of the unlabeled water samples at $r = .19$. With the labeled samples the correlation was .68.

An alternative explanation of this apparent difference in response to labeled and unlabeled objects is possible. It may be that where labels appear to have such strong effects, the attitude to the object is actually very low in centrality but high in direction. Such a case probably means that there is a fair amount of community consensus on the issue—which the person has come to accept—but that the issue has no particular importance to the person. It would mean, therefore, that the attitude is not very well-formed, and that it could not lead to very consistent behavior.

The sociology of motivational analysis leads us to still another consideration. The same act over time and in different social contexts changes its meaning, that is, its social definition. Attitude-consistent behavior at one time may be perceived as inconsistent at another time. Yesterday's radical may be today's impediment to progress, though neither his attitudes nor behavior have changed in consistency. Deutsch (1949, p. 49), who calls this the problem of "unrecognized locomotion," describes it: "To the extent that we do not take cognizance of how changes beyond our control affect our positions in relation to our goals, we are likely to behave in ways which are either inconsistent or irrelevant to our purposes. The incorrect assessment of present position is likely to lead to a faulty perception of the direction to one's goal."

Finally, informal evidence indicates that people sometimes intentionally act in an attitude-inconsistent manner. Such behavior, which may be an important condition for attitude change, may have its basis in either personal curiosity or an attempt to achieve novelty in an unstimulating environment. Inconsistent behavior may also be a primary means by which individuals test themselves and others.

Learning

The discussion thus far has focused on the condition of clarity in the relation of attitudes to behavior where, under this condition, the strategic problems become the determination of an attitude's expressibility and the nexus of intention to act. It is now appropriate to introduce the three assumptions hidden in this discussion. The first of these is the *learning assumption*. Even when a clear and expressible relation exists between an attitude and behavior, it is not necessary to assume that an actor knows how to behave in a consistent manner. The major determinant of attitude-discrepant behavior may be that an actor has not learned how to competently express his attitude in action. One determinant of the adequacy of such learning may be the level of direct or vicarious experience of the actor, if any, in such behavior situations. Under this condition of no or poor learning, inaction, inappropriate behavior, and sometimes ineffective behavior are defined by the observer as inconsistent acts. Certainly learning how to behave in a manner consistent with one's attitudes is a primary objective of socialization at all stages of the life cycle.

Accessibility

The second of the assumptions implicit in discussions of attitude-consistent behavior is the *assumption of opportunity and access*. Knowing how to behave in an appropriate manner is insufficient if the opportunity, access, or perceived access to the opportunity is nonexistent. For example, the study of ethnic intermarriage reveals that the best predictor of intermarriage is the opportunity to intermarry. For Negro-white marriages, for instance, opportunity is partly defined by the proportion of eligible mates, the degree of residential segregation, and the degree of status congruence (Heer, 1966).

Competence

Even knowing what is consistent and having the opportunity to engage in attitude-consistent behaviors is only one necessary condition for such behavior. Not only must an actor learn what comprises appropriate behavior, but he must learn how to use his skills and muster his personal resources for his actions to be effective. Thus the third assumption implicit in most past discussions has been an *assumption of skill and resource*. Patently, individuals vary in the skills they have developed and in the resources they can mobilize for behavior in any given situation. Inferences about behavior therefore must take into account such individual differences. An ostensibly inconsistent act may indicate only the actor's deficient skill, his lack of resources, or his inability to organize his resources for effective behavior. It is possible that inferences about behavior and consistency may be biased in the direction of more skillful individuals by the fact that they may emit more behaviors and/or perform more confidently and more effectively.

The research strategies indicated so far are of substantial consequence in establishing the attitude-behavior relation. Two widely discussed problems of crucial importance remain: the problem of situational analysis and the problem of multiple-attitude analysis.

Situational Analysis

In the absence of any well-established guidelines for such analysis, it seems reasonable to consider as separate problems those concerned with the structural, primarily physical characteristics of situations and those concerned with the social dimensions. The focus of structural analysis is, first, the study of the properties of situations and their interrelationships and, second, the study of the relation of these properties to behavior. Barker and his associates (1968) have developed an extensive language and research operations for structural analysis, but these have not yet been applied to the kinds of problems that concern us here. Hall (1963), through his proxemic analysis, has provided systematic procedures for assessing the effects of space on interpersonal behavior; and Sommer (1967) has recently reviewed this developing literature. For the social dimensions of situations, the most well-developed schemes now exist for the analysis of role behavior (e.g., Biddle and Thomas, 1966; Preiss and Ehrlich, 1966) and for the analysis of interaction processes (Borgatta and Crowther, 1965). Although the significance of role playing and role enactment for attitude change has been clearly demonstrated (Sarbin, 1964), attitude theorists have generally ignored role and related theories (and role theorists have generally ignored attitude variables).

Situational characteristics often are given theoretical consideration only if they are *perceived* by the actor, and sometimes they are considered only in terms of the actor's *attitudes* toward them. This strategy may be misleading. It remains to be demonstrated that the actor does in fact perceive and have an attitude toward situational properties and that such attitudes are of meaningful behavioral relevance. Although many situational variables are invariably perceived, other situational variables of behavioral importance, particularly the structural characteristics, probably are seldom perceived. Whatever the strategy of situational analysis in attitude research, the warrant for its priority should be clear. In the classic formulation of Lewin: Behavior is a function of the person and his environment.

Multiple Attitudes

A strategy for research on multiple attitudes is based on the assumptions that for some situations and objects more than one attitude will be evoked and that the behavioral strength of a set of attitudes may be formally determined. The research of Bayton, McAlister, and Hamer (1956), for example, has indicated that attitudes toward social class appear almost as important as race attitudes in determining the stereotypes assigned to Negroes. Triandis (1967) has demonstrated that the expression of behavioral intentions varies across the class, sex, ethnicity, occupation, and belief similarity of the attitude object. For example, behavior toward a Negro female physician may be directed primarily by one's attitudes toward Negroes, toward females, toward physicians, toward any two of these characteristics, or toward all three simultaneously. The development of a calculus of attitudes across attitude objects and situations should be considered as an item of high research priority.

CONCLUDING REMARKS

This discussion began by indicating that not all attitudes are behaviorally expressible or, at least, clearly expressible in interpersonal behavior. Some attitudes are deliberately not expressed in behavior, and I suggested that we examine the social and interpersonal conditions under which people are willing or unwilling to disclose their attitudes.

The exact behavior that complements a specific attitude is not always clear, and the presumed clarity of an act is itself a consequence of the perspective from which it is evaluated as well as the time that intervenes between act and evaluation. Knowledge of how to act consistently has to be learned, and not all actors are able to use their knowledge with equal competence. Beyond these conditions it still remains to be demonstrated that the actor has the opportunity to act appropriately. It seems that the actor's failure to act in a manner consistent with a given attitude could be a direct result of other situational constraints or a result of conflict with other relevant attitudes which are more important to the behaviors under analysis.

The specific effects that each of these intervening variables has on behavior remain to be determined. There should be no doubt, however, that the study of these variables and the relation of attitudes to behavior is of strategic significance in the development of social psychology. The question of these relations is, of course, a major instance of the classic problem of social psychology. Under what conditions, how, and to what degree do aspects of social structure and aspects of psychological structure determine interpersonal and intergroup behavior?

A READER'S GUIDE

In this book I am concerned with the study of prejudice almost exclusively. I thought it was necessary to devote a major part of the opening chapter to establishing the nature of the linkage of prejudice and behavior in order to dispell the naive critiques that have been directed toward attitude theory. It is my contention that except for those problematic situations where our role or self-identities are unclear, attitudes always precede action. What goes on in the minds of people can seldom escape social expression. I hope that in some future social psychology—maybe even a revision of this work—we will be able to present a series of discrete principles on the relation of ethnic prejudice to intergroup behavior. (There are in Chapter Five some hints as to what these principles might be.)

Each of the following three chapters is concerned with a different component of prejudice—stereotypes, personal and social distance, and affect. In each, but particularly in Chapters Two and Three, I try to examine first what I call the *societal* mechanisms for the maintenance of prejudice and then the *cognitive* mechanisms. This is followed by examining the organization of attitudes, that is, by looking at the *organizational* mechanisms that determine the internal structure of attitudes. The last grouping of principles in these chapters deal with the relation of social position to prejudice; these are what I call the *marginality* mechanisms.

In the final part of Chapter Four, I attempt to show the interrelationships of the three components of attitudes. Although the evidence is all supportive of my theory, just as in the case of the relation of prejudice and behavior there really isn't very much evidence.

In the final chapter I explore the principles by which prejudice is acquired and maintained.

By the end of the book I shall have introduced 22 basic principles (plus some corollaries) which I believe summarize and organize all of the existing research of quality on the nature of prejudice.

NOTE

1.   The discussion presented here is adapted from Ehrlich (1969).

Chapter Two

THE COGNITIVE DIMENSIONS OF PREJUDICE

The cognitive dimensions of prejudice have been traditionally subsumed under the singular label "stereotypes." "*Stereotypes*" as used in this book are a set of beliefs and disbeliefs about any group of people.[1] *Stereotype behavior* and, more conventionally, *stereotyping* are terms that refer to the structuring of the elements of belief statements about groups of people. A statement about the relation of the salience of a belief to the direction of a belief, for example, is a statement about stereotyping.

The study of stereotyping has no direct concern with the perceptual processes presumably underlying the perception of people and things. Although the perceptual apparatus, as a set of neurologic variables, is obviously implicated in the act of perception, I assume that the significant determinants of stereotyping as social psychological events are not to be found within the organism but in its environment. This basic strategy decision of social psychological inquiry guides my choice of variables here and throughout this work. However, the study of stereotyping alone cannot account for the fact that the stereotypes assigned to ethnic groups exhibit uniform and normative characteristics which have persisted through time. Such stability and consensus indicate that neither cognitive processes nor underlying perceptualist or personality dimensions can exclusively account for ethnic group stereotypes. To demonstrate the exclusive dependence of stereotypes upon individual psychological processes would require that these supporting psychological theories be able to adequately explain the existence of a relatively stable consensus on specific stereotypes and their assignment to specific groups.

If the same processes were to underlie, for example, the stereotyping of both Jews and Negroes, then the same stereotypes should more or less be assigned to both. If stereotypes are selectively assigned to them, it appears necessary to distinguish at least between stereotyping, as a general process, and the selection of the target and content of stereotypes, termed "stereotype assignment" (Ehrlich, 1962).

STEREOTYPE ASSIGNMENTS

Language Characteristics and Ethnophaulisms

To study stereotype assignments is to study the language of prejudice, for stereotypes provide a common language of discourse for prejudiced persons. As a special language, stereotypes function to reinforce the beliefs and disbeliefs of its users, and to furnish the basis for the development and maintenance of solidarity for the prejudiced. Stereotype assignments provide a vocabulary of motives for the action of prejudiced persons. They signal the socially approved and accessible targets for the release of hostility and aggression.

The language of prejudice, like any special language, has a small dictionary which consists of unique terms (ethnophaulisms) and terms of the natural language which are given a special usage. Although there has been little formal study here, there appears to be a primitive set of rules of formal usage (a grammar) and a more well-developed set of rules governing its social usage (i.e., the circumstances under which it may be spoken).

Natural language systems, at least of the Indo-European variety, have three structural characteristics that facilitate the development of a special language of prejudice. First, almost every word used to describe an individual may be used to describe a group. The transition from individual experience to group experience can be made with linguistic ease. Second, and particularly true of English, is that the use of collective nouns without qualification unambiguously encompasses the collectivity. The statement "Atheists are cynical," may be correctly transliterated "*All* atheists are cynical." Formal research on the effects of implicit quantifiers on verbal generalization has only recently begun (see Abelson and Kanouse, 1966). Third, the qualification of statements using collective terms requires greater verbosity and more complex construction in order to be precise. Thus for children and for verbally unskilled adults it is easier to talk about groups as one would talk about persons, and to do so in a categorical manner. There is also a semantic characteristic of the English language which appears to facilitate the development of race attitudes. This is the connotative meaning of skin color words. Gergen (1967, p. 397), reviewing the meanings of "black" and "white", writes:

After careful study of color symbolism in the Western tradition, Matthew Luckiesh lists the following as most commonly associated with black: woe, gloom, darkness, dread, death, terror, horror, wickedness, curse, mourning, and mortification. Walter Sargent adds to this list the attributes of defilement, error, annihilation, strength, and deep quiet. From his studies, Faber Birren concludes that "despair" is the major association elicited by black. Such attributes stand in marked contrast to those associated with white: triumph, light, innocence, joy, divine power, purity, regeneration, happiness, gaiety, peace, chastity, truth, modesty, femininity, and delicacy. Studies of color symbolism in the Bible, the works of Chaucer, Milton, Shakespeare, Hawthorne, Poe, and Melville also reveal a major tendency to use white in expressing forms of goodness, and black in connoting evil.

Williams (1966) and Williams and Carter (1967) systematically compared the meanings of color names (e.g., black), color-person concepts (e.g., black person), and ethnic concepts (e.g., Negro). Williams concluded that for his Caucasian subjects, color names and ethnic concepts had similar connotative meanings.[2] His subjects appeared to be most favorable toward Caucasians, next toward American Indians and Orientals, and least favorable toward Asiatic Indians and Negroes. Their evaluative ratings of colors followed the same order: white, yellow, red, brown, and black. The evaluation of color names, however, appeared to be more similar to the evaluation of color-person concepts than to ethnic concepts. Williams concluded by suggesting that the color adjectives may dominate the noun, and that the meaning communicated by the symbol "black person" is *black*-person rather than black-*person*.

Words and expressions unique to the language of ethnic prejudice have been designated as "ethnophaulisms." Roback (1944) coined the term without formally defining it; however, by following his direction, ethnophaulisms can be described as words or expressions that derogate ethnic groups. There appear to be three types. First are the disparaging group nicknames such as Chink, Mustard, or Pigtail for Chinese. Second are words or expressions that explicitly devaluate the ethnic group, for example, "to be in Dutch" (to be in trouble) or "luck of the Irish" (good fortune with the implication that it was undeserved). Third are words or expressions that have no explicit disparagement, but that function as mild derogations by using ethnic names irrelevantly. This is certainly a problematic subtype, although most words here were probably explicitly derogatory in origin. Two examples are jewbird, referring to any of several black cuckoos probably named for their prominent beaks, and Irish confetti, meaning bricks—especially when thrown in a fight.

To provide a detailed illustration, the current ethnophaulisms for Italians are presented.

Italians or persons of Italian descent are called dago, dino, eyeties, ginzo, greaseball, guin, guinea, italiano, ities, macaroni, meatball, Mediterranean Irish, paisano, Pinnochio, ringtail, spaghetti, spaghetti-bender, spaghetti-head, spic, spick, spig, wop. Names for southern Europeans which might also be applied to Italians include duke, ghin, gin, gingo, shike.

The Italian language is dago or wop.

Italy is the Land of de Spaghette, Macaroniland, Spaghettiland, Tally, Wopland.

Spaghetti, macaroni, and noodles are associated with dago, Italian special, wop food, wop special (all referring to pasta dishes), Italian hurricane or storm (spaghetti with garlic).

Other food associations include dago red (cheap red wine), Italian hero (a large sandwich made on a loaf of crusty bread sliced lengthwise with a variety of fillings including cheese, cold meats, peppers, onion, lettuce, tomato, and a dressing), Italian perfume (garlic), wophouse (an Italian restaurant).

Criminal and underworld associations include Black Hand, Mafia (criminal gangs primarily composed of Italians), dago bomb, guinea football, Italian football (a small, homemade bomb).

Musical instruments are the dago piano (accordion) and wopstick (clarinet).

The use of ethnophaulisms potentially presents considerable information to the social psychologist. It provides a linguistic indicator of past and present intergroup relations. It provides an indicator of the user's attitude, and, in doing this, should help us study the dimensions of situations and the characteristics of speaker-listener relations in which such usage is perceived as permissible. With the exception of a small study by Palmore (1962), ethnophaulisms have unfortunately received no systematic scientific attention. The potential of such study remains to be tapped.

Dictionary for the Classification of Ethnic Stereotypes

The structure of most natural language systems is of incredible flexibility. It is because of this that special languages and special usages can develop and proliferate. Nevertheless, communication is a social process and word usage is highly regulated. Thus within the language of prejudice there appears only a relatively small number of words incorporated from the natural language for the description of ethnic groups. The major norm governing the use of these words is assignment. For example, the word "lazy" is almost always assigned to Negroes, is optionally assignable to Americans, but is never assigned to Germans.

Whether in everyday language and interaction or in formal literature, the norms of assignment appear compelling. This is clear in the following analysis of the depiction of Germans in significant American literature (Flanagan, 1964, p. 113; key stereotype assignments italicized by the author):

Regardless of his social or economic status, the German is presented as *hardworking, energetic,* matching *physical durability* with a *determination to succeed.* He is *persistent* and *intractable* rather than intelligent, and his genius seems to lie in a *mastery of routine* and in *organization* rather than in persuasive leadership. It is perhaps significant that the novelists who have drawn German characters have preferred to show them as farmers, artisans, businessmen instead of as politicians, writers, or artists. The women are generally adept at the domestic arts, such as sewing and cookery, although they seldom have any sense of style; the men, once they have reached a modicum of success, settle into a routine in which the *pleasures of the table rank high.* It is notable that high blood pressure, strokes, and apoplexy usually bring about their decease.

Almost every novelist who has chosen to depict the German in the United States has emphasized not only the *clannishness* of the immigrants but their *loyal devotion to the fatherland.* Despite the harsh facts of economic life which frequently induced their departure, they recall with affection their old home and many of the ancestral ways. German customs and traditions are remembered, German proverbs are quoted, German songs are sung, and German foods are lovingly prepared. Where other nationals tended to assimilate fast and to disappear into the anonymous melting pot, the Germans clung to their group entity, well into the second generation. This practice brought about considerable ill feeling during the period of World War I and often made life difficult for those who were sincerely loyal to their adopted country. The stigma of German birth, the novelists seem to conclude, could be erased only by death.

No formal listing of ethnic group-descriptive words has yet been established. Table 1 presents a preliminary compilation. These 123 words are taken exclusively from the research literature on stereotypes and are probably representative though not exhaustive of American usage with American ethnic groups. By itself, such a listing provides little insight into the structure of stereotype assignments. What is required is a higher order dictionary, a metalanguage.

The 14-item dictionary presented here was compiled on the basis of a series of trial-and-error content analyses, stimulated in part by the coding scheme developed by Laffal (1965). Table 2 illustrates the application of the dictionary units to the words of Table 1.

TABLE 1. THE MAJOR STEREOTYPE TERMS FOR AMERICAN ETHNIC GROUPS

Aggressive (7)
Aimless (9)
Alert (2)
Ambitious (8)
Argumentative (7)
Aristocratic (4)
Arrogant (4)
Artistic (13)
Athletic (14)
Attention-
  seeking (4)
Bitter (4)
Boastful (4)
Brave (3)
Brilliant (2)
Casual (9)
Communistic (11)
Conceited (4)
Conservative (11)
Conventional (1)
Courteous (1)
Cowardly (6)
Critical (4)
Cruel (7)
Cynical (4)
Dark complexion (14)
Dark hair and
  eyes (14)
Dark-skinned (14)
Deceitful (6)
Democratic (11)
Dictatorial (4)
Disillusioned (4)
Dull (5)
Efficient (2)
Evasive (6)
Extremely
  nationalistic (4)
Extremist (11)
Faithful (3)
Free (11)
Freedom-loving (11)
Frivolous (9)
Fun-loving (9)

Generous (1)
Grasping (4)
Gregarious (1)
Happy-go-lucky (9)
Hard-working (8)
Honest (3)
Humorless (4)
Ignorant (5)
Imaginative (2)
Imitative (5)
Immoral (6)
Impulsive (9)
Individualistic (3)
Industrious (8)
Insecure (9)
Intelligent (2)
Jovial (1)
Kind (1)
Large (14)
Large noses (14)
Lazy (9)
Loud (4)
Loyal to
  family ties (4)
Materialistic (12)
Meditative (8)
Mercenary (12)
Methodical (8)
Musical (13)
Naive (5)
Neat (8)
Nonbeliever (6)
Oppressed (11)
Ordinary (1)
Ostentatious (4)
Passionate (10)
Persistent (8)
Pessimistic (4)
Physically
  dirty (14)
Pleasure-
  loving (10)
Poor (12)
Practical (8)

Prejudiced (4)
Progressive (8)
Quarrelsome (7)
Quick-tempered (7)
Quiet (4)
Radical (11)
Realistic (2)
Reserved (4)
Revengeful (7)
Rich (12)
Rude (4)
Scientifically minded (2)
Secure (8)
Self-secluding (4)
Sensitive (10)
Sensual (10)
Shrewd (2)
Skeptical (4)
Slanting eyes (14)
Sly (6)
Small (14)
Sophisticated (13)
Sportsmanlike (3)
Straightforward (3)
Strange (4)
Stubborn (4)
Stupid (5)
Suggestible (5)
Superstitious (5)
Suspicious (4)
Talkative (4)
Tradition-loving (4)
Treacherous (6)
Unimaginative (5)
Uninformed (5)
Unprincipled (6)
Unreliable (9)
Very religious (4)
Warlike (7)
Witty (2)
Yellow skin (14)

Note. Parenthetical numbers refer to dictionary categories cited in the text.

A PRELIMINARY DICTIONARY FOR THE CLASSIFICATION
OF ETHNIC STEREOTYPES

1. *Positive Relational Qualities.* Words coded here denote the target group's positive interpersonal qualities. Two types of words are coded here. Type 1 words depict the target group and its members as familiar or no different from others. Type 2 words emphasize those characteristics which make the group members desirable and attractive interpersonal partners.

    Examples: conventional, courteous, generous, gregarious, jovial, kind, ordinary.

2. *Positive Intellectual Qualities.* Words coded here denote the intellectual abilities and capacities for realistic and creative behavior of the target group and its members.

    Examples: alert, brilliant, efficient, imaginative, intelligent, realistic, scientifically minded, shrewd, witty.

3. *Positive Moral Qualities.* Words coded here depict target group values and/or member behavior as self-directed, sincere, and principled.

    Examples: brave, faithful, honest, individualistic, sportsmanlike, straightforward.

4. *Negative Relational Qualities.* Words coded here denote the target group's negative interpersonal qualities. Four types of words are coded here. Type 1 words depict the target group and its members as being strange or alien as opposed to familiar and native. Type 2 words emphasize the seclusion, ethnocentrism, and arrogance of the target group and its members. Type 3 words describe the target group and its members as embittered and disillusioned. Type 4 words emphasize those characteristics which make group members undesirable and unattractive interpersonal partners.

    Examples: aristocratic, arrogant, attention-seeking, bitter, boastful, conceited, critical, cynical, dictatorial, disillusioned, extremely nationalistic, grasping, humorless, loud, loyal to family ties, ostentatious, pessimistic, prejudiced, quiet, reserved, rude, self-secluding, skeptical, strange, stubborn, suspicious, talkative, tradition-loving, very religious.

5. *Negative Intellectual Qualities.* Words coded here denote the intellectual deficits, ignorance, or naivete of the target group and its members.

    Examples: dull, ignorant, imitative, naive, stupid, suggestible, superstitious, unimaginative, uninformed.

6. *Negative Moral Qualities.* Words coded here depict target group values and/or member behavior as immoral, deceptive, or unprincipled.

    Examples: cowardly, deceitful, evasive, immoral, nonbeliever, sly, treacherous, unprincipled.

7. *Conflict-Hostility.* The basic code criterion is the indication of aggressiveness, conflict, or hostility as descriptive of relations with the target group or as interpersonal characteristics of target group members.

   Examples: aggressive, argumentative, cruel, quarrelsome, quick-tempered, vengeful, warlike.

8. *Substantial.* Words coded here depict the target group and its members as possessing the qualities of continuity, industry, persistence, and direction.

   Examples: ambitious, hard-working, industrious, methodical, neat, persistent, progressive, meditative, practical, secure.

9. *Unsubstantial.* Words coded here depict the target group and its members as being capricious, fleeting, unreliable, unindustrious, and without direction.

   Examples: aimless, casual, frivolous, fun-loving, happy-go-lucky, impulsive, insecure, lazy, unreliable.

10. *Emotionality.* Words coded only here depict the emotionality and emotional sensitivity of the target group.

    Examples: passionate, pleasure-loving, sensitive, sensual.

11. *Political Characteristics.* All words referring to political forms, political attitudes, political activities, or the political relations of the target group with the dominant group are coded here.

    Examples: communistic, conservative, democratic, extremist, free, freedom-loving, oppressed, radical.

12. *Economic Characteristics.* All words referring to economic status, economic attitudes, economic activities, or the economic relations of the target group with the dominant group are coded here.

    Examples: materialistic, mercenary, poor, rich.

13. *Esthetic-Cultural Characteristics.* Words coded here relate to or deal with the arts and artistic appreciation or excellence in taste as generally associated with the quality of being cultured.

    Examples: artistic, musical, sophisticated.

14. *Physical Qualities.* All words referring to the physical qualities of the target group and its members are coded here. Three physical qualities are classified. Type 1 refers to directly visible and external physical characteristics such as color, physique, or physiognomy. Type 2 refers to physical qualities which are visible only in behavior such as athletic ability. Type 3 words refer to a present physical state such as clean or dirty.

    Examples: athletic, dark complexion, dark hair and eyes, dark-skinned, large, large noses, physically dirty, slanting eyes, small, yellow-skinned.

TABLE 2.   DISTRIBUTION OF DICTIONARY ENTRIES

	Number of Words	Percentage
1. Positive relational qualities	7	5.7
2. Positive intellectual qualities	9	7.3
3. Positive moral qualities	6	4.9
4. Negative relational qualities	29	23.6
5. Negative intellectual qualities	9	7.3
6. Negative moral qualities	8	6.5
7. Conflict-hostility	7	5.7
8. Substantial	10	8.1
9. Unsubstantial	9	7.3
10. Emotionality	4	3.2
11. Political characteristics	8	6.5
12. Economic characteristics	4	3.2
13. Esthetic-cultural characteristics	3	2.4
14. Physical qualities	10	8.3
Totals	123	100.0

The distribution of these presumably representative ethnic stereotypes is highly uniform across dictionary categories. The outstanding exception is category 4, Negative Relational Qualities. The redundancy of these negative characteristics along with the development of ethnophaulisms dramatizes both the content and the social functions of the language of prejudice.

Judgments of the validity of a classificatory scheme like this must be based on the new information the scheme enables one to discover and the ease with which the scheme (as a metalanguage) enables one to make statements of value. To test the validity of this scheme, two sets of data were reanalyzed. The first set comes from a study by Ehrlich and Rinehart (1965) in which the stereotype assignments produced by two similar college student groups were compared. One group was administered the 84-item Katz and Braly (1933) stereotype checklist. The other group was administered an unstructured questionnaire calling for them to write all descriptive words they thought appropriate to each target. The six ethnic targets were Turks, Russians, Negroes, Japanese, Jews, and Americans. Further details of this study are not relevant here; Table 3 presents an analysis of the dictionary entries as they appeared under the open and closed formats. The table displays both the degree to which the categories are used and the number of ethnic targets described differently within each category.

TABLE 3. DICTIONARY USAGE ACROSS SIX ETHNIC
TARGETS BY QUESTIONNAIRE FORMAT

Dictionary Category	Ratio of Use: Open to Closed	Number of Target Differences
1. Positive relational qualities	4–5	2
2. Positive intellectual qualities	4–6	2
3. Positive moral qualities	1–5	4
4. Negative relational qualities	5–6	1
5. Negative intellectual qualities	2–5	5
6. Negative moral qualities	3–4	4
7. Conflict-hostility	1–5	4
8. Substantial	4–6	3
9. Unsubstantial	1–4	3
10. Emotionality	0–6	6
11. Political characteristics	4–4	4
12. Economic characteristics	6–4	2
13. Esthetic-cultural characteristics	1–5	4
14. Physical qualities	5–0	5

Note. The ratios indicate the number of groups described by words of the stated category for the two question formats. The number of target differences indicates the number of ethnic groups described differently in the question formats for the stated category. *Source:* Ehrlich and Rinehart (1965).

As can be seen in Table 3, more targets are described in more categories under the closed format. This is in keeping with the findings of the original report. Striking absolute differences occur in ethnic group descriptions in the category of emotionality, which is never used by the open format subjects, and in the category of physical qualities, which are not options for the closed format subjects. Major differences of four or five out of six target group descriptions occur in the three negative categories, in conflict-hostility, and in the positive moral, the political, and the esthetic-cultural categories. It is clear that the dictionary is sensitive to the complex and subtle differences evoked by the two questionnaire formats which together elicited over 9000 stereotype assignments.

The second set of data to be examined are taken from two national surveys conducted in 1942 and 1966. The targets in these surveys were Germans, Japanese, and Russians. Given the intervening events, a comparison of these stereotype assignments over time should provide a further test of the sensitivity of the dictionary categories. The original percentages are displayed in Table 4, and Table 5 presents the changes that occurred by dictionary assignment. As we would expect, the Germans and Japanese

TABLE 4. STEREOTYPE ASSIGNMENTS OF GERMANS, JAPANESE, AND RUSSIANS FROM NATIONAL SURVEYS, UNITED STATES, 1942 AND 1966 (IN PERCENT)

Germans	1966	1942	Japanese	1966	1942	Russians	1966	1942
Hard-working	63%	62%	Hard-working	44%	39%	Hard-working	45%	61%
Intelligent	47	41	Intelligent	35	25	Warlike	24	14
Progressive	33	32	Artistic	31	19	Intelligent	23	16
Practical	23	21	Progressive	31	19	Progressive	19	24
Brave	19	30	Religious	20	18	Treacherous	18	10
Honest	19	10	Sly	19	63	Ordinary	16	25
Quick-tempered	18	25	Practical	17	9	Sly	15	7
Warlike	16	67	Brave	17	24	Cruel	13	9
Arrogant	16	31	Treacherous	12	73	Quick-tempered	13	10
Religious	12	7	Warlike	11	46	Practical	13	18
Ordinary	11	9	Ordinary	10	6	Radical	13	25
Cruel	10	57	Cruel	9	56	Arrogant	12	2
Conceited	8	32	Honest	9	2	Rude	11	6
Artistic	7	8	Arrogant	5	21	Brave	10	48
Treacherous	7	42	Aristocratic	6	21	Ignorant	10	20
Sly	7	21	Quick-tempered	6	21	Unimaginative	8	14
Aristocratic	5	8	Ignorant	4	16	Conceited	7	3
Rude	5	19	Radical	4	12	Dull	7	13
Radical	4	23	Conceited	3	27	Artistic	6	10
Unimaginative	4	8	Lazy	3	3	Honest	5	19
Ignorant	3	12	Rude	2	12	Religious	2	10
Dull	2	7	Unimaginative	2	7	Aristocratic	2	3
Lazy	2	1	Dull	1	4	Lazy	1	5
No opinion	6	6	No opinion	13	7	No opinion	13	18

Note. Columns add to more than 100 percent because many respondents chose more than one word. *Source:* Office of Public Opinion Research, July, 1942; American Institute of Public Opinion, June, 1966.

show increasing assignments of positive qualities and decreasing assignments of negative qualities. The Russian responses show the reverse pattern. Particularly dramatic is the decrease in the negative moral and conflict-hostility categories for both the Germans and Japanese. By contrast, for the Russians, these categories show a slight increase while the positive moral category displays a marked decline. Certainly the dictionary seems adequate to the problem of change.

As a descriptive device of considerable parsimony, the dictionary introduced here makes it easier to understand this facet of the language of prejudice. Whether the dictionary is employed as a frame for constructing new stereotype checklists or as the basis for classifying unstructured responses, it provides a level of manageability that this research area

TABLE 5. CHANGES IN THE STEREOTYPE ASSIGNMENTS
OF GERMANS, JAPANESE, AND RUSSIANS, 1942–1966,
BY DICTIONARY CATEGORY

Dictionary Category	Percentage Change: 1942–1966		
	Germans	Japanese	Russians
1. Positive relational qualities	+2.0	+4.0	−9.0
2. Positive intellectual qualities	+6.0	+10.0	+7.0
3. Positive moral qualities	−1.0	0.0	−26.0
4. Negative relational qualities	−10.2	−12.0	+4.5
5. Negative intellectual qualities	−6.0	−6.7	−7.4
6. Negative moral qualities	−24.5	−52.5	+8.0
7. Conflict-hostility	−35.0	−20.8	+5.6
8. Substantial	+1.4	+6.5	−8.8
9. Unsubstantial	+1.0	0.0	−4.0
11. Political characteristics	−19.0	−8.0	−12.0
13. Esthetic-cultural	−1.0	+12.0	−4.0

Note. For the original percentages for each year see Table 4. A "+" signifies an increase in the use of words in the stated category; a "−" indicates decreasing usage.

needs. The dictionary also provides the opportunity to test specific hypotheses about the relation of the language of prejudice to other forms of intergroup behavior, as discussed later. Thus the dictionary provides both a facile means for making statements about ethnic stereotypy and a means (to be indicated) for testing hypotheses, that is, for making new statements.

THE DETERMINANTS OF STEREOTYPE ASSIGNMENTS: SOCIAL PROCESSES

Three fundamental principles of cognition characterize the relation between objects and belief.[3]

1. *Principle of distinction.* Social objects are distinguishable on the basis of the belief statements associated with them.
2. *Principle of diffusion.* Belief statements about social objects are widely diffused in a society.
3. *Principle of consensus.* There is high consensus on the belief statements associated with specific social objects.

The transposition of these general principles into specific statements about stereotype assignments is simple and direct.

1a. The assignment of stereotypes to the major ethnic groups in American society is relatively distinct and exclusive.

2a. Knowledge of the stereotypes assigned to the major ethnic groups in American society is highly diffused.

3a. There is high consensus on the assignment of specific stereotypes to specific groups.

Supporting evidence, which in full would represent almost all research in this area, includes Centers (1951), Duijker and Frijda (1961), Ehrlich (1961), Ehrlich and Rinehart (1965); Ehrlich and Van Tubergen (1971), Johnson (1944), Kátz and Braly (1933, 1935), Meenes (1943), Morsh and Smith (1953), Prothro and Melikian (1955), Ringer (1967), Vinacke (1949), and Williams (1964).

The primary institutions for the diffusion of knowledge in society are the family and the school. These major agencies of socialization present, authenticate, and legitimize the use of ethnic stereotypes. The priority and crucial significance of the family is well documented: the transmission of ethnic stereotypes occurs as early as age 3. A discussion of the family and other supporting mechanisms is presented in chapter 5. For the moment we need only the following corollary to our first principle:

2b. The primary contexts for the diffusion of knowledge of ethnic stereotypes, and for the legitimation of such knowledge, are the family and the school.

The initial media for the transmission of ethnic stereotypes is interpersonal. Through the life cycle, mass media become increasingly important. What the relative balance is between the interpersonal and the mass media for transmitting ethnic stereotypes remains to be determined. MacKinnon and Centers (1958), for a limited example, find that most adults report that their major sources of beliefs about Russia come from newspaper, radio, and television.

2c. Consensual ethnic stereotypes are copied in the mass media of communication and the media of mass education.

Studies in serious literature (e.g., Rosenberg, 1960; Howe, 1949; Gross and Hardy, 1966), popular fiction (e.g., Berelson and Salter, 1946), movies and television (e.g., McManus and Kronenberger, 1946; Scotch, 1960), and even pictorial illustrations in mass circulating magazines (e.g., Shuey, 1953) provide considerable documentation. Glock and Stark (1966) demonstrate the diffusion of negative Jewish stereotypes in the Christian-American media of mass religion.

Klineberg (1963) reviewing 15 current and popular children's readers, concludes:

> In summary, then, life in the United States as it is portrayed in these children's readers is in a general way easy and comfortable, frustrations are rare and usually overcome quite easily, people (all white, mostly blonde and "North European" in origin) are almost invariably kind and generous. There are other kinds of people in the world, but they live in far-off countries or in days gone by; they evidently have no place on the American scene (p. 77).

Larrick (1965), in a more detailed analysis, studied all trade books published for children in 1962, 1963, and 1964. Of the 5206 books published in that period, only 6.7% contained one or more Negroes. The majority of the books portraying Negroes, however, place them outside the United States or before World War II. Fewer than 1% of all of the children's books told a story about American Negroes today.

In a study of over 1000 elementary school textbooks of the nineteenth century, Elson (1964) provides an invaluable documentary on the diffusion of ethnic stereotypes in the educational media:

> Each race and its subdivisions—nationalities—are defined by inherent mental and personal characteristics which the child must memorize. . . . And these traits are used to determine the rank of each race and nation. . . . The American, as the ideal man, is of the white race, of Northern European background, Protestant, self-made, and if not a farmer at least retaining the virtues of his yeoman ancestors (p. 340).

Analyses of contemporary textbooks and curriculum materials document the pervasiveness of stereotype assignments and their low rate of change (e.g., Harris, 1963; Marcus, 1961; Olson, 1963; Sloan, 1966; and Wilson, 1944, 1946, 1949). Blom, Waite, and Zimet (1967) and Waite (1968) engaged in content analyses of first-grade reading textbooks published between 1965 and 1966. The purpose of their analyses was to compare the new, multiethnic series of readers with the more traditional texts. In all, they analyzed 820 stories that were deliberately multiethnic and 1307 stories in which, presumably, there was no deliberate intent to represent ethnic others. In general, they found that even in the multiethnic series there were very few significant characters who were other than white Anglo-Saxon. The stories generally depicted a single Negro family living in a happy, stable, white suburban neighborhood.

Stereotypes of women, as a subordinate group in American society, are also diffused in the media of communication and education. Martin (1971,

p. 238) concludes her review of "the image of women in American fiction" with a set of rhetorical questions summarizing her findings:

Why have our novelists persisted in ignoring . . . examples of strong women, reinforcing instead the image of women as forlorn, helpless creatures, who are certain to be destroyed or hopelessly embittered unless they devote themselves exclusively to their domestic lives and duties as wives and mothers? Why have novelists persisted . . . in perpetuating the tradition of the fallen woman consistently punished for her frailty? Why have novelists insisted that heroines can redeem themselves only if they forgo sexuality?

Carol Ehrlich(1971) examined the six major and current sociology textbooks on marriage and the family and found the following:

Such texts, despite their claims to be compilations of the accumulated knowledge of social science, are—with respect to the female—primarily collections of folklore and social stereotypy. Areas where major questions remain unanswered (and sometimes unasked) were treated by all writers as if folklore were fact. The female as viewed by the American male sociologist of the family belongs at home, ministering to her husband and children and forswearing all other interests (p. 430).

Ehrlich ironically concludes her review by quoting one of the sociologists she studied: "Whichever way the society goes, there will be scientific justification for the trend somewhere in the sciences of human behavior."

Since ethnic stereotypes reflect the established relations of ethnic groups, knowledge of these stereotypes is widely diffused in society. Consensus presumably is a consequence of these distinctive relations and the diffusion of this knowledge. Perhaps, as an hypothesis, it might be suggested that increases in the distinctive character of particular intergroup relations and/or the importance of that relation to a group will result in an increase in diffusion and in consensus.

Established group relations change slowly. The processes of establishing intergroup linkages, although we don't understand them well, do appear to be slow-moving. To the extent that ethnic group relations remain relatively constant, we should expect a relatively stable consensus on ethnic stereotypes. Crises in ethnic group relations, such as war, should result in marked changes in ethnic group stereotypy. The following principles summarize the existing knowledge of stability and change in ethnic stereotype assignments. We start with the basic principles.

4. *Principle of stability*. Belief statements associated with social objects are highly stable.

Stereotypes about ethnic groups appear as a part of the social heritage of society. They are transmitted across generations as a component of the accumulated knowledge of society. They are as true as tradition, and as pervasive as folklore. No person can grow up in a society without having learned the stereotypes assigned to the major ethnic groups. But while ethnic stereotyping has been a constant in folklore, in literature, and in history, we should not overlook the fact that within societies the primary targets of stereotype assignments have changed over time. Even where targets remained stable, the content of assigned stereotypes stand in a reciprocating relation: as intergroup relations change, intergroup imagery changes. In cycle, changes in intergroup imagery affect changes in intergroup behavior. These reciprocal effects may be stable or they may spiral in an increasingly negative or positive direction.

One of the traditional arguments for the explanation of stereotype assignments is based on the properties of the target. In its essential form, this argument holds that some of the inherent properties of the target determines—or in its less stringent form, set limits—on the content of assigned stereotypes. The argument is without empirical confirmation. Ethnic characteristics which are defined as distinctive, and thus become a central part of stereotype assignments, are defined as such as a result of ethnic group relations. The significance of ethnic characteristics and differences is a matter of social definition, not a matter of inherent qualities. The limits set on stereotype assignments, similarly, are a primary consequence of the intergroup relationship. Campbell (1967) suggests an hypothesis which emphasizes the importance of the intergroup relationship in the origin and maintenance of stereotypy: "The greater the real differences between groups on any particular custom, detail of physical appearance, or item of material culture, the more likely it is that that feature will appear in the stereotyped imagery each group has of the other" (p. 821).

5. *Principle of change.* Belief statements associated with social objects change as the relation of people to the objects changes.

In their specific application:

4a. Ethnic stereotype assignments are relatively stable historically within and across societies.

5a. Changes in ethnic stereotype assignments follow changes in established ethnic group relations.

Strong supporting evidence is found in the natural experimental studies which have measured ethnic stereotypy at periods before and after organ-

ized warfare. Seago (1947), for example, administered the Katz-Braly stereotype checklist to cross-sectional specimen groups of college students
every year from 1941 to 1945 using Americans, Germans, Japanese, and
Negroes as targets. With the advent of the war, the stereotype assignments of the experimental targets Germans and Japanese decrease on an
index of favorability, recovering slightly by 1945. By 1966, recovery
seems virtually complete, as our dictionary analysis demonstrates (see
Table 5), reflecting the re-establishment of friendly intergroup relations.
In contrast, for the control targets, Negro stereotype assignments display
the same index of favorability (highly unfavorable) in 1945 as they did in
1941. While the index value for American stereotypes declines in favorability, it still remains highly favorable.[4]

Controlled experimental research by Sherif, Harvey, White, Hood, and
Sherif (1961) provides further and important confirmation. These researchers assessed the stereotypes assigned by the members of two groups
of boys following the experimental inducement of intergroup conflict and
following the inducement of intergroup cooperation. At the end of the
conflict condition the stereotype assignments were consensually unfavorable, but by the end of the cooperative condition they were consensually
favorable for both groups. The differences, as a result of the changing
group relations, were highly significant. Further support can be found in
Buchanan (1953), Child and Doob (1943), Diab (1962), Dudycha (1942),
Fernberger (1948), Gilliland and Blum (1945), Gundlach (1944), Jahoda
(1959), Katz and Braly (1933, 1935), Marx (1967), Meenes (1943, 1950),
Morsh and Smith (1953), Prothro (1954), Prothro and Melikian (1955),
Prothro and Miles (1952), Remmers (1943), Ringer (1967), Schoenfeld
(1942), Sherif and Sherif (1953), Stagner and Osgood (1941), and Zeligs
(1947).

Social objects are not necessarily dispersed in a uniform manner in society. Persons in different geographic locations, in different "ethclass"[5]
locations, and in different roles vary in the degree to which social objects
are visible to them. (The mass media, of course, cut across most social locations and tend to minimize differences in direct visibility.) Correla-
tively, we know that American ethnic groups are distributed in a mani-
festly nonuniform manner partly as a consequence of original settlement
and partly as a matter of organized discrimination. Neither the determinants of visibility nor the effects of visibility are well established. Probably the major determinants of visibility are absolute and relative size,
physical distinctiveness, and cultural distinctiveness. The effects of visibility are also a matter of some conjecture. Since visibility is a major variable
in this study of prejudice, the following principles are very important.

6. *Principle of visibility*. Under conditions of stability, the greater the visibility of a social object, the greater the distinctiveness, diffusion, and consensus of belief statements associated with the object.

6a.   Under conditions of stable group relations, the greater the visibility of an ethnic group, the greater the distinctiveness, diffusion, and consensus of stereotypes assigned to the group.

6.1.   Under conditions of change, social objects become temporarily more visible.

6.1a.   Under conditions of change, ethnic groups become temporarily more visible.

Evidence of any value is hard to come by. If we equate population size and density with visibility, though this is clearly not the best of assumptions, we can see that at least three studies reporting regional differences in stereotype behavior provide support (Sims and Patrick, 1936; Chase, 1940; Pettigrew, 1959). Thus Pettigrew's comparative analysis indicates a greater consensus and distinctiveness in Negro stereotype assignments for southern as compared to northern American respondents. Regional differences, however, are ephemeral and in themselves of no scientific consequence. Since 1945, intergroup imagery in the South has become almost indistinguishable from Northern imagery (see Pettigrew, 1966).

Changes in visibility are implied by changes in the relation of people to a social object. Almost any change in intergroup relations should increase the visibility of an ethnic group. Assuming that war increases visibility, certainly a safer assumption than the foregoing one, we can by reference to Table 5 obtain further supporting evidence. Using the median value for each column as an index of consensus, we can see that while the value for Russians hardly changes (1 %), the consensus on stereotype assignments for both Germans and Japanese was twice as great in 1942 as in 1966 (21 versus 10–11 %). This analysis also makes it clear that short-term changes in the visibility of an ethnic group may have no long-term effects on the other variables of stereotype assignment. Since the visibility effect was here determined by a world war, the potency of our principle of stability is again established.

These five principles considered jointly suggest five new hypotheses about stereotype assignment.

2d.*   The greater the distinctiveness of ethnic stereotype assignments, the greater their diffusion in society.

3b.*   The greater the distinctiveness of ethnic stereotype assignments, the greater the consensus on their assignment.

3c.*   The greater the diffusion of ethnic stereotype assignments, the greater the consensus on assignment.

4b.*   The greater the distinctiveness, diffusion, and consensus on stereotype assignments, the greater the stability of the assignment.

5b.*   Changes in the established relations between ethnic groups will decrease the stability of stereotype assignments and modify their distinctiveness and their levels of diffusion and consensus.

STEREOTYPE ASSIGNMENTS AS A PSYCHOLOGICAL PROCESS

The assignment of stereotypes to ethnic groups is best understood through the analysis of ethnic group relations. However, to understand how a specific ethnic person is assigned ethnic group stereotypes requires a different order of analysis.

All social objects can be grouped and classified. It may not even be an exaggeration to assert that all social objects *are* grouped and classified. Surely the social environment is far too complex for people to react to the unique qualities of everything they encounter. Shared classifications of social objects represent both individual and societal responses to the management of this complexity. These shared classifications may be termed *social categories*. Although social categories entail specifiable criteria for the classification of social objects, these criteria are not always easily recognized or articulated by their users. Race, religion, and nationality, for example, are social categories. They represent classifications of people based on distinctive, easily recognized, and easily articulated criteria shared by members of society. Their universality may in part be a consequence of their ease of application.

The process of establishing a social object as a member of a social category involves minimizing its individual differences and maximizing its categorical properties. To categorize a social object implies that the criterial similarities are more important for that object and like objects than any differences among them. This minimax operation makes it easier to store knowledge and to recall it. The use of social categories narrows the amount of information that a person needs to have about someone in order to act. Paradoxically, while categorization narrows the amount of information necessary for action, it also expands the scope of information about an object. Thus you may need very little information to decide that a person is Jewish, but once you assign him to this category you now (ostensibly) know a great deal about him—which is to say that you think you know a great deal about Jewish persons.

Two general principles are operative here.

7. *Principle of categorical placement.* The categorization of a social object is contingent on its codability.

Codability may be defined as the degree to which social objects can be easily and precisely classified into social categories. The codability of a category can be determined by measuring the amount of information about an object that is required to assign it to a category. By following Bruner (1957), whose writings on cognition are basic to the present discussion, it can be seen that the greater the codability of a social object, the less information is needed to assign it to a social category. The placement process is contingent on the joint effects of the object's characteristics, the criteria of classification, the object's eligibility for other social categories, and the context in which the object appears (cf. Bruner, 1957; Brown, 1965, Chapter 7; Jones and Gerard, 1967, Chapter 4). In its applied form, then, Principle 7 becomes:

7a. Ascribing ethnic group membership to an individual is contingent on the joint effects of that person's characteristics, the criteria of ethnic classification, his eligibility for other social categories, and the social context in which he appears.

Generally, where social categories are of societal importance the basis of categorization is formally established by law. Examples of this may be found in the history of American immigration policies (Jones, 1960), in the laws concerning miscegenation (Mayer, 1961), in the attempts of people to classify American triracial groups (Berry, 1963), and even in the intragroup problems of defining membership through law (Galanter, 1963). The everyday principles of ethnic group ascription appear to be based on criteria of skin color, physiognomy, surname identification, and self-reported identities. Little formal research has been addressed to the subjective aspects of ethnic categorization.

An important experimental study, though not in an ethnic group context, is provided by Guskin (1962). The researcher presented films of a subnormal 10-year-old girl and boy to 42 college students. Half the students were told that both children were retarded, the other half were told only that they were school children. The filmed boy displayed some obvious physical symptoms; the girl had none. After viewing the films, students rated the children on an adjective scale: confident-timid, strange-normal, capable-helpless, unintelligent-bright, and clumsy-skillful. Analysis of variance indicated that the boy was rated as more subnormal than the girl *only* when the retarded label was assigned. The girl's rating stayed essentially the same under both conditions. It seems a valid inference from these data that the ascription of subnormality could have an effect only when the object's characteristics were in some sense perceived as relevant and validating.

At the very least, it is clear that categorical placements are well regulated in society. This leads to the following.

7.1.   *Corollary of veridicality.* All categorical placements must satisfy some test of accuracy.

7.1a.   All persons assigned ethnic membership must satisfy some social criteria of membership.

Situational characteristics are of considerable significance in categorical placement. The situation provides the context and cues for assessing the person's characteristics, the applicability of the classificatory criteria, and the person's eligibility for other categorical assignments. Riddleberger and Motz (1957) explored situational effects with constructed photographs of Negroes in "conventional" (jazz trio, rural slum, large family) and "non-conventional" (mainly intergroup) settings. The pictures were paired so that the same Negro face appeared once in a conventional and once in a nonconventional setting. There were four faces and eight situations. The photographs were displayed to 60 freshman and sophomore college students who scored extremely high or low on the anti-Negro subscale of the California Ethnocentrism scale. After a 10-second exposure, the students were asked to describe what they saw and how people in the picture might have met. Then they were asked to supply descriptive words about the pictured Negro and a pictured white. The two major and relevant findings were that (1) the same Negro was described differently in the conventional and in the nonconventional settings and (2) regardless of the subject's level of prejudice, those high and low *both* described the Negro in the stereotyped setting with twice the frequency of negative stereotypes than they did in describing the Negro in the nonconventional setting.

Almost no research has explored systematically the effects of competing social categories on the categorical placement of people, and no meaningful statement is possible yet. In one of the few studies of this problem, Bayton, McAlister, and Hamer (1956) administered a stereotype checklist to both Negro and white college students. The subjects were asked to check the items they thought descriptive of "upper-class white Americans, upper-class Negroes, lower-class white Americans, and lower-class Negroes." From this data, it is quite clear that class represented to their subjects a meaningful category of stereotype assignment. This excerpt from their Table 2 displays the class-race interaction nicely:

Responses of 92 white subjects to . . .

Lower-class whites		Lower-class Negroes	
Trait	Percentage	Trait	Percentage
Happy-go-lucky	20	Superstitious *	66
Materialistic *	20	Lazy	39
Ignorant	19	Physically dirty	34
Lazy	19	Unreliable	34
Loud	19	Musical *	30
Rude *	19	Loud	26
Unreliable	17	Ignorant	26
Pleasure-loving	16	Happy-go-lucky	24
Physically dirty	15	Ostentatious *	19
Practical *	14	Pleasure-loving	17

Seven of the ten stereotypes are the same in both arrays. But the distinctive components of the Negro stereotype—superstitious, musical, and ostentatious—as contrasted with those unique to the white listing—materialistic, rude, and practical—emphasize the salience of these characteristics in the stereotype of the American Negro. (The relative salience of the stereotypes assigned can further be seen in the range of endorsement they receive, 14–20% for the lower-class white and 17–66% for the lower-class Negro.)

Although Bayton's interpretation that "there was little evidence of purely race-linked stereotyping," is questionable, his research does indicate that class may be a significant alternative to ethnicity as a basis for the categorization of persons. Ethclass may, in fact, be the most important of contemporary American social placements.

The second principle and its corollary probably have their origin in motivational theory. Leeper (1965, p. 60) provides the analog: "Active motives tend to modify sensory perceptions, particularly in the direction of making relevant things stand out focally." From our perspective, we arrive at the next principle.

8. *Principle of categorical dominance.* If a social object is cast in a social category, then initial response will be determined more on the basis of its categorical characteristics than its individual characteristics.

8.1. *Corollary of categorical response.* The less knowledge available about a categorized social object, the greater the likelihood that it will be assigned the characteristics of its social category.

The principles of dominance and response are also directly applied.

8a. If a person is assigned ethnic membership, then initial response will be made more on the basis of the stereotypes assigned to that ethnic group than to the individual.

8.1a. The less knowledge available about an ethnic person, the greater the likelihood that person will be assigned those stereotypes associated with the ethnic group.

An experiment directly testing the effects of the categorical dominance of ethnic identity is reported by Tajfel, Sheikh, and Gardner (1964). The researchers had 25 students observe the behavior of ethnic persons in two sessions. For the first session, a male Canadian and a male Indian (from India) individually discussed their views about films. In the second, two other Canadian and Indian males were interviewed about their favorite books. Each person appeared in front of the class for 8 minutes, and following their appearance they were rated on 25 semantic differential scales. A second group of subjects, not exposed to the testing sessions, were administered the same 25 scale items and were asked to select those which they thought most characteristic of the two ethnic groups. The major stereotype of Canadians was then defined as the seven most and least frequently assigned adjectives, while the Indians were defined by the nine highest and lowest assignments.

The ratings of the subjects in the first group were then scored by determining the mean difference between their ratings of the high- and low-characteristic adjectives. Both the Indians and Canadians were rated more similarly on the highly assigned stereotypes than on those of low assignment. The researchers conclude: "Evidence was presented indicating a minimization of the differences between members of an ethnic group on traits which subjectively characterize that group. It is clear that stereotypes were operating in both instances to reduce judged differences between individuals within an ethnic group."

Categorical placement is most frequently induced in experimental research through naming. Given this mode of experimental placement, the principles of categorical dominance and response have been well confirmed. Razran (1950) displayed photographs of 30 attractive and ethnically nonspecific white girls' faces to 150 students. Judgments of liking, beauty, intelligence, character, ambition, and entertainingness were elicited from the students. Two months later, they were exposed to the same photographs, this time with ethnic surnames attached. Five were assigned Jewish surnames (e.g., Goldberg), five were assigned Italian surnames (e.g., D'Angelo), five were assigned Irish surnames (e.g., Kelly), and the remaining were given Anglo-Saxon surnames (e.g., Adams, Clark,

Chase). Few changes were reported as occurring in the photographs with the Anglo-Saxon surnames. Judgments of *liking* and *character* significantly decreased for the Italian and Jewish labeled photographs, and the rating of ambition significantly increased with the Jewish labels.

Secord (1959) demonstrated that the identification of a photograph as that of a Negro was sufficient to evoke the characterization of that individual by the stereotypes commonly assigned to Negroes. He presented, under differing conditions and to a variety of subject groups, a series of 10 photographs scaled to range widely from markedly Negro to markedly Caucasian. The strength of the categorical response to the experimenter's identification of the photographs as Negro was found to be independent of the Negroid-Caucasoid features of the photographed person, of the subject's affective response to the photograph, and of the subject's level of prejudice. The categorical response weakened when the photographs were so Caucasoid that they could not be spontaneously identified by subjects as Negro. Even then, highly prejudiced subjects still accepted the experimenter's placement and continued to respond categorically.

Further evidence supporting the principles of placement and dominance in stereotype assignments can be found in Clarke and Campbell (1955), DeFleur and Westie (1959), Gardner and Taylor (1969), McDavid and Harari (1966), Ringer (1967), Secord, Bevan, and Katz (1956), Sherif (1935), and Ziller and Behringer (1965).

STEREOTYPING

Stereotyping refers to the way in which stereotype assignments are cognitively structured. Three complex principles of structure, differentiation, and organization will be introduced here.[6] (The discussion of these is directed primarily toward social scientists, although all readers should try to work through these materials.)

18.   *Principle of elemental structure.* The elements of a belief/disbelief system are individually established in ordinal relations. In its applied form, this principle asserts: *The stereotypes assigned to a target group are ordinally related.*

The specific elements were essentially introduced in Chapter One. They are repeated here with their application:

POSTULATE OF SALIENCE. Beliefs and disbeliefs can be located on a scale of salience.

The stereotypes assigned to a target group vary in the degree to which they characterize the group.

POSTULATE OF INTENSITY. Beliefs and disbeliefs can be located on a scale of intensity.

The stereotypes assigned to a target group vary in the degree to which they are accepted or rejected.

POSTULATE OF DIRECTION. Beliefs and disbeliefs can be located on a scale of evaluation.

The stereotypes assigned to a target group vary in the degree to which they are favorable or unfavorable.

POSTULATE OF CENTRALITY. Beliefs and disbeliefs can be located on a scale of importance.

The stereotypes assigned to a target group vary in the degree to which they are important.

These postulates are purely descriptive, though obviously necessary. They provide the background for us to examine the structure of stereotypes. This is not a simple task since the results of research on stereotype assignment have displayed considerable variation as a consequence of research procedure.[7] Nevertheless, a number of important and powerful generalizations seem to have emerged from the study of intergroup and interpersonal imagery.

The four major elements—direction, intensity, salience, and centrality—lead to six statements of simple structure. The evidence for these statements, however, is sparse, so only the bivariate possibilities are considered.

Direction, Directionality, and Intensity

The original investigation of the relation of direction to intensity comes from the search for the "principal components of scalable attitudes" and, in particular, from the search for a zero point in attitude scaling (Stouffer, et al., 1950). In this pioneer statement, Suchman (pp. 213–277) presents a detailed analysis of the relation of intensity to what he calls content. However, the "content" of Suchman's and subsequent investigations is equivalent to direction. Manifest content is always ignored. In the original research and its replications content is operationally defined by various metricizations of directional responses. Cantril (1946) recognized the difference between content and direction and attempted to establish formally "a distinction between the intensity of an attitude and its direction." His analysis, although using somewhat different research operations, is equivalent to Suchman's.

The basic mode of analysis is the cross-tabulation of subjects' intensity and directional responses. With a high order of regularity, the graphic rep-

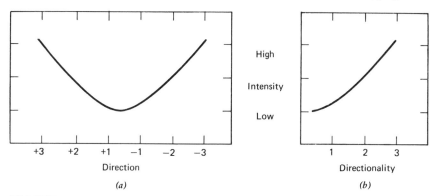

FIGURE 1.   Idealized curves of the direction-intensity and directionality-intensity relations.

resentation of this relation is manifest as a U- or slightly curtailed as a J-shaped curve. In idealized form this is presented in Figure 1*a*. This finding has been achieved in numerous replications (Stouffer, et al., 1950; McDill, 1959; Campbell, 1962; Komorita, 1963), and provides our first corollary of structure.

18.1.   Direction and intensity are associated in a U-shaped relation.

In applied form, although untested, this corollary seems tenable.

18a.*   The greater the favorability or unfavorability of stereotype assignments, the more strongly they will be accepted or rejected.

If we shift our focus from direction to directionality, this relation changes shape in an interesting manner. Directionality ignores the poles. Positive and negative are treated equally, and measurement is based on the magnitude of direction responses (i.e., the degree of favorableness-unfavorableness). Using a standard 6-point answer format, the two measures can be illustrated as follows:

Answer Option	Scoring for Direction	Scoring for Directionality
Strongly favorable	+3	3
Moderately favorable	+2	2
Slightly favorable	+1	1
Slightly unfavorable	−1	1
Moderately unfavorable	−2	2
Strongly unfavorable	−3	3

Insofar as the intensity-direction relation is U-shaped, it should be symmetrical. The intensity-directionality relation, then, should represent that U folded over, as seen in Figure 1*b*. This leads to the second corollary of structure.

18.2. Directionality and intensity manifest a monotonic relation expressed by a positively accelerated curve.

This corollary may be stated in applied form as follows.

18.2a.* As stereotype assignments become increasingly evaluative, they are accepted or rejected with greater intensity.

It appears from the earlier research that increases in the magnitude of direction responses occur at a slightly faster rate than increases in intensity. The two forms of the relationship displayed in Figure 1 are thus curvilinear. However, no empirical tests of this departure from a straight line have been attempted.

Direction, Directionality, and Salience

To explore the relations among these elements, Ehrlich and Van Tubergen (1971) constructed a 56-item Jewish stereotype checklist and a 69-item Atheist checklist. The checklists utilized a 7-point scale of salience, asking the respondent to indicate the degree to which each word applied to the target group. The subjects' responses were factor-analyzed, and the subjects were assigned to three directionally consistent Jewish types and two directionally consistent Atheists types (more about this later). These positive and negative types were then examined for their differences in salience. The major relevant findings, as hypothesized and confirmed, were that salience and direction are independent, but that as salience increases, directionality increases. In an independent replication of their work using a different research design (also reported in Ehrlich and Van Tubergen, (1971), the researchers failed to reconfirm their hypothesis. Positive stereotypes were found to be more salient than negative stereotypes.

Fishbein and Raven (1962) attempted to distinguish operationally between "belief" and "attitude." Using as their attitude objects racial prejudice, extrasensory perception, and atomic fallout, they had subjects respond on a 7-point semantic differential rating form to five adjective pairs defining belief and five pairs defining attitude. The belief pairs were probable-improbable, possible-impossible, likely-unlikely, existent-nonexistent, and true-false. Their operations for belief are highly congruent with our definition of salience. Further, they define attitude by adjective pairs which approximate our definition of direction: good-bad, sick-healthy, harmful-beneficial, wise-foolish, and clean-dirty. For all three attitude objects, they found, in our language, that salience scores were not significantly correlated with direction scores. In a subsequent experiment, reported in the same article, Fishbein and Raven demonstrated by means of a simple attitude change design that it was possible to independently manipulate direction and salience. These findings provide the next corollaries.

18.3.*   The salience of a belief is independent of its direction.

18.3a.*   There is no necessary relation between the degree to which an assigned stereotype is thought to characterize a target group and whether it represents a favorable or unfavorable evaluation of that target.

18.4*   As the salience of a belief increases, its directionality increases.

18.4a.*   The more an assigned stereotype is thought to characterize a target group, the more strongly it will be evaluated.

Direction and Centrality

There is no research that directly tests the relation between these elements. The basic question is this: Are the most central beliefs or disbeliefs that an individual holds about ethnic targets likely to be related to direction or to the magnitude of direction? It seems likely that direction is independent of centrality. Being a segregationist, for example, can be just as important to some people as being an integrationist can be to others. There seems to be meaningful hypothetical argument relating centrality to direction.

If directionality and centrality were independent, it would imply that a person's important beliefs need not be those that are directionally strongest, or, vice-versa, directionally strongest beliefs need not be those that are most important to a person. In this case the alternative hypothesis— directionality and centrality vary together so that important beliefs are more likely to be directionally strong—appears more cogent. Thus we have the following hypotheses.

18.5.*   The centrality of a belief is independent of its direction.

18.6.*   As the centrality of a belief increases, its directionality increases.

Intensity and Salience

In the replication study reported by Ehrlich and Van Tubergen (1971), the researchers had their subjects respond to four sets of Atheist stereotypes and three sets of Jewish stereotypes on a 5-point scale of salience and a 6-point scale of intensity. The rank correlations between these responses was positive and moderately high. For the Jewish stereotypes, the tau between intensity and salience was .70 ($p<.001$); for the Atheist stereotypes, it was .56 ($p<.001$). On the basis of these findings we may hypothesize further.

18.7.   As the salience of a belief increases, its intensity increases.

18.7a.   The more an assigned stereotype is thought to characterize a target group, the more intensely it will be accepted or rejected.

Intensity and Centrality

It follows from Corollaries 2 and 6 that the more central a belief, the more intensely it should be endorsed. One study provides empirical confirmation. Rokeach (1963) presented to 70 students 9 belief statements ranging in centrality from statements like "Death is inevitable" to "It is wrong to smoke." The subjects were asked to rank these statements in the order of which "they would be most reluctant to relinquish under any circumstance." The subjects were then asked to indicate how strongly they agreed with each of the statements. Although this mode of measuring centrality is not the most direct, the two arrays of response, centrality ranks and ranked intensity of agreement, correlated .73, $p<.05$ (computation from Rokeach's Table 1).

18.8.   As the centrality of a belief increases, its intensity increases.

18.8a.   The more important an assigned stereotype is, the more intensely it will be accepted or rejected.

Salience and Centrality

The alternative relationships are either (1) the importance of a belief is independent of the degree to which it characterizes a target or (2) the more characteristic a belief is, the more important it is. Since many highly salient characteristics of objects are also commonplace, the independence alternative seems more cogent.

18.9*   The centrality of a belief is independent of its salience.

It is manifest in this analysis that salience and centrality appear to be the major structural elements and that they appear to be independent of each other. However, very little research has been directed toward them; perhaps this analysis will establish their research priority. In contrast, directionality and intensity covary, and both are a function of salience and centrality. It may be that they are redundant.

Consider, then, that the early research on Likert scaling established that analytically and empirically derived weights for intensity were equivalent to arbitrary weights (Murphy and Likert, 1938; Rundquist and Sletto, 1936). This was a boon to early researchers. The use of arbitrary weights simplified the task of constructing summated rating scales. But from today's perspective we may well ask why empirical weights are not better. After all, the arbitrary weights merely assign a direction (agree-disagree), and usually two or three rank orders (e.g., in common practice, we find strong, moderate, slight).

Consider, second, that reducing intensity scales to direction scales produces almost equivalent forms. Korn and Giddan (1964) display a correlation of .94 between a 2-point and a 6-point answer format for the Dogmatism scale. Rokeach and Norrell (1966) report .92 for the Dogmatism scale, and .91 for the Gough Rigidity scale. Komorita (1963), using two 14-item forms of a measure of attitudes toward racial integration-segregation, established correlations of .97 and .96 between 2-point and 6-point versions of the two forms. In addition, using alternate forms of a measure of attitudes toward socialized medicine, Komorita reports the direction-intensity correlations to be .92 and .94.

Third, consider a more recondite factor Ehrlich (1964) compared the responses of two randomized groups of subjects on five sets of items. The contents of six items were unfavorable stereotypes of Jews; six more items comprised unfavorable stereotypes of Negroes; twelve items were stereotypic statements of policemen, six of which were favorable and six unfavorable. Srole's 5-item Anomia scale was also used. One group of subjects was presented with the standard 6-point response scale, while the second group was administered a 6-point scale augmented by separate "no opinion" and "can't decide" answer options.

One of the hypotheses being tested was that subjects who presumably had no opinion or who couldn't decide, when exposed to a forced response format, would choose those options showing the least intensity ($+1$ and -1 on a standard format). This hypothesis was not confirmed, and its disconfirmation strongly indicates that the basis of response was not intensity.

Peabody (1962) distinguished four scoring categories in order to examine the relation of direction to intensity (which he terms "extremeness"):

$$C \text{ (the composite score)} = PX - (1 - P) Y$$

where P is the proportion of responses in a positive direction, X is the mean intensity of positive responses, and Y is the mean intensity of negative responses.

He provides this example: "A subject makes 10 responses as follows: $+2$, $+2$, $+2$, $+2$, $+3$, $+1$, -1, -1, -2, -3. If the responses are scored as they stand, then $P = .60$, $X = 2.00$, $Y = 1.75$, and $C = +.50$" (p. 66).

Through a complex analysis of covariance, Peabody then attempted to determine the degree to which the composite score was determined by direction and/or intensity. Using a variety of scales and items (including the F-scale, the Dogmatism scale, a measure of conservative attitudes, anti-Jewish attitudes) the author administered his questionnaires to small specimen sets of 88 American and 75 English college students. His analysis indicated that 70–80% of the composite score variance was attributable to direction scores, 10% to intensity scores, and 10–20% involved the covariation of direction and intensity scores. The correlation of C scores with direction scores ranged across scales and subject groups from .87 to .97. The C scores range of correlations with the intensity of positive responses was .03 to .56, and with the intensity of negative responses it was −.06 to −.47.

These data, as the author indicates, provide justification for scoring scale items dichotomously, that is, by direction of response. With respect to intensity scores, Peabody suggests two hypotheses. First, that they may have some independent correlation with other forms of behavior, and thus be psychologically meaningful (cf. Berg, 1967). Second, he proposes that intensity scores may actually represent nothing more than the way people use response scales, that is, response error.

Consider, finally, an external criterion. The preceding arguments were concerned primarily with the operating characteristics of intensity scales. Does using an intensity scale lead to predictions different from those found using direction only? Korn and Giddan (1964) compared the correlations of the 2-point and 6-point Dogmatism scale with 5 independent measures. The maximum difference was .06. Rokeach and Norrell (1966) compared the correlations of 2- and 6-point versions of both the Dogmatism and Rigidity scale on 33 measures. The maximum difference was .08.

This evidence is not definitive. Indeed, so much is invested in scales of intensity that extensive and replicated efforts are demanded. For the moment we can say only that our standard intensity scales with their range from strong agreement to strong disagreement are equivalent to measures of direction and directionality. The intensity with which a belief statement is accepted or rejected may be a quasi-variable. It may, in fact, provide nothing more than an imperfect indicator of direction.

The principle of structure and its corollaries are focused on the interrelationships of the elements of beliefs and disbeliefs. Now we consider the organization of beliefs and disbeliefs, independent of their elemental properties.

19. *Principle of differentiation.* Belief/disbelief systems vary in their differentiation.

19a.   The number of stereotypes assigned to a target group varies by target.

Although this assertion is embarrassingly obvious, the degree of differentiation appears to be an important component of belief/disbelief systems. We shall see shortly the manner in which differentiation is systematically related to the elements of beliefs and disbeliefs. The next principle involves the directional organization of stereotypes. It was suggested by an early finding, derived from Gestalt psychology, that an individual's beliefs tend to be consistent in direction (Asch, Block, and Hertzman, 1938). It appears, in more contemporary dress, as Osgood and Tannenbaum's (1955) principle of maximal simplicity.

20. *Principle of elemental organization.* Sets of beliefs and disbeliefs are psychologically established in systemic relations and tend toward directional consistency.

20a.   The stereotypes assigned to a target group tend to be directionally consistent.

To say that a set of units is systemically related has three implications. First, it means that all of the units that comprise the system stand in some determinate relation to each other. The relations that obtain at any given time we generally talk of as the "state of the system." The second implication of this conceptual strategy is that any change involving any unit of the system has consequences for the entire system. Third, the state of a system is always in equilibrium (current attitude theorists talk of balance). Equilibrium or balance does not mean that systems are static and unchanging—this is a common misconception. Balance means, especially in the case of belief/disbelief systems, that as the state of the system changes, the orderly relations of its units are preserved.

The implications and significance for the study of prejudice of the principle of organization and its related corollaries are not well developed. They appear to have their most significant application in the analysis of attitude change.

In focusing on the description of ethnic imagery, most stereotype research has obscured the existence of directional consistency. The output of the descriptive research is typically a summary table pointing to the percentage of persons who, at some given time, assign a set of stereotypes to some ethnic target. Table 4 is a standard example. Even if you accept only the major assignments, say, those agreed to by 10% or more of the sampled persons, it is clear that even these are *not* directionally consistent.

The stereotype assignments viewed in such aggregate tables do not represent a test of the principle of directional organization. Aggregate tables are inconsistent primarily because they sum together consistent people whose consistency is in opposite directions. By means of illustration, consider that we have four people, each of whom holds three beliefs about a target group.

Person 1	Person 2	Person 3	Person 4
Reserved Ordinary Realistic	Reserved Dull Realistic	Radical Honest Realistic	Radical Brilliant Individualistic

Now individually each person holds a set of beliefs that is not too extreme in direction and is reasonably consistent. However, consider the difficulties of interpreting this summary:

Realistic. 75%
Radical. 50%
Reserved. 50%
Brilliant 25%
Dull 25%
Honest. 25%
Individualistic 25%
Ordinary. 25%

Of course, if we stick to describing the content of stereotypes and the degree of uniformity in stereotype assignments, then we can avoid the interpretive difficulties. However, earlier researchers, in trying to make sense of evaluative inconsistencies in aggregate stereotype assignments, assumed that these inconsistencies reflected the personality characteristics of prejudiced *persons* who are presumably able psychologically to endorse contradictory beliefs. This had led even some contemporary theorists to conceptualize prejudice as a rigidly endorsed set of beliefs (e.g., Allport, 1954; Cooper and McGaugh, 1963; Krech, Crutchfield, and Ballachey, 1962; Simpson and Yinger, 1965).

The directional consistency of stereotypes was demonstrated by Ehrlich and Van Tubergen (1971) by analytic procedures that had not previously been applied to the study of ethnic stereotypes. In the first of a series of replicated studies, they had their college student subjects respond to stereotype checklists with Jews and Atheists as targets. The checklists used a 7-point scale of salience, asking the respondent to indicate the degree to which each word applied to the target group. The analytic procedure, inverse factor analysis (Q), used the respondent, not the response, as the basic unit for generating a matrix of correlations. The results of the factored matrix are groups of subjects whose patterns of response are similar. The researchers found two groups of Atheist stereotypes, one positive and one negative, and three groups of Jewish stereotypes, two negative and one positive. In an independent replication study, this time using a procedure of paired comparisons, the researchers demonstrated that the directionally consistent stereotypes isolated in the first study could be reproduced by other methods of analysis.[8]

A further illustration of directional consistency can be observed in the report of Schuman and Harding (1964). In two samples, one of college students and the other of Boston residents, the researchers administered a questionnaire consisting of 48 pairs of generalizations about 7 target groups. The questionnaire design provided for separate scores by direction and by rationality: half the statements were favorable and half were unfavorable; half the statements were rational and half were irrational. The authors summarize their findings (and express their surprise at the occurrence of directional consistency) thus:

> The actual *anti-pro* correlations are negative in both samples, and quite strongly so: −.47 in the Boston sample, −.61 in the special college sample. In accordance with the classic view, most individuals high on the *anti* scale are low on the *pro* scale. But *not* in accord with the classic view is the finding that individuals low on the *anti* scale are *high* on the *pro* scale: those who reject irrational statements against ethnic groups tend to *accept* irrational statements in favor of ethnic groups. It is thus the dimension of favorableness-unfavorableness, not the dimension of rationality-irrationality, that mainly distinguishes among people in our samples (pp. 360–361).

In the two preceding studies, the directionality of stereotype assignments was inferred by the researchers rather than the subjects. The verification of the principle of directional consistency will require the further demonstration that the stereotypes assigned to a target tend to be directionally consistent *from the perspective of the subjects themselves*. The central issue in continued research concerns the manner in which evaluations are integrated into a belief-disbelief system.

At present there is an inordinate proliferation of models and theories that have been developed to explain how information about people is integrated into an individual's system of beliefs and disbeliefs. None of these have been tested in a context of study of ethnic stereotype assignments. A full discussion of the issues can be found in Abelson et al. (1968, Section IV, Part D); informative tests of some of the competing models appear in Anderson (1971) and Warr and Smith (1970).

The principle of directional consistency does not imply that people only form systems of univalent beliefs and disbeliefs. It does assert, however, that belief/disbelief systems tend toward univalence, and it implies that ambivalent systems are thus unstable. There can be no doubt that the dominant set of ethnic stereotypes uncovered in American research are negative (see Tables 1 and 2). It may be that negative information about persons and categories of people is a *culturally* or even *psychologically* stronger input than positive data.[9] In a laboratory study of impression formation Richey, McClelland, and Shimkunas (1967) provided limited evidence to suggest that when negative and positive information about a person are presented in equal amounts, the negative inputs dominate. Pastore (1960) in a questionnaire study tested the hypothesis that it is more difficult to change a disliked person into a liked person than it is to change a liked person into a disliked person. His questionnaire contained a capsule description of a hypothetical person who was attributed five traits. Half the subjects were presented with five favorable characteristics, and half were presented with five unfavorable characteristics. Subjects were then asked to rate the possibility, difficulty, and circumstances for the five traits changing to their opposite. For all the ratings, the subjects' responses significantly indicated that it is more difficult for a disliked than for a liked person to change. The hypothesis was thus confirmed and again suggests that negative characteristics may be more compelling than positive characteristics in stereotyping.

In two slightly varying studies, Irwin, Tripodi, and Bieri (1967) had their subjects rate persons they liked, felt neutral toward, or disliked. For the subjects of both studies they found that disliked persons elicited significantly greater response differentiation than liked persons. The authors propose a *vigilance* hypotheses:

> From an adaptive point of view, one could argue that the individual should differentiate more finely among negative, potentially threatening figures in his social environment so as to be able to isolate and identify these potentially dangerous individuals (p. 444).

Another confirmation of the vigilance hypotheses appears in Turner and Tripodi (1968). This hypothesis is clearly derivative from the cynicism and projectivity hypotheses of Adorno et al. (1950) in which the highly prejudiced person is presumed to view the world as a jungle in which men are basically evil and dangerous. And neither of these views are unlike the "sense of threat" hypotheses that appear thematically in current sociological writings including Blalock (1967), Blumer (1961), Pierson (1950), and Williams (1964).

The linkage of the structural elements to the two organizing principles can be accomplished in a relatively straightforward manner. From the preceding discussion we should expect that highly differentiated belief/disbelief systems would be characterized by beliefs and disbeliefs whose structural properties were of higher magnitude. The principle follows in its basic and applied forms.

20.1.   As a belief/disbelief system increases in differentiation, the magnitudes of direction, intensity, salience, and centrality of its component beliefs and disbeliefs will increase.

20.1a.   The more stereotypes a person assigns to a target group, the more these will be evaluative, intense, salient, and important to him.

Robb (1954) in his ethnographic survey of anti-Semitism in a London working-class suburb provides data indicating that intensity and differentiation follow the predicted pattern. Robb, however, suggests that qualitative changes also occur as intensity and differentiation increase:

There are some interesting changes in stereotype as one progresses from the more to the less anti-Semitic. Those who are rated [highest] for anti-Semitism are most inclined to accuse Jews of the more heinous crimes, of being firebugs, swindlers, warmongers, and traitors. They also state that Jews have too much political and economic power, occupy the best houses, are lazy, cowardly, selfish, and (surprisingly) great eaters of poultry. Physical appearance and personal habits are practically never mentioned, nor are speech, Communist affiliations, or qualities as employers. On the whole the description refers to matters well outside the realms of reality and the personal experience of the man concerned.

The stereotypes of the less anti-Semitic persons follow:

[They] are reasonable in the sense that some people (both Jewish and gentile) could easily be found to whom many of these descriptions would apply. Taken individually they are all well within the range of experience of the ordinary man and they lack that air of extravagant phantasy typical of the plottings and high life described [above] (pp. 98–100).

From the corollaries of structure it follows that directional consistency would increase as directionality, salience, intensity, and centrality increase.

20.2.   Increases in the directional consistency of a belief/disbelief system are a direct function of increases in the magnitudes of the direction, intensity, salience, and centrality of its component beliefs and disbeliefs.

20.2a.   The more evaluative, intense, salient, and important a set of stereotypes are to a person, the greater their directional consistency.

Only the relation between centrality and directional consistency has been empirically tested. Sherif and Hovland (1961) and Sherif and Sherif (1967) provide and summarize an extensive number of confirming replications.

Finally, it follows that increases in differentiation lead to increases in directional consistency. No empirical evidence is available.

20.3.* As a belief/disbelief system increases in differentiation, it increases in directional consistency.

20.3a.* The more stereotypes a person assigns to a target group, the greater their directional consistency.

The character of the relation between the social processes of stereotype assignment and stereotyping depicts in a fundamental sense the interdependency of the social psychological perspective on the sociological. From the standpoint of a social psychology of prejudice, we can never lose cognizance of the individual as a member of society. The stability or changing character of ethnic group relations, the distinctiveness, diffusion, and consensus on ethnic stereotype assignments are a part of the individual's social heritage. Even the structure of stereotypes—their direction, their intensity of expression, their presumed salience, and even, within limits, their centrality—are socially defined and regulated. The crucial problem is, of course, determining how the social processes of stereotype assignment affect the structure of stereotyping.

As much as contemporary social psychology has come to adopt the position that biological factors are necessary but not sufficient conditions for the determination of human behavior, so it should have adopted (and is moving toward) a societal analog. Biological structure and social structure provide the limits for human behavioral expressions, but neither is exclusively determinative of social behavior—except under conditions of pathology. This limiting strategem applied to the present concern leads to another principle.

20.4.* As consensus on the beliefs and disbeliefs associated with social objects increases in society, individual variability in their structural properties will decrease.

20.4a.* Increases in consensus on stereotype assignments result in the decreasing variability, across individuals, of direction, intensity, salience, and centrality responses.

Conversely, we might expect that as the magnitude of direction, intensity, salience, and centrality increases across people, consensus will increase.

20.5.*   As the magnitudes of the structural elements of beliefs and disbeliefs associated with a social object increase across people, consensus on these beliefs and disbeliefs will increase.

20.5a.*   Increases in the magnitude of the direction, intensity, salience, and centrality responses of people to ethnic targets will result in increasing consensus on stereotype assignment.

Although neither of these principles has received direct empirical test, they are easily testable, even with existing data. Operationally, we should be able to examine existing national surveys and observe that as the percentage of people who report specific beliefs and disbeliefs about an ethnic group increases over time, the variability of direction, intensity, salience, and centrality estimates should decrease. In the laboratory the manipulation of consensus is already an established technique, and it could be adapted easily for a test of this hypothesis.

These two principles together emphasize the reciprocal character of the sociological and social psychological study of prejudice. A third principle, also an hypothesis, displays a one-directional effect.

20.6.*   As the visibility of social objects in society increases, individual variability in the structural properties of beliefs and disbeliefs about these objects should decrease.

20.6a.*   As the visibility of ethnic groups increases, the variability of direction, intensity, salience, and centrality responses across individuals should decrease.

These three hypothesized principles are without empirical confirmation. They are, however, consistent with (although not directly implied by) other confirmed principles presented here. Although additional consistent statements could be adduced, these appear the most cogent and the most novel.

All of these principles adumbrate what is to come. In the following chapter, they are applied to the conative dimension of prejudice, behavioral intentions. Before we turn to that, a new order of problems should be considered.

THE MARGINALITY MECHANISMS

The principles of the social and the psychological processes of stereotype assignment apply equally to ethnic and nonethnic individuals, to minority group members and members of the dominant groups in society. People, however, unlike other objects of cognition, react to the beliefs and disbeliefs that others hold of them. Their own beliefs and disbeliefs are determined partly by their reactions. In turn, their reactions partly determine how they are cognized. Presumably this reciprocity is stable if ethnic group relations are stable, and changes with changing ethnic group relations. Certainly one of the findings that the neophyte student of prejudice finds most surprising is embodied in the first principle of marginality.

21. *Principle of ethnic group congruity*. The belief statements held by ethnic persons about ethnic targets other than their own are congruent with those consensually associated with those targets in society.

Thus we can see that Negroes' beliefs and disbeliefs about Jews are no different from those of white Christians about Jews. Similarly, the Jews' beliefs about Negroes differ little from those of other white Americans. Support for this has been well established for the major American minority groups and by a full range of research procedures (Bayton, 1941; Bayton and Byoune, 1947; Bayton, McAlister, and Hamer, 1956; Brink and Harris, 1964; Clarke, 1949; Marx, 1967; Meenes, 1943; Prothro and Jensen, 1952; Sappenfield, 1944; Sheppard, 1947; Simmons, 1961; Simpson, 1959; Sklare and Vosk, 1957; Williams, 1964; Vinacke, 1949).

Not only do ethnic persons develop a congruent set of beliefs and disbeliefs about other ethnic groups in society, they develop within their own subsociety a set of beliefs and disbeliefs about the majority group members themselves. These appear to be incongruent with majority self-imagery (although research here is sparse), but they do reflect the established intergroup relationship. The processes of stereotype assignment follow naturally the basic principles established.

21.1. *Corollary of reciprocity*. Within the ethnic subsociety the assignment of stereotypes to dominant group targets follow the principles of stereotype assignments (1–6).

In its full scope, the corollary has not been tested. Partial confirmation appears in Cothran (1951), Fichter (1958), Fishman (1955), McDaniel and Babchuk (1960), and in the materials cited in support of the basic principle of congruity. Cothran (1951) provides illustrative material, concluding from a content analysis of novels by Negro writers that "white characters are most frequently depicted unfavorably; that Negroes possess not only pejorative conceptions of white character traits, but also they categorize whites into 'social types' which likewise tend to be unfavorable; and that the unfavorable conceptions of white people are in effect counter-conceptions" (p. 256).

Clarke (1949) in an impressionistic analysis presents a graphic image of Jewish beliefs about Gentiles:

The nucleus of the stereotype *goy* is, of course, his omnipresent anti-semitism . . . it is his nature. . . . The Gentile family is a strained, loveless complex without devotion. . . . Children are spoiled with possessions and kept from achieving maturity . . . are precocious and well-mannered . . . dull and rude. The Gentile personality has a characteristic, stylish reserve. The Gentile does not often confide. . . . He is without curiosity about his friends. . . . He is decently mannered, stingy, fathomlessly hypocritical; he is inarticulate, humorless, and incapable of love. . . . In business [he] is unscrupulous in dealing with Jews, . . . slow-witted, conservative, and unimaginative. The Gentile drinks enormously, but without savor. . . . He sets a sparse, inept table. . . . He cannot relax, or spin out a pleasure. The Gentile feels that marriage with a Jew is an act of blood pollution . . . (pp. 547–548).

A second corollary has received almost no systematic research inquiry, although most of the materials cited above provide consistent supporting evidence. In the same manner that ethnic persons come to learn the stereotypes associated with other ethnic targets in society, so they come to learn the stereotypes assigned to themselves. Here a strong displacement effect occurs and the self-imagery of the target group shifts in a positive direction. One illustration can be found in a small-scale study by Johnsen (1969). Examining the mutual stereotype assignments of college females and males, the researcher observed that both sexes assigned more favorable stereotypes to themselves than they assigned to the opposite sex.

21.2. *Corollary of directional displacement.* The belief statements held by ethnic persons about their own group tend to be similar but more favorable than those held by others about them.

The final principle is based on the observation that minority persons tend to display lower levels of prejudice (on omnibus measures) than do majority persons.

22. *Principle of marginal perspective.* Marginal persons manifest more favorable stereotype assignments of other target groups than do the more socially integrated.

Only one study appears to involve a test of the effect of marginality on stereotyping. Using semantic differential ratings of the concepts White and Negro, Proenza and Strickland (1965) found that Negro college students were more favorable to the concept White than white college students were to the concept Negro. The principle is adequately tested in the context of behavioral intentions and social distance, and it will be discussed more fully then.

NOTES

1. Actually few scholars have proposed any formal definition of stereotype. In keeping with the word's etymology, however, most persons have emphasized the idea of a *rigidly* held set of beliefs. Whatever its etymologic virtues, this emphasis is conceptually inelegant and empirically false. For a brief statement on the origins of "stereotype" see Gordon (1962, pp. 3–6). The issue of rigidity and other mechanisms for the maintenance of prejudice are discussed in Chapter Five.

2. Negro subjects evaluated color names in the same manner as Caucasians, but their evaluations of color-person and ethnic concepts were different.

3. For a statement to qualify as a principle I have applied the following set of criteria: (1) It must be a generalization of comprehensive scope. (2) It must be verifiable. (3) It must be consistent with existing scientific knowledge and with the other principles to be adduced. Any statement that satisfies these criteria but lacks strong empirical support is marked with an asterisk (*); all other statements should be regarded as well-confirmed. The complete set of principles to be introduced are presented in summary form in the Conclusions of Chapter Five.

4. Intragroup stereotype assignments become more positive during intergroup conflict and less positive following conflict. This may reflect an increase in the mutual visibility of group members. See Principle 6.

5. "Ethclass" is defined as the conjunction of ethnicity and class (Gordon, 1964).

6. The discontinuity in the numbering of the principles is deliberate. New principles will be introduced in succeeding chapters. For those who want the full picture, see the conclusion to Chapter Five.

7. The research operations of importance appear to be (1) the structure of the answer format, checklist or open; (2) the number of targets; (3) the number of items on structured formats; (4) the response scale; and (5) the order of presentation. Discussions of these issues can be found in Anderson (1965), Anderson and Barrios (1961), Asch (1946), Beilin (1963), Bjerstedt (1960), Bruner, Shapiro, and Tagiuri (1958), Cahalan and Trager (1949), Duijker and Frijda (1961), Ehrlich and Rinehart (1965, 1966), Eysenck and Crown (1948), Haire and Grunes (1950), Kelley (1950), Luchins (1957), Reigrotski and Anderson (1959), Saenger and Flowerman (1954), Van Den Berghe (1966), and Wishner (1960).

8. The authors also obtained directionally clear results using the conventional, direct factor analytic procedure (*R*). Directional clarity appeared, too, in an earlier direct factor analytic study by Prothro and Keehn (1957) of German, Italian, and Turkish stereotype assignments. The direct analyses, as Ehrlich and Van Tubergen point out, mainly provide descriptions of ethnic imagery and do not facilitate subsequent data analysis, nor do they always correspond with inverse analyses.

9. Although I shall shortly propose an hypothesis suggesting the greater strength of negative beliefs, it will remain to be demonstrated that it is not a consequence of cultural and learned adaptations to a Western, urbanized environment.

Chapter Three

THE CONATIVE DIMENSIONS OF PREJUDICE

The conative or behavioral dimensions of prejudice have been traditionally subsumed under the label "social distance." The concept of social
distance was introduced by Park (1924), who described it as "the grades
and degrees of understanding and intimacy which characterize personal
and social relations generally" (p. 339). Bogardus (1925) operationalized
the concept in the following year, beginning an influential program of research that extends almost half a century (Bogardus, 1968). The original
social distance scale employed 39 ethnic targets and confronted each subject with this judgmental task:

> According to my first feeling reactions I would willingly admit members of
> each race (as a class, and not the best I have known, nor the worst members)
> to one or more of the classifications . . .
>   To close kinship by marriage
>   To my club as personal chums
>   To my street as neighbors
>   To employment in my occupation in my country
>   To citizenship in my country
>   As visitors only to my country
>   Would exclude from my country

Stimulated by this innovative and facile technique, social scientists have
applied the social distance scale or relatively minor variants to ethnic minorities, social classes, and occupational groups, among other social categories. Social distance research has generated approximately one new
scientific report a month since 1926.

Although most of the research that succeeded Bogardus' pioneering efforts labeled the most diverse operations as indicators of social distance,

Poole (1927) provided an early but neglected foundation for an important distinction:

It is necessary to distinguish between two kinds of distance which characterize association. The first may be called social distance, the degree of intimacy which group norms allow between any two individuals. Groups differentiate between individuals on the basis of race, age, sex, official position, nationality, etc. . . .

Persons seeking to satisfy their wishes strike up various degrees of intimacy with one another; these degrees of intimacy are personal distances in so far as they are free from the dictates of social norms and contain merely the element of individual welfare and satisfaction. These distances are popularly known by such terms as acquaintance, friendship, mutual understanding, speaking terms, Platonic love, etc. Personal distances are bounded only by the possibilities of association, the limits of intimacy. . . .

The relation between social distance and personal distance shows the often observed difference between the individual and the group, the part and the whole. As the group exists only in the individuals who make it, so social distance exists only in the degree of personal distance which it requires. As a result there can be no social distance where there is no personal distance (pp. 115–116).

Today we can distinguish at least four different phenomena that have been studied under the rubric of ethnic social distance:

1. *Manifest norms* of behavior—inferences of social distance derived from rates of actual behavior, for example, intermarriage rates or indices of residential segregation.

2. *Idealized norms* of behavior (values)—indicators of the expressed preference for specified modes of intergroup behavior such as, the desirability, in principle, of intermarriage or of open housing.

3. *Social norms* of behavior (social distance)—indicators of the expressed legitimacy and conventionality of specified modes of intergroup behavior, including the acceptability of intermarriage and the legitimacy of open housing.

4. *Personal norms* of behavior (personal distance)—indicators of the expressed intention to engage personally in specified modes of intergroup behavior, for example, would intermarry, would live in open housing.

The study of manifest norms falls properly in the study of intergroup behavior and does not concern us here. The study of idealized and social norms falls within the purview of social psychology, and represents the study of values and of social distance. As areas of inquiry they are undeveloped, and their relation to the behavioral component of ethnic attitudes remains to be established. (Studies of the idealized and social norms of behavior provide a minor semantic problem for the student of prejudice since both are often described as studies of social distance. Worse still is the fact that most studies called social distance are really studies of personal distance.)

The understanding of the regulation of social and personal distance in intergroup and interpersonal behavior requires, in part, a theory of norms, but none is available. Although there are many schemes for the classification and study of norms, most have been developed as general schemes, and—perhaps because of their lack of concern with content—appear inapplicable to our domain of inquiry. Particularly provocative schemes can be found in the writing of Anderson and Moore (1957), Gibbs (1965), and Wright (1963).

Failure to develop an adequate conceptualization of the norms of intergroup behavior has resulted in a conspicuous production of unrelated research. The problem of analysis encountered here is not new in form. It is really a problem of failing to establish and consistently work within a single domain of inquiry. In content, the major problem is that of distinguishing social norms of behavior from personal intentions to behave in some specified manner. These general norms of behavior traditionally have been designated in the literature as *social distance*, and this convention is followed here. Behavioral intentions, the conative component of attitudes, are referred to in this context, again in keeping with conventional use, as *personal distance*.

Whatever the relation between norms of behavior and personal intentions to behave, that is, between social distance and personal distance, these represent two distinct components of prejudice and intergroup behavior. Blurring this distinction (usually by calling everything social distance) makes it difficult for us to interpret and build cumulatively on past research and analysis.

Although the study of stereotypes is almost fully an American enterprise, the study of social distance is so ethnically rich, and the findings so consistent, that a strong claim can be made for their cross-cultural generality. Specimen groups have been studied in every major American city and have included the major American ethnic groups as well. Outside the United States, specimen groups have been drawn from Armenia, Australia, Belgium, Canada, Egypt, Ethiopia, Finland, Germany, Great Britain, Greece, India, Iraq, Italy, Japan, Jordan, Kenya, Lebanon, The Netherlands, New Zealand, Pakistan, The Philippines, South Africa, Spain, Sweden, Switzerland, Syria, Tanzania, Thailand, Turkey, and Uganda.

NORMS OF SOCIAL DISTANCE

Two propositions summarize the major data concerning the norms of prejudice. The first proposition is really the obverse of the principle of distinction.

Behavioral norms are directed toward persons associated with the major social categories in a community or society. In Western, industrialized societies these categories are age, sex, race, class (occupation, education, income), religion, nationality, ideology (particularly political, economic, and religious beliefs), and some aspects of personal appearance and interpersonal qualities.

Brooks (1936) was perhaps the first to explore systematically the effect of changing a property of the target on the distance displayed toward the target. On separate test administrations, subjects were asked to complete a modified Bogardus scale indicating their distance (from intermarriage through exclusion from citizenship) for 12 ethnic groups. Alternative ratings were made for each of the 12 groups, with one modification being that the group be considered as having a college education and the other being that the group be considered as having a sixth-grade education or less. The results indicated that education had a clear, though not very strong, effect on social distance. Six of the 12 groups changed their distance rank, and two groups shifted one scale point on this 6-point scale of distance.

Just (1954), in a subsequent demonstration of this principle, examined the social distance responses of a specimen set of 1713 American Mennonite secondary school and college students. Three modified social distance scales were used. One measured distance toward 30 nationality groups; the second toward 34 non-Mennonite religious groups; and the third toward 26 Mennonite groups. A comparative analysis of scale results indicated that religion was a more important determinant of distance than was nationality for American Mennonites.

The most systematic research here was produced in the program of Triandis and his associates. Triandis and Triandis (1960) began with a novel social distance scale using 16 stimulus-person constructs. The 16 people were chosen so that they had characteristics consisting of combinations of one of two characteristics of race (Negro-white), occupation (high prestige or low prestige), religion (same as the subject or different from that of the subject), and nationality (with high-low social distance from Bogardus' studies). For instance, one of the stimuli was, "A portuguese Negro physician of the same religion as you"; another was, "A white Swedish truck driver of a different religion." The stimuli were chosen according to a factorial design; this permitted the estimation of the percentage of the total variance in social distance scores controlled by each of the characteristics (race, occupation, religion, nationality).

The results of this study indicated that about 77% of the variance in the social distance scores was accounted for by race, about 17% by occupation, 5% by religion, and 1% by nationality. The subjects for the study were American college students.

In their subsequent research, using the categories of race, occupation, religion, and nationality in studies conducted in the United States, Germany, Japan, and Greece, Triandis and Triandis (1965) reported striking differences in the importance of these categories as determinants of social distance. This can be seen in the following summary of their data:

Rank Importance for Social Distance

	Race	Occupation	Religion	Nationality
Americans	1	2	3	4
Germans	3	1	2	4
Japanese	2	1	4	3
Greeks	2	3	1	4

Variations in the societal importance of these social categories is apparent. In Greece, the major emphasis was placed on religion, followed by race and occupation. In Germany, the major concern was on occupation, followed by religion, race, and nationality. In Japan, the emphasis was again on occupation, although it was much less than in Germany, and the next most important factor, race, was much more important than in Germany. In the United States, where Triandis and his associates conducted five replications, the most potent factor in personal distance was race, followed by occupation, religion, and nationality. Ames and Sakuma (1969), in a factor analysis of Bogardus' 1966 national data, also report that race appears as the strongest determinant of personal distance.

Although these findings are of limited generality, they do serve to illustrate this proposition quite well. The full range of social categories would probably look something like this:

Ethnic distance
    Race
    National origin

Nationality
Regionality
Socioeconomic distance
    Age
    Sex
    Education
    Occupation
    Class
Belief distance
    Religious beliefs
    Political beliefs
    Other beliefs
Interpersonal distance
    Physical qualities
    Interpersonal competence
    Level of reciprocal interaction

Almost all researchers in this area have based their efforts on a common presumptive framework which may prove misleading. One major presumption has been the prior selection of target groups and persons. In almost all formal social distance research the investigator has provided the subject with a list of targets; these have been primarily ethnic targets—distinguishable by nationality, national origin, race, region, and religion.

There are at least three problems of differing seriousness that may be concomitant with this procedure of research. First, *inadequate* forced response format prejudice questionnaires probably increase the level of instrument error and result in the increased rejection of others (Ehrlich, 1962a). Second, the relevance of ethnicity for interpersonal or intergroup behavior is strongly variable by person and across situations. Third, if target characteristics other than ethnicity are important, and/or they are important in qualitatively different ways, then generalizations based on the study of ethnic social distance may be highly limited in scope.

To adequately study behavioral intentions, the investigator must identify those persons and social categories which are phenomenally *relevant* for the actor. The basic problems are to determine (1) who the others are that actors conceive as targets for different types of behavior and (2) the factors that influence this differential selection of targets. The investigation of these problems is a major research priority since the framework of past research has so distorted them.

As a means toward the resolution of this problem, Table 1 presents a coding scheme for the analysis of targets of personal distance. It follows, in part, the stereotype scheme presented in Chapter Two. In a preliminary test of this coding procedure, Ehrlich (unpublished ms., 1969) administered open-ended questionnaires to a specimen sample of 97 undergraduates at the University of Iowa. The questions elicited their targets of categorical rejection and intimate acceptance ("With what kinds of persons could you possibly engage in the behaviors listed above?" One listing was the couplet "look down upon, be prejudiced against"; the other listing was, "date seriously, fall in love with.") Subjects were asked to "write in as many types, categories, or groups of persons" with whom they "probably could" and with whom they "probably could not" do this. Responses were coded by the scheme presented in Table 1.

TABLE 1. A SCHEME FOR THE CLASSIFICATION OF TARGETS OF PERSONAL-SOCIAL DISTANCE

1. *Socioeconomic Categories.* All words referring to the target person's socioeconomic characteristics (income, education, economic status, occupation, residence, social class).
2. *Ethnic Categories.* The major set of words to be coded here are those referring to the target's ethnic characteristics (nationality, national origin, region, race, religion). Included within this set are ethclass designations, ethnophaulisms, and "minority group" designations. A second set of words to be coded here are those referring to "background" similarity or dissimilarity.
3. *Social, Political, and Moral Deviant Categories.* All words which primarily distinguish the target person as a social, political, or moral deviant in contrast with distinguishing him on his socioeconomic or ethnic distinctiveness.
   a. *Political Deviant Categories.* All words which primarily distinguish the target person as a political deviant in contrast with distinguishing him or her on the basis of socioeconomic or ethnic distinctiveness.
   b. *Moral Deviant Categories.* All words which primarily distinguish the target person as a moral deviant in contrast with distinguishing him or her on the basis of socioeconomic or ethnic distinctiveness.
   c. *Other Deviant Categories.* All words which primarily distinguish the target person as a social deviant in contrast with distinguishing him or her on the basis of socioeconomic or ethnic distinctiveness.
4. *Other Social Categories.* All words which primarily distinguish the target person by *social location* rather than by socioeconomic, ethnic, or deviant characteristics. Types of social locations include kinship networks, interpersonal (friendship) networks, membership in voluntary or formal organizations, or membership in ostensive groups (e.g., sports-car lovers, social climbers, married persons).

5. *Physical Qualities.* All words referring to the physical qualities of the target person are coded here. Three physical qualities are classified.

Type 1 refers to directly visible and external physical characteristics such as color, physique, physiognomy, and age.

Type 2 refers to physical qualities which are visible only in behavior, such as athletic ability.

Type 3 words refer to a present physical state, such as clean or dirty.

6. *Positive Relational Qualities.* Words coded here are those which denote the target person's positive interpersonal qualities independent of his or her physical or categorical (socioeconomic, ethnic, deviant, or other) characteristics. Six types of words are coded here.

Type 1 words depict the target person as familiar or no different from others.

Type 2 words emphasize those characteristics which make the target person a desirable and attractive interpersonal partner.

Type 3 words are those that depict the target person's moral qualities, such as sincere, self-directed, or principled.

Type 4 words depict the substantiality of the target person—as possessing the qualities of industry, persistence, and direction.

Type 5 words denote the intellectual abilities and capacities for realistic and creative behavior of the target person.

Type 6 words describe the target person in terms of his artistic ability or appreciation, or his excellence in taste as generally associated with the quality of being cultured.

7. *Negative Relational Qualities.* Words coded here denote the target person's negative interpersonal qualities independent of his or her physical or categorical (socioeconomic, ethnic, deviant, or other) characteristics. Eight types of words are coded here.

Type 1 words depict the target person as being strange or alien as opposed to familiar and native.

Type 2 words emphasize the seclusion, ethnocentrism, and arrogance of the target person.

Type 3 words describe the target as embittered and disillusioned.

Type 4 words emphasize those characteristics which make the target person an undesirable and unattractive interpersonal partner.

Type 5 words depict the target person's moral qualities as immoral, deceptive, or unprincipled.

Type 6 words depict the unsubstantiality of the target person, for example, capricious, unreliable, unindustrious, and without direction.

Type 7 words denote the intellectual deficits, ignorance, or naivete of the target person.

Type 8 words depict the target person as uncultured.

8. *Cannot Classify.*

The 97 respondents listed a total of 1537 targets for these two situations. It was possible to classify all but 16 of these responses into one of the seven substantive categories. In these data, interpersonal qualities predominated as a stated basis for the rejection or acceptance of intimate behavior. In contrast, ethnic status appeared to be a slightly more important determinant of rejection than of acceptance. These initial data indicated, moreover, that ethnicity is used by college students as a stated basis for rejection of both prejudice and intimacy more often than for acceptance of these intentions. Further, the range of targets given by respondents suggested that persons may differ considerably among themselves in the manner in which they characteristically classify others.

This provisional research appears promising and illustrates the need for a more microscopic perspective on the objects of personal distance.

The second proposition summarizing our knowledge of the norms of prejudice may also be construed as an obverse of the principle of distinction.

Social norms and behavioral intentions appear to be organized around classes of behavior that are societally defined as important. These behavioral classes probably are intimate (marital) acceptance, friendship acceptance, positional acceptance, rejection-hostility, and (possibly) emotional expression, the management of physical distance, and the management of self-disclosure.

In the first attempt at analyzing classes of behavior, Westie (1952, 1953) distinguished, on an a priori basis, four components of social distance and devised appropriate scales for their measurement:

1. Residential Distance, the degree of residential proximity the respondent will permit a target group.

2. Position Distance, the extent to which the respondent is willing to have target group members occupy positions of prestige and power in the community.

3. Interpersonal-Physical Distance, the degree to which respondents are averse to physical association with target group members or with physical objects with which they have been in contact.

4. Interpersonal-Social Distance, the degree of proximity permitted in interpersonal interaction.

The items ranged from casual interpersonal contacts to intimate friendship.

The major attitude-objects for each scale were target persons in eight different occupations: doctor, lawyer, big-business executive, banker, owner-manager of a small store, bookkeeper, machine operator, and ditch digger. In the first study the target group was Negro and the subjects were white (Westie, 1952). In the second study, whites were the target group and Negroes the subjects (Westie and Howard, 1954).

The findings of both studies were similar and both established the contingency of personal and social distance on the classes of behavior being examined. (An important determinant of distance, which will be discussed later, was the relative status difference between subject and target.)

Despite this lead, and probably because Westie himself focused on status rather than on the components of prejudice, it was not until 10 years later that Triandis (1964) demonstrated the multidimensionality of the conative component of ethnic attitudes. In the initial study, Triandis introduced the technique he called the "behavioral differential." The basic elements that define this procedure are the variations that characterize the stimulus (target) persons and the stimulus behaviors. Subjects are asked to respond by indicating what behaviors they are likely or unlikely to engage in with stimulus persons. A sample format for an item is:

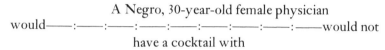

A Negro, 30-year-old female physician
would——:——:——:——:——:——:——:——:——would not
have a cocktail with

In the first study, stimulus persons were judged against two samples of 31 behaviors. Through a series of factor analyses, Triandis isolated five factors. Since that initial study, Triandis and his associates (1967) have produced substantial, replicated evidence to support the conclusions, among other major findings, that social distance is comprised of at least three and possibly seven organized components. These behavior classes can be fairly easily labeled. The most stable appear to be intimate acceptance, friendship, positional acceptance, and categorical rejection.

Intimate acceptance appears to be defined by such behaviors as readiness to love, fall in love with, date seriously, physically love, marry. *Friendship acceptance* is defined by willingness to be partners with, eat with, gossip with, permit to do one a favor, teach, be on a first name basis, accept as an intimate friend, and so on. *Positional acceptance* appears to be defined by willingness to obey, ask an opinion of, be commanded by, invite to one's club, not treat as a subordinate, depend upon, enjoy meeting, praise, admire, elect to political office, and the like. Finally, *categorical rejection* is defined by intention to exclude from one's neighborhood, prohibit from voting, not invite to one's club, not accept as a close kin, hate, look down upon, avoid, be an enemy of, and so on.

Through his cross-cultural and programmatic research, Triandis not only established the existence of classes of behavioral intentions, but the fact that the number of classes changes with the society and, to a lesser degree, with the personality characteristics of individuals. Methodologically, his work also reaffirmed the sensitivity of such research to sampling procedures. Changes in the content and number of behaviors, targets, and target characteristics presented usually yielded somewhat different factor structures.

The full implications of construing social distance and behavioral intentions as multidimensional remain to be assayed.

THE DETERMINANTS OF SOCIAL DISTANCE NORMS

Norms represent a special class of beliefs. By conventional definition, norms are beliefs about appropriate or acceptable behavior. It should come as no surprise, then, that the basic principles of cognition that were introduced in the preceding chapter appear here with the same priority.

1. *Principle of distinction.* Social objects are distinguishable on the basis of the belief statements associated with them.

2. *Principle of diffusion.* Belief statements about social objects are widely diffused in a society.

3. *Principle of consensus.* There is high consensus on the belief statements associated with specific social objects.

The transposition of these general principles into specific statements about norms of ethnic distance can be made with the same facility displayed earlier.

1a. Norms of behavior concerning the major ethnic groups in society are relatively distinct and exclusive.

2a. Knowledge of the norms associated with the major ethnic groups in American society is highly diffused.

3a. There is high consensus on the norms associated with specific ethnic groups.

Support for these principles can be found in virtually every study in which two or more ethnic targets were represented. The evidence for these principles, however, is more inferential than direct. It may be that norms of ethnic distance are not as distinctive or as diffused as are ethnic stereotypes. Levels of consensus appear quite high, and recent examples can be seen in Williams (1964), Glock and Stark (1966), Marx (1967), Ringer (1967), and Lever (1968). Summary materials relative to all three principles appear in Stember (1966) and Schwartz (1967).

2b.   The primary contexts for the diffusion of knowledge of distance norms, and for the legitimation of such knowledge, are the family and the school.

2c.   Norms of social distance are copied in the mass media of communication and the media of mass education.

No research has been directed to the contexts in which knowledge of distance norms is diffused among adults, and the children's socialization data which do provide confirming evidence will not be presented until Chapter 5.

Studies in serious literature, popular fiction, movies, television, and of the educational media, which so densely populate the literature of stereotypes, are rare in this domain. Since norms of behavior are seldom displayed directly in the mass media today, they are less readily observable. Barcus and Levin (1966) provide the first major content analysis of social distance since Berelson and Salter (1946). The researchers sampled short stories from "majority-oriented" and "Negro-oriented" magazines published in 1964 and 1965. Their story sample was drawn from *Saturday Evening Post, Ladies' Home Journal, McCall's Playboy, True, Negro Digest, Bronze America,* and *Elegant.* Each role relation depicted in the story (e.g., engaged couple, neighbor-neighbor, employer-employee, customer-customer) was coded on an 8-point scale of social distance ranging from a score of 1 for intimate distance (husband-wife) to a score of 8 for a relationship of subordination (servant-master). Their basic findings are:

	Median Distance	
	Majority Fiction	Negro Fiction
Ingroup distance	1.4	1.5
Intergroup distance	4.0	4.2

It is clear that ingroup and intergroup distances are as well established in the fiction of society as in the structure of society.

Even pictorial illustrations may assert normative patterns. Cox (1970) analyzed the occupational placements of Negroes appearing in advertisements in six general, mass-circulating magazines in 1967–1968. In all, Cox examined over 12,000 ads; approximately 2% pictured identifiable Negro persons. Comparing the occupational statuses of the Negro and white persons pictured, and comparing his data with those reported by Shuey, King, and Griffith (1953) for 1949–1950 magazines, Cox displays a not unexpected pattern of results:

	Negro		White	
Occupational Category	1949–1950	1967–1968	1949–1950	1967–1968
Skilled	6%	71%	93%	97%
Unskilled	94	29	7	3

Flora (1971) analyzed male-female behavior in the short stories of two working-class-oriented women's magazines (*True Story* and *Modern Romances*) and two middle class-oriented women's magazines (*Redbook* and *Cosmopolitan*). As in the case of majority-minority relations, the relations of men and women were depicted with women being socially acceptably passive. Female dependence was seen as desirable in 51% of the middle-class and 30% of the working-class stories. Female dependence and passivity were the focus of the story line in 69% of all of the stories. The resolution of the plot in the majority of the stories involved the female "achieving" her proper dependent status, affirming or reaffirming her subordinate position.

In a study concerned with the analysis of educational media, Gordon and Shankweiler (1971) investigated the content of the 18 best-selling marriage manuals, 1950–1970, as they dealt with sexual behavior. Male dominance was the primary prescription for adjustment.

2d.* The greater the distinctiveness of social distance norms, the greater their diffusion in society.

3b.* The greater the distinctiveness of social distance norms, the greater the consensus concerning them.

3c.* The greater the diffusion of social distance norms, the greater the consensus concerning them.

Every class of behavioral norms may vary in distinctiveness and exclusivity of assignment. Norms of categorical rejection or of intimate acceptance, for example, are probably more distinctive than are those norms involving matters of more casual or routinized relations. These norms may, therefore, be hypothesized to display greater diffusion. No present data exist to test these hypotheses or the implications of distinctiveness and diffusion for increasing consensus.

The following principles summarize the existing knowledge of stability and change in norms of ethnic distance.

4. *Principle of stability*. Belief statements associated with social objects are highly stable.

4a. Norms of social distance are relatively stable historically within and across societies.

5. *Principle of change.* Belief statements associated with social objects change as the relation of people to the objects changes.

5a.   Changes in social distance norms follow changes in established ethnic group relations.

Inspection of Bogardus' data from 1926 to 1966 provides a fascinating view of the stability and pattern of change characterizing American ethnic relations. Table 2 presents all ethnic groups used by Bogardus in each of the four time periods studied. Table 3 presents a more quantitative view of the changes displayed in Table 2.

TABLE 2.   SOCIAL DISTANCE RANKS OF AMERICANS, 1926–1966

Target Group	1926	1946	1956	1966
English	1.0	3.0	3.0	2.0
Americans (U.S., white)	2.0	1.0	1.0	1.0
Canadians	3.5	2.0	2.0	3.0
Scots	3.5	5.0	7.0	9.0
Irish	5.0	4.0	5.0	5.0
French	6.0	6.0	4.0	4.0
Germans	7.0	10.0	8.0	10.5
Swedish	8.0	9.0	6.0	6.0
Hollanders	9.0	8.0	9.0	10.5
Norwegians	10.0	7.0	10.0	7.0
Spanish	11.0	15.0	14.0	14.0
Finns	12.0	11.0	11.0	12.0
Russians	13.0	13.0	22.0	22.0
Italians	14.0	16.0	12.0	8.0
Poles	15.0	14.0	13.0	16.0
Armenians	16.0	17.5	18.0	19.0
Czechs	17.0	12.0	17.0	17.0
Indians (Amer.)	18.0	20.0	19.0	18.0
Jews	19.0	19.0	16.0	15.0
Greeks	20.0	17.5	15.0	13.0
Mexicans	21.0	23.5	26.0	26.5
Japanese	22.0	28.0	24.0	23.0
Filipinos	23.0	22.0	20.0	20.0
Negroes	24.0	27.0	25.0	26.5
Turks	25.0	23.5	21.0	24.0
Chinese	26.0	21.0	23.0	21.0
Koreans	27.0	25.0	28.0	25.0
Indians (India)	28.0	26.0	27.0	28.0

Source. Adapted from Bogardus (1958, 1966).

The pervasiveness of social distance norms can be seen clearly in the stability of the rankings across all four time periods. The extremely high correlations that assess the magnitude of these rankings provide strong confirmation for the principle of stability. The rank correlations, all greater than .92, are presented in the top half of Table 3.

TABLE 3. THE DISTRIBUTION AND
INTERCORRELATIONS OF AMERICAN
SOCIAL DISTANCE RANKS 1926–1966

	Mean	Median	Range of Scores		
			Low	High	Spread
1926	2.14	1.94	1.06	3.91	2.85
1946	2.12	1.94	1.04	3.61	2.57
1956	2.08	2.09	1.08	2.83	1.75
1966	1.92	1.98	1.07	2.62	1.56

	Rank Correlations			
	1926	1946	1956	1966
1926	—	.95	.94	.92
1946		—	.96	.92
1956			—	.98

Source. Adapted from Bogardus (1958, 1966).

The bottom half of Table 3 adds another perspective. Whereas the targets of social distance norms have remained in a highly stable order, the directionality of the distance responses displays considerable curtailment. Mean social distance response has decreased slightly while the range of rejection has decreased sharply.

Two other views of time changes in the magnitude of rejection that characterizes American ethnic relations can be found in two reviews of national survey materials. Schwartz (1967) extrapolated from the earlier survey results the approximate year in which 90% of the white population could be expected to accept associative norms of social distance toward Negroes. The extrapolations were based on the assumption that the rate of change observed in past surveys would be constant. Her results indicate the relative slowness of change. For example, the acceptance of integrated schools by 90% is dated 1981, and the willingness to live next door to a Negro is dated 1986. Stember (1966) presents a review of national survey data on Jewish social distance from 1938 to 1962. Figure 1

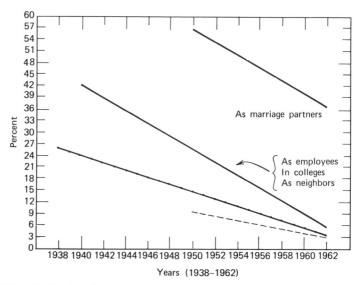

FIGURE 1.   Rejection of Jews, 1938 to 1962. (Adapted from Stember, 1966.)

reproduces the trend lines displayed in his review. These data provide a picture of rather rapid change, and these changes in norms appear to follow the pace of Jewish mobility in American society (cf. Gutman, 1966).

Other supporting evidence from American studies can be found in Glock and Stark (1966), Marx (1967), Prothro and Miles (1953), and Ringer (1967). Confirmation can also be found in longitudinal data from South Africa and the Arabian countries. Lever (1968), comparing his 1964 social distance ranks with those almost 30 years earlier (MacCrone, 1937, 1938), reports a correlation of .91 for English-speaking subjects, .94 for Afrikaans-speaking South Africans, and .90 for Jewish South Africans. Prothro and Melikian (1952), with a sample of mainly Christian Lebanese college students (from the American University of Beirut), found that nationality was a more important determinant of their social distance responses than religion. Dodd's (1935) earlier study of a sample of Arab Near Eastern students found the reverse, that is, that religious group membership was more important than nationality as a determinant of social distance. This change over the 18 years that intervened between the two studies highlights a new facet of our principle of change by pointing to changing criteria for the categorization of targets. As the Arab countries became more concerned with their national identities and international relations, so nationality became the primary basis for the codification of people (see also Brown, 1969).

Although neither the causes nor the consequences of ethnic group visibility has been established vigorously, it does seem that here, as in the case of stereotype assignment, visibility is of major significance. The principles of visibility follow.

6. *Principle of visibility*. Under conditions of stability, the greater the visibility of social objects, the greater the distinctiveness, diffusion, and consensus of belief statements associated with the object.

6a.   Under conditions of stable group relations the greater the visibility of an ethnic group, the greater the distinctiveness, diffusion, and consensus on social distance norms.

6.1. *Principle of visibility*. Under conditions of change, social objects become temporarily more visible.

6.1a.   Under conditions of change, ethnic groups become temporarily more visible.

The principle of visibility asserts only that increases in visibility will result in a greater polarization of social distance, that is, in greater distinctiveness, diffusion, and consensus on norms of social distance. The direction of polarization cannot be explained by changes in visibility, nor does it seem likely that changes in visibility can determine direction.

Visibility is generally inferred from some relational aspect or property of ethnic groups such as size, physical distinctiveness, spatial distance, or accessibility. In American society, for example, social distance norms appear much more confined by social location than do stereotypes. The variations in location affecting distance, quite independent of the target, appear to be region of the country and socioeconomic status. Regionality appears to be a direct indicator of size and distribution of ethnic populations in the United States. The highly distinctive locations, through 1960, of Jews (northern, particularly northeastern, and almost exclusively urban) and Negroes (primarily rural and southern) has provided a quasi-experimental context for testing visibility hypotheses. (These locational differences have changed and are still changing.)

Perhaps the first report of regional differentiation in Jewish social distance was made by Harlan (1942). Using as a measure of social distance the subject's approval or disapproval of 12 incidents involving anti-Jewish behavior (e.g., admission to medical school, interreligious dating, fraternities, college quotas, student voting, social clubs, roommates), Harlan found that Southern students displayed lower social distance than did Northern students. Further, Harlan reported that rural and small-town subjects displayed lower social distance toward Jews than did urban and metropolitan subjects. In contrast, subjects with parents in business and professional occupations displayed higher social distance toward Jews than did subjects whose parents were skilled or clerical workers or farmers. Thus the relatively lower visibility of Jews in the South and in rural and small-town settings appears to lead to a lower diffusion and lower consensus on distance norms; in contrast, the greater accessibility of Jews in business and professional occupations appears to lead to greater diffusion and consensus. A related finding with a sample of Louisiana white adults is presented by Prothro (1952), who reported the occurrence of very high social distance toward Negroes with low social distance toward Jews.

Pettigrew (1959) compared the responses of Northern (New England) and Southern (North Carolina and Georgia) white samples on a Negro social distance scale. Southern subjects displayed significantly greater social distance. In a further analysis, he compared social distance scores of those who lived in the two low Negro percentage towns sampled with those living in high Negro percentage communities. As expected, whites living in high Negro percentage communities displayed greater social distance.

Generally confirming evidence of the effects of region and size on social distance can also be found in Kelly, Ferson, and Holtzman (1958) and Williams (1964). Research demonstrating the effects of size on manifest norms of behavior are redundant, and Blalock (1967, Chapter 5) reviews much of this research. Ehrlich (1962b) provides a unique test using anti-Jewish behavior as the dependent variable.

In general, higher socioeconomic status entails slightly lower levels of the acceptance of negative stereotypes and a greater likelihood of positional acceptance (but not intimate acceptance). There are no data relating affective responses to socioeconomic status, and I would expect there to be no general relationship. To assert, then, that increases in socioeconomic status have any major effect on levels of prejudice is a serious overstatement. The present focus on relative, rather than absolute, status differences is based on the assumption that absolute status is of minor significance. Status, as an index of position within a social structure, becomes significant in the study of prejudice only when we consider the relative status arrangements.[1]

Accessibility, as one indicator of visibility, can be inferred from status distance. The smaller the relative status distance, the greater the accessibility of persons; the greater the accessibility, the greater the visibility. (Whether accessibility makes an independent contribution to prejudice or is itself only an indicator of visibility is an open question. There are no data and the question warrants test.) Harlan's finding of a direct association between occupational status (of parents of students) and high social distance to Jews has been replicated and extended by Williams (1964). Williams, summarizing his case studies of several cities, concludes, "Persons who work in relatively high-status occupations tend to be more prejudiced toward Jews, whereas those in lower status occupations are the more likely to have feelings of social distance toward Negroes and Mexican-Americans" (p. 65).

Physical distance, which could be defined as a facet of accessibility, can also be operationally construed as an indicator of visibility. Physical distance (as manifest particularly by ecological barriers, or by residential or social segregation) may be the primary mechanism of the maintenance of the stability and diffusion of norms of intergroup behavior. In large measure, the manifestation of physical distance has been regulated by law, for example by community law in the case of residential segregation or by the constitutions of voluntary associations in the case of social segregation.

It is difficult to study the effects of physical distance on social distance since independent measures of the two variables are not readily available. In an extensive test involving 50 members in each of 10 tribes in Kenya, Uganda, and Tanzania, Brewer (1968) was able to operationalize physical distance as "the sharing of a common border." Thus she was able to compare four levels of physical distance (adjacent border, separation by one tribe, separation by two tribes, more remote) with the subjects' scores on a four-item scale of social distance. Adjacent outgroups were responded to with significantly lower social distance. The average intratribe correlation between physical and social distance was .54.

Willis (1966) performed a minor analysis of speaking distance (physical distance while standing and conducting a conversation), which suggested that with age and sex controlled, conversations between Negro and white were conducted at slightly greater speaking distances than were withingroup conversations.

Physical distinctiveness or dissimilarity should also increase visibility. Although no direct tests have been conducted, we can observe in Table 2 that the bottom quartile of ethnic groups through 1966 are those who depart most strikingly from the skin coloring and body builds of top quartile groups. On the bottom are Russians, Japanese, Turks, Koreans, Mexicans, Negroes, and Indians.

Finally, we should consider the effects of change and the assumption that almost any change in intergroup relations will increase the visibility of an ethnic group. Bogardus' data, as presented in Table 2, provide a particularly facile means for testing the principle of visibility. With the advent of World War II, we should expect to observe, in the 1946 ranks, increases in social distance for Germans, Italians, and Japanese. Following the war, as established group relations are resumed, social distance should decrease toward these groups. The reverse pattern should, of course, obtain for Russians. Similarly, we should expect the Korean War to have its manifestation in Table 2 by an increase in distance toward Koreans from 1946 to 1956 and decrease by the 1966 reading. All of these postfactum hypotheses are confirmed by the data of Table 2.

Two derivative principles remain to be introduced. Neither has received empirical test, but they are consistent with the available evidence.

4b.* The greater the distinctiveness, diffusion, and consensus on social distance norms, the greater the stability of these norms.

5b.* Changes in the established relations between ethnic groups will decrease the stability of distance norms and modify their distinctiveness and their levels of diffusion and consensus.

Finally, it seems likely that special properties of norms may be an important component of their polarization, that is, their increased distinctiveness, diffusion, and consensus, although this is still speculation. These properties may in fact be unique to behavioral norms and not generalizable to stereotypes or to norms concerning the display of affective reactions.

In an attempt at replicating the structures of behavioral intention isolated by Triandis, Ehrlich and Van Tubergen (1969) used two procedures of factor analysis. By the first procedure, similar to the original, they produced a successful replication. By the second procedure (Q-factor analysis), they failed to obtain comparable results. Instead of obtaining a structured set of intentions to behave, they obtained a structured set of behaviors that were distinguished by negative loadings—behaviors which their subjects intended *not* to perform. This analysis appeared to indicate that although the subjects were uncertain of the behaviors they probably would engage in, they were quite clear as to what behaviors they perceived as proscribed and so would not engage in. The researchers concluded with the hypothesis that proscriptive norms of intergroup behavior may display greater polarization than prescriptive norms. Prescriptive norms, they argued, may depend for their application on specific situational circumstances. Proscriptive norms, in contrast may be situationally bound, that is, they may be applicable in virtually all situations.

A direct test of this hypothesis, as well as the formulation of hypotheses relating the properties of norms to their social determinants, remain to be accomplished.

THE COGNITIVE BASIS OF PERSONAL DISTANCE

The assignment of ethnic group membership to a given individual usually precedes the development of a set of behavioral intentions directed toward that individual. Sometimes, of course, interpersonal relations develop before ethnic identity is clear. But this means that the individual was placed originally in the wrong category, and that without this error no relationship might have developed. A good illustration of this can be found in Mayer's (1961) study of Jewish-gentile intermarriage where the author shows that many persons who intermarried probably would not have begun dating had they been aware initially of their partner's ethnic identity. The general principle of categorical placement and its applied statement were introduced in Chapter 2.

7. *Principle of categorical placement.* The categorization of a social object is contingent on its codability.

7a. Ascribing ethnic group membership to an individual is contingent on the joint effects of that person's characteristics, the criteria of ethnic classification, his eligibility for other social categories, and the context in which he appears.

Once the placement has been made, a repertoire of behaviors is open to the actor. It seems likely that normative constraints on personal distance follow the same principle.

7b. If a person is assigned ethnic group membership, then personal distance will be contingent on the joint effects of the prevailing norms of intergroup behavior (social distance), the person's other characteristics, his eligibility for other social categories, and the situational context in which he appears.

Two studies illustrate the complexity of personal distance decisions. Shim and Dole (1967) provide evidence to indicate that physical disability (without two legs) is almost as important a determinant of personal distance as being Negro. More important than these placements (to their sample of Hawaiian college students) were the positive intellectual and relational characteristics of the stimulus persons being judged. Persons who lacked competence or empathy were more likely to be rejected than were disabled persons or Negroes on their omnibus scale of distance.

Long, Ziller, and Thompson (1966) presented 40 white male and 40 white female college students with 16 stimulus persons and asked that they estimate their likelihood of becoming close friends with them. They were told to assume that each person was the same sex as themselves and that they would be in close contact in their jobs. Likelihood ratings were made on a 6-point scale, and the stimulus persons were constructed from four factors of two values each: (1) race—Negro, white; (2) education —college graduate, grade school education; (3) health—healthy, chronically ill; (4) age—old, young.

Highest ratings for friendship acceptance were for the healthy, educated, white, young person, and these factors appeared to be important to the subjects in that order. Race, as a basis for same-sex friendship at work, was clearly less important than health and education. The relative effects of these characteristics, however, was a contextual matter. "If the stimulus person was a Negro, for example, whether or not he was educated, healthy, or young made less difference than did these qualities in relation to a white person. Likewise age, health, and race made more difference among the educated; education, age, and race among the healthy; and education, race, and health among the young" (p. 108).

The principle of categorical dominance and its corollary of categorical response illustrate the nature of the relation between social distance and personal distance. Neither of these has received any precise test, but both are consistent with (if not implied by) the existing literature.

8.   *Principle of categorical dominance.* If a social object is cast in a so-cial category, then initial response will be determined more on the basis of its categorical characteristics than its individual characteristics.

8a.   If a person is assigned ethnic membership, then the initial distance accorded him will be more on the basis of his ethnic membership than on his other characteristics.

8.1.   *Corollary of categorical response.* The less knowledge available about a social object, the greater the likelihood that it will be assigned the characteristics of its social category.

8.1a.   The less knowledge available about an ethnic person, the greater the likelihood that he will be responded to in accordance with the pre-vailing norms of social distance appropriate to his ethnic category.

Studies of personal distance have provided a coherent complex of find-ings that lead to the introduction of a new principle that was not sug-gested by the research on stereotype assignment.

12.   *Principle of categorical congruity.* The greater the perceived similarity between social object and the actor classifying it, the greater the likelihood it will be assigned the characteristics of the actor's own so-cial category.

12.1.   *Corollary of ethnic congruity.* The greater the perceived simi-larity between an ethnic person and the actor, the lower the personal dis-tance.

Rokeach (1960) postulated in his theory of cognitive structure that all beliefs are organized along a continuum of similarity-dissimilarity. Partly on the basis of this postulate he hypothesized that similarity and dissimi-larity of belief were the major determinants of the acceptance and rejection of others. In the first test of this hypothesis, Rokeach, Evans, and Smith

(1960) administered to 201 white northern and southern college students an experimentally designed questionnaire. Subjects were asked to respond on a 9-point scale ranging from "I can't see myself being friends with such a person" to "I can very easily see myself being friends with such a person" to three pairs of statements dealing with eight different beliefs. An example of one set of pairs follows:

> *Type R:* Race varied, belief held constant
> a. A white person who believes in God
>   1 2 3 4 5 6 7 8 9
> b. A Negro who believes in God
>   1 2 3 4 5 6 7 8 9
> *Type B:* Belief varied, race held constant
> a. A white person who believes in God
>   1 2 3 4 5 6 7 8 9
> b. A white person who is an atheist
>   1 2 3 4 5 6 7 8 9
> *Type RB:* Race varied, belief varied
> a. A white person who believes in God
>   1 2 3 4 5 6 7 8 9
> b. A Negro who is an atheist
>   1 2 3 4 5 6 7 8 9

Separate scores were computed for each subject on each of the eight issues. As one would expect, whites were preferred as friends over Negroes, and people who agree were preferred more often than those who do not. More important, however, was the finding that Negroes whose beliefs were congruent with the subject were preferred over whites whose beliefs were dissimilar. This was true for both northern and southern students.

In a second study, using Hebrew school students 7 to 16 years of age and a different set of belief statements, the rearchers replicated their basic finding that belief congruity was a more important determinant of friendship acceptance than ethnicity.

Additional replications varying subjects, targets, and measures of distance can be found in Anderson and Cote (1966), Insko and Robinson (1967), Rokeach and Mezei (1966), Rokeach (1968), and Smith, Williams, and Willis (1967).

In a different manner of demonstration of the effect of perceived similarity on social distance, Rokeach (1960) studied six groups of college students. Grouping was by religion (Catholic, Episcopalian, Presbyterian, Lutheran, Methodist, and Baptist), and the groups ranged in size from 26 to 166. Subjects were presented with the following mimeographed list:

Atheist
Baptist
Catholic
Episcopalian
Jewish
Lutheran
Methodist
Mohammedan
Presbyterian

Blank lines followed the list, and the subject was asked to write the name of his or her own religion on the first line, the name of the religion most similar to it on the second line, with the least similar religion being written on the last line. Subjects were also administered a five-item scale of personal distance which was repeated for each of the nine religions they ranked.

Following this procedure, the social distance scores were plotted against the similarity ranks for each of the six groups. The same results, a positively accelerated curve, were obtained for every group. As religions were perceived as increasingly dissimilar, the level of personal distance toward them increased.

In two studies, Smith, Williams, and Willis (1967) repeated the original design by Rokeach, Smith, and Evans (1960). One sample consisted of 119 white college student subjects, the other sample was of 167 Negro college students. Subjects responded to 192 pairs of statements constructed around eight beliefs and race and sex. Each of the statements was rated with the same 9-point scale of friendship acceptance-rejection used by Rokeach and his associates. The pairs were of six types:

Type R: Difference in race only
Type S: Difference in sex only
Type B: Difference in belief only
Type RB: Difference in both race and belief
Type SB: Difference in both sex and belief
Type RS: Difference in both race and sex

The basic finding that belief was a more important determinant of friendship choice than race was replicated for both samples. (There was one minor reversal.) This study added to our knowledge, however, the additional finding that sex was the least important of the determinants of friendship acceptance. Neither variations by sex of the stimulus person nor sex of the subject were important. Further, there were no significant interaction effects. That is, the sex of the stimulus person made only a negligible difference in the magnitude of preference for agreers over disagreers or in the magnitude of preference for Negroes over whites or whites over Negroes. Correlations in friendship acceptance of the two sexes, independent of race or belief, ranged in the middle and high .90s.

Byrne and his associates have conducted extensive research on the problem of belief congruity from a learning theory perspective. In his developing theory, Byrne has proposed that the perceived similarity and dissimilarity of categorical attributes may be conceptualized as interpersonal rewards and punishments. Thus each similar belief can be seen as rewarding, and each dissimilar belief is seen as punishing. In his first study, Byrne (1961) tested and confirmed his central hypothesis: a stranger known to have attitudes similar to one's own will be better liked than a stranger who does not.

The basic design of Byrne's research has three stages. First, subjects are administered the experimental measure, usually an attitude scale. Second, after a period of several weeks, they are engaged in the experiment. The experimental manipulation, under the guise of a study of interpersonal judgment, is to present the subject with the scale identical to the one originally administered. The subject is informed that it has been completed by another subject. The scale is actually prepared by the experimenter who manipulates, according to the specific study design, the proportion of statements that agree with those obtained from the subject himself. Third, the subject is asked to evaluate the person who allegedly completed the scale in terms of his intelligence, knowledge, morality, and adjustment, and on the probability of liking that person and the probable enjoyment of working together.

In two subsequent studies by Byrne and Wong (1962) and Byrne and McGraw (1964), the relative effects of race and belief were explored. Although their experiments did not yield uniform results, Byrne concluded for both studies that "a subject high in prejudice will respond positively to a Negro stranger providing that this stranger is completely similar to himself concerning attitudes about a relatively large number of topics. Conversely, a subject low in prejudice will respond negatively to a Negro stranger who expresses a sufficiently large proportion of dissimilar attitudes" (Byrne and McGraw, 1964, p. 211).

Although further research has not involved the manipulation of ethnicity, Byrne, Clore, and Worchel (1966) have demonstrated a congruity effect for similarity in socioeconomic status and Byrne, Griffit, and Stefenick (1967) have demonstrated the effect for similarity in personality scale response.

Triandis and Davis (1965), in a complex design involving 140 variables and 300 college student subjects, attempted an independent replication that questions aspects of both Rokeach's and Byrne's work. Their questionnaire involved 12 semantic and 15 behavioral differential scales using as target persons the eight combinations generated by the characteristics Negro-white, male-female, and for or against civil rights legislation. Their analysis suggested the hypothesis that ethnicity was a more important determinant of personal distance where the behaviors involved friendship and marital acceptance. In the case of nonintimate behaviors, belief was more important than ethnicity, whereas belief and ethnicity appeared equally important for behaviors that were intermediate in intimacy.

Although the data of Stein, Hardyck, and Smith (1965) and the extensive study by Stein (1966) support the belief similarity hypothesis, both studies indicate that intimate behaviors and highly visible behaviors may be sensitive to determinants other than the congruity of beliefs.

It should be apparent that belief similarity is only a special case of categorical congruity. In some cases, we should expect that belief similarity would *not* be the criterion for assigning a person to the same category as the actor. First, some beliefs, similar or dissimilar, are irrelevant to given situations. Presumably only beliefs that are relevant for the classification of persons in given situations would affect personal distance. For example, the fact that two people like parakeets is a shared belief that could affect their behavior in only the most circumscribed of situations. Second, belief similarity is only one criterion for categorical placement. Novak and Lerner (1968) provide an especially cogent illustration. College student subjects were asked to evaluate a partner who was presented by the experimenter as similar or dissimilar to the subject on two sets of attitude scale responses. The partner was also presented as being either normal or emotionally disturbed. Following the presentation of the partner's characteristics, subjects rated his attractiveness and similarity to themselves, and they indicated their willingness to interact with him. The findings of the study showed that subjects were more willing to interact with "normal" others when they were attitudinally similar than when they were different. When the partner was categorized as emotionally disturbed, subjects were less willing to interact with a similar but disturbed person. In this case, interaction was preferred with the normal partner even though he was attitudinally dissimilar. Presumably, the attitude similarity of an emotionally disturbed other is a personally threatening bond. Taylor and Mettee (1971) in a replication using a somewhat different design try to explain the avoidance of a similar but "obnoxious" other as an "anxiety-reducing" act. From these studies we can see that considerable effort will have to go into determining which criteria of placement operate in specified intergroup and interpersonal situations.

PERSONAL DISTANCE

The complex principles of structure and organization have received very little direct research in this context, although as we saw in the preceding chapter they have been tested in area of stereotyping. From the work of Triandis and his associates, which we reviewed earlier in the chapter, we may conclude that the principles of differentiation (19) and elemental organization (20) are confirmed. Further, the literature of personal and social distance does not yield any contradictory evidence.

Rather than reiterate the entire set of statements here, only their application to the study of personal and social distance is presented. (The full set of statements appears in the concluding section of Chapter 5.)

18.* *Principle of elemental structure.* The elements of personal distance are established individually in ordinal relations.

19. *Principle of differentiation.* The number of behavioral intentions associated with a target group varies by target.

20. *Principle of elemental organization.* Behavioral intentions associated with a target group are systemically related and tend toward directional consistency.

20a.* The more intentions a person directs to a target group, the more these will be evaluative, intense, salient, and important to him.

20b.* The more evaluative, intense, salient, and important a set of behavioral intentions are to a person, the greater their directional consistency.

20c.* The more behavioral intentions a person directs to a target group, the greater their directional consistency.

20d.* Increases in consensus on social distance result in the decreasing variability, across individuals in personal distance, that is, direction, intensity, salience, and centrality responses.

20e.* Increases in the magnitude of the direction, intensity, salience, and centrality responses of people to ethnic targets will result in increasing consensus in social distance.

THE MARGINALITY MECHANISMS

The maintenance of social and personal distance, like stereotype assignment, is a reciprocal process. The norms of social distance between groups are also learned early, and ethnic persons are not excluded from this part of the social heritage.

21. *Principle of ethnic group congruity.* The norms of social distance expressed by ethnic persons about target groups other than their own are congruent with those consensually associated with those targets in society.

21.1. *Corollary of reciprocity.* Within the ethnic subsociety, the expression of norms of social distance follows the basic principles of distinction, diffusion, consensus, stability, change, and visibility (1–6).

21.2. *Corollary of directional displacement.* Target group members displace themselves to positions of least personal and social distance while otherwise maintaining the normative pattern of distance.

Few tests of any rigor support this principle and its corollaries. Since relatively few studies have utilized both ethnic and dominant group samples, or several ethnic group samples, most support must be drawn by comparing data across studies. Williams' (1964) multisample and multicommunity studies, however, do provide direct and supporting evidence. An estimate of the magnitude of congruity and direct evidence of displacement can be derived from Lever (1968). In a probability sample of 1884 white adult residents of Johannesburg, South Africa, Lever demonstrated that in three ethnic subsamples—English-speaking South Africans, Afrikaans-speaking residents, and Jews—each ethnic group displaced its own group to the most accepted position among 15 target groups studied. The rank correlations (my computations) for each pair of groups not counting the pair itself were .94 for the English- and Afrikaans-speaking, .89 between the Jews and the English-speaking, and .82 between the Jews and the Afrikaans-speaking. Further confirming evidence can be found in Anderson and Cote (1966), Bogardus (1928), Derbyshire and Brody (1964), Fagan and O'Neill (1965), Hartley (1946), Just (1954), Rokeach (1968), Rokeach, Smith, and Evans (1960), Stein (1966), Triandis, Davis, and Takezawa (1965), and Westie and Westie (1957).

The principle of marginal perspective was introduced with little discussion in Chapter Two. It has received no test in application to stereotype assignment, but it has received extensive—though indirect—testing in application to social distance.

22. *Principle of marginal perspective.* Marginal persons manifest a lower acceptance of norms of social distance and less personal distance toward ethnic targets than do the more socially integrated.

Inasmuch as social and personal distance represent normative behavior, we should expect that persons who manifest articulated and well-formed patterns of social distance will be generally conforming and uncritical of normative standards and values. There are no rigorous, direct tests of this principle. Triandis, Davis, and Takezawa (1965) do conclude from their comparison of American, German, and Japanese students that "The high social distance scorer is conforming and uncritical of the values imparted to him by his culture, conservative, and intolerant of ambiguity" (p. 548). Seeman (1956) also provides minor supporting evidence. In the absence of any direct measure of marginality, one technique of assessing this proposal is to compare the distance behavior of persons occupying social positions that differ in their social integration. Following this strategy, we may make a series of predictions of the social distance of selected criterion groups.

To begin, it seems reasonable to assume that minority groups in a society are marginal to that society. This is not a new presumption, and Seeman (1956) and Barron (1967) provide reviews of this mode of conceptualizing minority status. On this basis we should expect that minority group members would display a lower acceptance of social distance norms than members of the dominant groups in society. (We should not expect, however, a perfect association here, since some minority persons are well integrated into society or into minority subsocieties.) Confirming evidence, for Negro subjects, appears in Broom and Glenn (1966), Edlefsen (1956), Proenza and Strickland (1965), Prothro and Jensen (1952), Radke-Yarrow, Trager, and Miller (1952), and Williams (1964). Disconfirmations appear in Fagan and O'Neill (1965), Gray and Thompson (1953), and Landis, Datwyler, and Dorn (1966). For Jewish subjects no disconfirmations appear, and confirming evidence can be found in Goodnow and Tagiuri (1952), Lever (1968), Pettigrew (1960), and Triandis and Triandis (1960).

Another body of evidence relates to church membership and attendance in the United States. In general it appears that church members display greater acceptance of social distance norms than do nonmembers. Similarly, persons whose church attendance or religious activities follow conventional American practices display greater social distance than those detached from such conventional behavior. Direct supporting research includes Brown (1967), Kelly, Ferson, and Holtzman (1958), Photiadis and Biggar (1962), Williams (1964). Indirect support through studies using omnibus measures of prejudice include Adorno et al. (1950), Allport and Kramer (1946), Allport and Ross (1967), Feagin (1964), Maranell (1967), Rokeach (1960), Stember (1961), Stouffer (1955), Wilson (1963).

Finally, Williams (1964) presents a unique datum demonstrating that independent voters, as contrasted with persons voting with major political parties, display lower social distance.

The principle of marginal perspective leads to one of the most puzzling findings in the social distance literature. Ames, Moriwaki, and Basu (1968) analyzed the 1966 social distance data collected by Bogardus (Bogardus, 1968). Their analysis replicated the earlier findings. While the rank correlation between male ($n = 1144$) and female ($n = 1239$) responses was .98, females displayed greater distance for 23 of the 25 ethnic groups on the checklist. This high correlation between men and women across social distance ranks appears to be quite general. At the same time, the greater dissociative distance displayed by women is also a well-replicated finding. Similar reports for both minority and majority women can be found in Bogardus (1959), Brown (1967), Cowgill (1968), Edlefsen (1956), Just (1954), Landis, Datwyler, and Dorn (1966), Pettigrew (1960), Sinha and Upadhyay (1960), Triandis, Davis, and Takezawa (1965), Triandis and Triandis (1960), and Williams (1964). Partial support appears in Fagan and O'Neill (1965), Lever (1968), and Pettigrew (1959), while only two inconsistent studies have been reported, Kelly, Ferson, and Holtzman (1958) and Turbeville (1950). Williams (1964), in his analysis, goes on to show that a sex difference remains even with consecutive controls for age, marital status, education, intergroup contact, and voluntary association membership.

The persistent differences in the directionality of social distance responses must derive from the differential role requirements of women in Western society. Passivity, compliance, and the protection of conventional moral standards still represent major role demands on women. Thus, as a social category women should display greater social integration than men. As sex role definitions change, so the observed differences in social distance should change. An appropriate hypothesis, derived from the principle of marginal perspective, is: Men and women who reject traditional sex role definitions display lower ethnic distance than those who accept such definitions.

NOTE

1. The interaction between absolute and relative status does seem likely. I expect that the higher the absolute status of actor *and* target, the less the effect of status difference on the level of social distance.

Chapter Four

AFFECT AND THE STRUCTURE OF PREJUDICE

This chapter covers two problems: the affective dimension of prejudice and the structure of attitudes. In principle, each should have a chapter of its own; in fact, so little research has been done on affect or on the interrelationships of the affective, conative, and cognitive dimensions of prejudice that placing each subject in a separate chapter would almost be misleading.

AFFECT AND EMOTION

The hypothesis that beliefs and behavioral intentions are supported by affective states of the same direction and magnitude has until very recently come from two types of nonsystematic observation. First, when a person verbally expresses a strong negative or strong positive attitude toward some human group, or defends such an attitude in the face of contradiction, he or she commonly displays behavior which is interpreted by others as emotional. Second, emotionally charged words and phrases used in attitude scales are often selected by subjects as descriptive of their attitudes toward certain human groups. An appropriate illustration, if any is required, can be seen in this excerpt from a feature by Elizabeth Dilling, in a journal of hate, *Common Sense* (May 15, 1965; p. 4):

Today—The TALMUD on CHRIST
    The TALMUD teaches that Mary, Mother of Christ, was a whore and adulteress who spawned Him by a Roman soldier, Pandera. That Jesus tried to seduce women, had intercourse with animals, was a betrayer, a fool. That one should always speak against Him unless this might endanger Pharisees in general. That He deserved FIVE sadistic deaths; namely: Sinking in dung to the

armpits and strangling; sinking in dung to the armpits and boiling lead poured down His pried open mouth; decapitating; stoning to death; and Crucifying as a "blasphemer" of Pharisaism—which He certainly WAS!

The TALMUD and MORALS

Sodomy in general is sanctioned, and, in particular, with dead bodies, little tots, neighbors' wives, and with one's own wife. The adult man who rapes baby girls under three, is held to be blameless and pure, in book after book of the TALMUD. A baby girl three years and one day old may be acquired as a wife "by coition."

Non-Pharisees rank as "the people who are like an ass—slaves who are considered the property of the master". . . . The nonhuman "gentile" may be killed, cheated, his wages withheld, etc., just as long as this does not endanger fellow Pharisee "humans."

Psychologists commonly assert that emotions "presuppose" or "are associated with" or "are determined by" bodily, visceral, or physiological reactions. Even social psychologists tend to assume an underlying physiological basis for affective responses. Perhaps the basis for these reductionist tendencies can be illustrated in this statement by Arnold (1969), a leading psychophysiological theorist of emotion: "All action tendencies result in the activation of a whole pattern of voluntary and involuntary muscles, of glands of internal and external secretion. But only in the case of emotion is the activation of the autonomic nervous system and the organs it innervates really conspicuous" (p. 184).

Within the context of the study of attitudes, I regard emotion and affect as separate concepts referring to events of a different order and requiring different theories for explanation and different strategies for analysis. I shall define affect as the feeling experienced about a given object or class of objects and an affective state as the set of feelings held about a given object or class of objects.[1]

The distinction between affect and emotion derives mainly from three assumptions about the relation of affect and physiological arousal:

1. Any specific report of an affective state may or may not be accompanied by some form of autonomic arousal. The persistence of that state over a continuous period of time or its recurrence over many time periods may lead to some differentiated physiological patterns being associated with that state.

2. Conversely, some forms of autonomic arousal may or may not be accompanied by the report of a specific affective state. The persistence or recurrence of a set of physiological responses may come to be associated over time with a specific affective state.

3. As a consequence, affective responses to an attitude object may sometimes lead to autonomic arousal and autonomic arousal may sometimes lead to affective responses, but neither should be construed as a sufficient condition for the other.

One possible qualification to this assumptive structure may be that after an association has been established, an extreme state of affective or physiological arousal may be sufficient to produce the other. The popular meaning of emotion, which makes good sense in this conceptual scheme, defines an emotional state as the conjunction of specific affective responses with a specific pattern of physiological responses. Schacter (1965) argues similarly "that an emotional state may be considered a function of a state of physiological arousal and of a cognition appropriate to this state of arousal" (p. 76).

At present, we know very little about emotional states as defined above. However, the creative experimental research of Stanley Schacter, which has involved the independent and simultaneous manipulation of physiological and cognitive variables, has provided a new impetus for extended inquiry separating the attitudinal and physiological components of behavior. Schacter and his associates (Schacter, 1965, 1967) have shown that the same physiological state, induced by the controlled administration of a sympathomimetic drug, could lead to such different affective states and behaviors as euphoria, amusement, fear, anxiety, and even no affect at all. The basis of this differential response to the similar states of physiological arousal were the beliefs that subjects held about their bodily state and the social situation in which they were located.

A number of studies have been specifically concerned with the relation of physiologic responses to ethnic stimuli or performance on ethnic attitude scales. Almost all of the research relating physiological autonomic responses to prejudice has involved the galvanic skin response (GSR). (None of the studies, unfortunately, have used a measure of the affective dimension of prejudice.) The GSR is a measure of electrodermal reactivity, that is, the resistance or conductance of the skin to the flow of electric current. A fall in skin resistance is associated with the secretions of the sweat glands. Increased sweating is under the control of the sympathetic system, and in response to attitudinal stimuli is taken as an indicator of emotional involvement. GSR measurements are generally made on bodily areas which are relatively independent of normal thermoregulatory sweating.

Probably because the early research on the relation of GSR to attitudes was not very promising (e.g., Abel, 1930; Chant and Salter, 1937), the first attempt to examine the relation of prejudice to GSR is relatively recent. Rankin and Campbell (1955) recruited 40 white male subjects to participate in what was represented as a word association test with GSR being recorded. Two experimenters, one black and one white, alternated in making simulated readjustments of a dummy apparatus attached to the subjects left wrist while a right-arm apparatus remained in effect. A highly significant difference in GSRs to the two experimenters was found.

The studies of J. B. Cooper represented another landmark.[2] In the first study (Cooper and Singer, 1956), each potential subject was given both a rating scale and a ranking scale containing the names of 20 alphabetically listed ethnic groups. Subjects who participated in individual GSR sessions later on were those who had indicated strong positive and negative attitudes. Four brief evaluative statements were composed, each written so that the name of any group could be inserted into it. Two of the statements placed the named group in a derogatory light, and the other two placed the named group in a complimentary light. For a given subject, the name of his most liked group was inserted into one of the derogatory statements, and the name of his most disliked group was inserted into one of the complimentary statements. The names of the groups the subject had ranked in positions 10 and 11, the middle positions, were inserted into the two remaining statements—one complimentary and one derogatory. The order of presentation of the statements and the insertion of ranked group names were randomized from subject to subject. The equipment operator knew neither the content nor strength of the subject's attitude toward any group. One of the derogatory statements was: "People can be divided into two groups: the good and the bad. Close to the bottom of the list are the ———. They certainly can be said to have caused more trouble for humanity than they are worth." One of the complimentary statements was: "The world over, no single group of people has done as much for us, for our civilization as the———. The world will undoubtedly come to recognize them as honest, wise, and completely unselfish." The other statements were similar to these. Subjects were instructed not to reply verbally to any of the statements. After a subject had been balanced in, a trial statement, which incorporated the name of the group the subject had ranked in position 9, was read. Following this, the four statements were read.

Each subject's laboratory session was treated as an experiment. Intrasubject rather than intersubject comparisons were made. The problem was simply reduced to that of determining in how many experiments the critical stimuli evoked relatively greater responses than did the neutral stimuli. For 14 of the 20 subjects GSRs were greater to derogatory statements containing the names of groups toward which they had expressed strong positive attitudes. However, for 19 of the 20 subjects, GSRs were greater to complimentary statements containing the names of disliked groups than those containing the names of neutrals.

A second study (Cooper and Siegel, 1956) was then designed and run as a partial replication of the first, dealing only with negatively directional attitudes. The same rating and ranking scales were administered to 176 college students, 31 of whom gave extremely low ratings to the groups they ranked lowest. Of these, 23 were available for individual experimental sessions. In this series of experiments, the statements were all complimentary. The results of these second study experiments were almost identical to their counterpart in the first study. Twenty of the 23 subjects' GSRs were greater to statements containing the names of the most disliked groups than to statements containing the names of neutral groups.

In a third study (Cooper and Pollock, 1959) the design was reversed. Instead of predicting from paper and pencil scale results to GSR magnitude, the researchers predicted from GSR magnitudes to scale results. Their basic hypothesis was that an excessive GSR to a complimentary statement concerning a group would identify that group as the object of a negative attitude. In this study subjects were *not* first screened and selected on the basis of attitude scale results. Nothing was known of a subject's attitudes prior to his coming to the laboratory. GSR sessions came first, and subjects responded to nine complimentary statements about nine groups. Approximately one week after the laboratory sessions, subjects were administered a paired comparison scale, containing the names of the groups used in the GSR sessions.

Their first analysis dealt with the following question: "How frequently would the group named which evoked the greatest GSR be below the scale median?" The answer was 81% of the time. The second analysis was exactly like the first, except that, instead of the single greatest GSR, the two greatest GSRs were identified and the same prediction was made with respect to both being ranked below the paired-comparison median. In this instance, 41 of the 53 subjects gave below the median paired comparison scores to *both* of their highest GSR group names. When the nine stimulus groups were ranked according to both GSR magnitude and paired comparison position, a positive relationship was found. The Spearman rank coefficient was .82.

The relation of electrodermal reactivity to ethnic attitudes has now been investigated in fewer than a dozen studies. The findings are relatively consistent. However, the original finding by Rankin and Campbell (1955), that the physical contact of white subjects with a black experimenter resulted in greater GSRs than similar contact with a white experimenter, was not replicated in a more controlled study by Poirer and Lott (1967).

The basic findings can be summarized briefly:

1. Continued physical contact of white subjects with a Negro experimenter (in the context of adjusting dummy apparatus) resulted in decreased GSR responsiveness (Rankin and Campbell, 1955; Poirer and Lott, 1967).

2. Highly ethnocentric persons (measured by an omnibus scale that included multiple ethnic targets) displayed greater GSRs as a result of physical contact with a Negro experimenter than did persons of low ethnocentrism (Porier and Lott, 1967).

3. Strongly directional beliefs evoked greater GSRs when contradicted than did beliefs of moderate directionality (Cooper and Singer, 1956; Cooper and Siegel, 1956; Cooper and Pollock, 1959; Dickson and McGinnies, 1966).

4. Strongly negative ethnic beliefs evoked greater GSRs when contradicted than did strongly positive ethnic beliefs (Cooper and Singer, 1956; Cooper and Pollock, 1959).

5. Persons with a high personal distance toward Negroes produced greater GSRs when exposed to photographic slides of Negroes and whites than did persons with low personal distance (Westie and DeFleur, 1959).

6. Persons highly prejudiced toward Negroes (measured by an omnibus scale) displayed greater GSRs when exposed to photographs of Negroes or Negros and whites in interaction than did persons of low prejudice (Vidulich and Krevanick, 1966).

Although these studies indicate a direct association between a physiological variable and ethnic attitudes, none of them establishes a firm link between attitude and emotion as defined here. Not only will other physiological variables have to be examined in their relation to affect, as well as to the cognitive and conative components, but a theory of emotion in which these relations are articulated has yet to be developed.

Other physiologic indicators of ethnic attitudes that have been studied include finger pulse volume (Westie and DeFleur, 1959) and pupil response (Woodmansee, 1970). None of these variables was significantly related to attitudes toward Negroes. Summaries of other research dealing with interpersonal attitudes and behavior as related to GSR are presented in Shapiro and Crider (1969).

THE LANGUAGE OF AFFECT

Affect is denoted in language by certain categories of words. These categories refer to relatively well-articulated (distinctive, consensual, widely diffused) experiences common to persons within a given society. Although facial responses and other body gestures that communicate affect may vary considerably across societies, very little is known about cross-cultural developments of the language of affect.

Formal research on the language of affect is rare, and as yet there has been only one application of this approach to the direct measurement of the affective dimension of ethnic attitudes (Ewens, 1969). Nowlis (1965), in a review of 15 factor analyses of checklists of words denoting affect, reported the possibility of 12 categories of affect. The categories and examples of the words defining them (in order of their frequency of occurrence in the 15 analyses) were:

1. *Aggression:* defiant, rebellious, angry, furious, ready to fight.
2. *Fatigue:* drowsy, dull, sleepy, tired, sluggish.
3. *Concentration:* careful, contemplative, attentive, serious, efficient.
4. *Surgency:* carefree, playful, witty, lively, talkative.
5. *Social Affection:* affectionate, forgiving, kindly, warm-hearted, sociable.
6. *Anxiety:* clutched-up, fearful, jittery, tense, nervous.
7. *Skepticism:* skeptical, suspicious, dubious.
8. *Egotism:* egotistic, self-centered, boastful, aloof.
9. *Sadness:* sad, blue, lonely, down-hearted, sorry.
10. *Vigor, general activation:* active, energetic, vigorous, bold, strong.
11. *Elation:* overjoyed, elated, pleased.
12. *Nonchalance, general deactivation:* bored, nonchalant, leisurely.

Davitz (1969) in a series of studies and analyses also reported 12 categories. Although there is some overlap with Nowlis' categories, the two sets are rather different. As a result of a higher order analysis, however, Davitz provides a classification by direction of affect. His positive affect grouping contains four clusters:

Activation: admiration, amusement, awe, cheerfulness, delight, elation, enjoyment, gaiety, happiness, hope.
Moving Toward: affection, love.
Comfort: contentment, determination, friendliness, gratitude, reverence, serenity.
Enhancement: confidence, inspiration, pride.

Two negative groupings were isolated. The first is marked by a general deactivation and disengagement:

Hypoactivation: boredom, depression.
Moving Away: apathy.
Discomfort: grief, pity, sadness.
Incompetence-Dissatisfaction: guilt, remorse, shame.

The second negative classification is quite different:

Hyperactivation: anger, fear, panic.
Moving Against: contempt, dislike, hate.
Tension: disgust, frustration, impatience, irritation, jealousy, nervousness, resentment.
Inadequacy: anxiety.

As you look across the three categories, you can see that each comprises the same four dimensions: various levels of activation; the direction of the given state (toward, away, against); the hedonic tone associated with it (comfort, discomfort, tension); and what Davitz called the individual's competence in relating to his environment.

The classificatory schemes of Nowlis and of Davitz apply to the study of affect in general, and they were not derived with specific reference to the targets of prejudice. Because of their generality, they would no doubt undergo considerable change in their application to the study of attitudes.

THE NORMS OF AFFECTIVE RESPONSE

The expression of affect is as socially regulated, as normative, as the assignment of stereotypes or beliefs about appropriate or acceptable behavior. Although few social scientists would deny the normative basis of affective response, not a single piece of research has been directed explicitly to the basic principles that have been so well-confirmed in the studies of the cognitive and conative components of prejudice. Following are the basic hypotheses concerning the norms of affective response.

1. *Principle of distinction.* Social objects are distinguishable on the basis of the belief statements associated with them.

1a.* Norms of affective responses concerning the major ethnic groups in society are relatively distinct and exclusive.

2. *Principle of diffusion.* Belief statements about social objects are widely diffused in a society.

2a.* Knowledge of the affective responses associated with the major ethnic groups in American society is highly diffused.

2b.* The primary contexts for the diffusion of knowledge of affect norms, and for the legitimation of such knowledge, are the family and the school.

2c.* Norms of affective response are copied in the mass media of communication and the media of mass education.

2d.*   The greater the distinctiveness of affect norms, the greater their diffusion in society.

3.   *Principle of consensus.* There is high consensus on the belief statements associated with specific social objects.

3a.*   There is high consensus on the affective responses associated with specific ethnic groups.

3b.*   The greater the distinctiveness of affect norms, the greater the consensus concerning them.

3c.*   The greater the diffusion of affect norms, the greater the consensus concerning them.

4.   *Principle of stability.* Belief statements associated with social objects are highly stable.

4a.*   Affect norms are relatively stable historically within and across societies.

4b.*   The greater the distinctiveness, diffusion and consensus on affect norms, the greater the stability of these norms.

5.   *Principle of change.* Belief statements associated with social objects change as the relation of people to the objects changes.

5a.*   Changes in affect norms follow changes in established ethnic group relations.

5b.*   Changes in the established relations between ethnic groups will decrease the stability of affect norms and modify their distinctiveness and their levels of diffusion and consensus.

6.   *Principle of visibility.* Under conditions of stability, the greater the visibility of social objects, the greater the distinctiveness, diffusion, and consensus of belief statements associated with the object.

6a.*   Under conditions of stable group relations, the greater the visibility of an ethnic group, the greater the distinctiveness, diffusion, and consensus on affect norms.

THE COGNITIVE DETERMINANTS OF AFFECTIVE STATES

The coding of individuals establishes the basis for subsequent response, and the principles of categorical placement, dominance, and the corollary of response are well confirmed by the research of stereotypes and social distance. The principles, as applied to the study of affect have received little formal attention.

7.   *Principle of categorical placement.* The categorization of a social object is contingent on its codability.

7a.   Ascribing ethnic group membership to an individual is contingent on the joint effects of that person's characteristics, the criteria of ethnic classification, his eligibility for other social categories, and the context in which he appears.

7b.   If a person is assigned ethnic group membership, then the affective response will be contingent on the joint effects of the prevailing norms of affect, the person's other characteristics, his or her eligibility for other social categories, and the situational context in which the person appears.

8.   *Principle of categorical dominance.* If a social object is cast in a social category, then initial response will be determined on the basis of its categorical characteristics more than on its individual characteristics.

8a.* If a person is assigned ethnic membership, then the initial affective response will be on the basis of ethnic membership more than on the person's other characteristics.

8.1.   *Corollary of categorical response.* The less knowledge available about a social object, the greater the likelihood that it will be assigned the characteristics of its social category.

8.1a.* The less knowledge available about an ethnic person, the greater the likelihood that response will be in accordance with the prevailing norms of affect appropriate to the ethnic category.

The work of Schacter and his associates, discussed earlier, provides partial confirmation for the principle of categorical placement, as does the name-labeling experiment of Razran (1950) described in Chapter 2. Obviously, much more systematic work is needed.

Although studies have shown that the situational context is an important determinant of the manner in which people code the affective state of another, relatively little research has been accomplished demonstrating the effects of context on specific affective states. Studies on the recognition of affective states are reviewed in Frijda (1969) and Tagiuri (1969).

One of the possibly unique determinants of affective response, which is still consistent with the placement principle, is the effect of physiological cues. Valins (1967) tested and confirmed the hypothesis that people vary in the reliance they place on physiologic cues in determining their own affective response:

It was hypothesized that emotional and unemotional individuals differ with respect to the utilization of internal sensations as cues. In comparison to unemotional *Ss*, emotional ones were expected to make more use of information concerning their internal reactions. *Ss* who were psychometrically classified as emotional or unemotional were shown 10 slides of seminude females while hearing a tape recording of sounds that were allegedly their heart beats. To 5 of the slides they heard a marked change in their "heart rates"; to the other 5 they heard no change. It was found that relatively emotional subjects labeled nudes as attractive or unattractive depending upon whether they thought their hearts had reacted. This effect was significantly less marked for unemotional subjects. These individual differences were still apparent 2 mo. later when subjects were allowed to choose photographs of the nudes as rewards (p. 458).

THE STRUCTURE OF PREJUDICE

The three components of an attitude—cognitive, conative, and affective—together with the elements that characterize them are interrelated. These interrelationships are of three kinds. First, the relationships among the elements are the same (or hypothesized to be the same) for each component. For example, increases in centrality have the same effect on directionality regardless of which component we are observing. Second, within any component a change in the magnitude of one element will bring about a change in most of the other elements within the component. The direction of these changes has been, of course, the subject of most of the principles in this book. Third, a change in the magnitude of the elements of one component will affect the magnitudes of the elements of both of the other components; this is one of the concerns of this section.

It should be clear, then, that an attitude is a complex system; that is, it is made up of three subsystems. Given this complexity, it is sometimes not clear to those new to thinking about complex systems what the meaning of attitude *structure* is.

Since an attitude is a hypothetical construct, its structure can be observed only through a set of research operations. It may be helpful to illustrate the idea of structure before defining it. If I wanted to measure completely a person's attitude toward Piraneans, I would administer an attitude scale that assessed all of the DISC elements—direction, intensity, salience, centrality—for each component. (I would have built the items of my scale by assembling statements of belief, intention, and affect which varied in their polarization, i.e., in the degree of distinctiveness, diffussion, and consensus with which they characterized Piraneans.) A person's performance on the scale would be derived from the number of statements accepted or rejected within each component along the continua of the DISC elements. The scale, then, would yield 12 readings; for example, the magnitude of direction for belief, intention, and affect; the magnitude of intensity for each, and so on.

The structure of an individual's attitude toward Piraneans, then, is described by the magnitude of each element for each component at the time of measurement. The structure of an attitude may therefore be defined as the state of its system at a given point in time. The "state of the system" is the magnitude of each element for each component. An attitude may be said to be stable to the degree that it maintains the same structure over time.

Two principles which were the model for the principles of elemental structure and organization can now be introduced:

16. *Principle of attitude structure.* The components of an attitude are established in ordinal relations.

16a. Cognitive, conative, and affective responses vary in their relative strength by attitude object and across persons.

16b. For any given person, the relative strength of the components varies by attitude object.

17. *Principle of attitude organization.* The components of an attitude are systemically related and tend toward directional consistency.

We begin the substantive analysis by examining three studies of attitude structure. The work of Ewens (1969) represents the most careful attempt at assessing the interrelations of the components of prejudice and at examining the different ways they relate to indicators of intergroup behavior. Ewens constructed three 20-item checklists on the basis of the direction and salience of the items. He described his procedure for building the affect checklist as follows:

Affect Toward Negroes. The words used in this 20-item adjective checklist were taken from a larger list obtained by Stanley L. Saxton (1968). Saxton began with a set of 648 words taken from the dictionary which were believed to express feelings. In a series of administrations, he was able to narrow this list down to 42 words which respondents identified as expressing their feelings toward Negroes in several selected hypothetical situations.

A sample of 122 students from a social science core course at The University of Iowa was asked to evaluate these 42 words according to how well each term described their feelings toward Negroes (salience) and how favorable or unfavorable each term was as a description of feelings toward Negroes (directionality). Each word was given a salience score of one to six. A score of six indicated that the respondent felt the word to be completely descriptive of Negroes, and a score of one indicated that the term was not at all salient. The words were also given a directionality score of one to seven, with low scores indicating negative feelings toward Negroes. On the basis of these directionality scores, the words were then divided into tertiles. Each of the words in the upper and lower tertiles was given a score which was the product of its salience and directionality scores. . . . The 10 words in each of these lists with the highest salience-directionality scores were selected for the final checklist.

Respondents in the present sample were asked to indicate for each term how much they felt that it applied to Negroes as a target group. Scores of one to seven were assigned to each word. A score of seven meant that the word applied unquestionably to Negroes, whereas a score of one meant that the word did not at all apply to Negroes. A final score was arrived at for each respondent by subtacting his score for the negative affect words from his score for the positive affect words. A constant of 60 was then added to the scores to eliminate negative numbers. This meant that the scale could range from 0 to 120 with higher numbers indicating pro-Negro feelings and lower scores indicating anti-Negro feelings (pp. 62–63).

Similar procedures were followed in constructing the stereotypes and behavioral intentions checklists; the words for these scales came from Ehrlich and Van Tubergen (1969, 1971). The items employed are presented in Table 1. All three scales displayed reliabilities of approximately .85.

TABLE 1.   CHECKLIST ITEMS BALANCED FOR DIRECTION AND SALIENCE FOR MEASURING ATTITUDES TOWARD NEGROES

Stereotypes	Behavioral Intentions	Affect
1. —Alert	1. —Accept help from	1. —Affectionate
2. —Ambitious	2. —Admire ideas of	2. —Aggravated
3. —Athletic	3. —Approve of	3. —Agreeable
4. —Boastful	4. —Ask opinion of	4. —Alarmed
5. —Conceited	5. —Avoid	5. —Angry
6. —Courteous	6. —Be an enemy of	6. —Annoyed
7. —Honest	7. —Be friendly to	7. —Antagonistic
8. —Industrious	8. —Be loyal to	8. —Confident
9. —Intelligent	9. —Be on first-name basis	9. —Contemptuous
10. —Intolerant	10. —Be prejudiced against	10. —Disagreeable
11. —Kind	11. —Be proud of	11. —Friendly
12. —Lazy	12. —Be unfriendly to	12. —Hostile
13. —Loud	13. —Dislike	13. —Indignant
14. —Musical	14. —Fear	14. —Intimate
15. —Quarrelsome	15. —Feel superior to	15. —Intolerant
16. —Quick-tempered	16. —Hate	16. —Jovial
17. —Radical	17. —Help	17. —Loving
18. —Revengeful	18. —Look down upon	18. —Outgoing
19. —Rude	19. —Respect	19. —Sympathetic
20. —Sportsmanlike	20. —Treat as subordinate	20. —Tolerant

Source. Ewens, 1969. (Responses are elicited on 6-and 7-point scales.)

Ewens then administered the three scales to a specimen set of 83 persons as part of a laboratory study of the relation of ethnic attitudes to behavior. Using *tau* as his measure of association, he reported that scores on the affect scale correlated .46 with stereotyping and .43 with personal distance. The stereotypes and personal distance scales correlated at .29, and all coefficients were significant beyond the .05 level of confidence.

Eight weeks after the subjects completed the scales they were individually contacted and asked to participate in a laboratory study. The study procedures, which are described in further detail in Chapter 5, involved the subjects in videotaping a talk on Negro-white relations. Following the recording, they were presented with a legal release form which would permit the study sponsor to broadcast the tape on their college and hometown radio and television stations. In addition, the subjects were presented with a series of forms by the study sponsor (a fictitious civil rights action agency) asking the subject whether or not he or she would want to engage in other activities. These activities involved a peaceful protest march, speaking on civil rights with a mixed ethnic team at a local church or civic organization, the endorsement of a strong pro-Negro newspaper statement, or devoting an afternoon to interviewing for a survey on racial attitudes. The subject had to sign his or her name, give hometown and college addresses and telephone numbers, and to indicate willingness to engage in each of these activities in either hometown or the college community.

Given these operations, the researcher was then able to correlate each component score with each of the 12 behavioral commitments. The stereotype scores yielded only two significant correlations: the personal distance scores yielded significant correlations for 7 of the 12 actions; and the affect scores were significantly correlated with 9 of the 12 actions. The overall *tau* correlations with all 12 actions were .13 with stereotypes, .28 with personal distance, and .35 with affect (the latter two were significant beyond the .05 level).

Ewens' research not only demonstrated the relative ease by which all components may be assessed by the same method, but it demonstrated two also theoretically crucial findings:

1. All three components are positively correlated.
2. Each component may have a different relationship to specific behaviors.

The significance of these data is discussed in detail at the conclusion of this section.

The second study to be reviewed is Ostrom's (1969) analysis of the structure of attitudes toward the church. Ostrom utilized four types of scale to measure each component—summated ratings, equal-appearing intervals, scalogram, and a self-rating scale. Using the scores obtained from three samples of students, he was able to determine that the average correlation for each component with itself across methods was .62, while the average intercorrelation of each component with the other two across methods was .59. The differences in the strength of the correlations among the three components appeared to by negligible.

For one specimen set of 189 students, Ostrom administered a questionnaire to determine (1) the frequency of church attendance, (2) the amount of money donated, (3) the amount of time spent in church-related activities, (4) whether the subject had ever studied or (5) discussed the possibility of studying for the ministry, (6) the amount of time spent in religious meditation, and (7) the amount of time spent talking about the church and its activities; (8) as a final behavioral measure, the last page of the questionnaire contained an invitation to attend a discussion of the results of the study and its "contribution to the church in modern society." If the respondent was interested he had to sign his name and address on the page, tear the page off, and hand it in separately (to preserve anonymity). The researcher then correlated each response by each component for all scales. The mean correlations for each component, averaged over the four scaling methods, with the eight behavior reports was highest for behavioral intentions. The conative and affective components were higher than the cognitive for all eight items, and the conative was higher than the affective for five of eight behaviors. The mean correlations ranged from .01 to .60.

Ostrom's findings corroborate those of Ewens: Component scores are positively correlated, and each component has a different relation to specific behaviors. Ewens found affect to be the best predictor of civil rights activities, and Ostrom found behavioral intentions the best predictor of church-related activities.

Kothandapani (1971) replicated Ostrom's study investigating attitudes toward contraception and its relation to an individual's use or nonuse of contraception. Across all four scaling techniques component scores all displayed moderate to strong positive correlations with contraceptive behavior. The median correlations (point biserial) for affect and behavior was .59; for belief and behavior, .67; and for intentions and behavior the correlations were almost uniform, approximately .81.

The only other studies employing indicators of all three components are Morse and Allport (1952) and Campbell and McCandless (1951). In the Morse and Allport analysis, the highest correlation (r) between components is that between the cognitive and conative, .72; affect correlated .42 with the cognitive and .64 with the conative. Campbell and McCandless reported correlations (r) between affect and personal distance as .87 and affect and stereotype assignment as .77. Their correlations were derived from measures using five different ethnic targets.

The third study, Rosenberg (1960), is the only experimental demonstration of the interrelationships among the elements of different components. Rosenberg provided evidence from two experiments indicating that a change in the direction of affect can result in changing the centrality of beliefs and the centrality of behavioral intentions toward an object. Changes in affective state were produced through hypnotic suggestion. The measures of centrality were rating scales: value importance, here labeled belief centrality, and perceived instrumentality, here labeled conative centrality. The subjects completed the scales before and after their hypnotic session. The experimental subjects were commanded to feel differently toward the attitude object. For example, "When you awake you will be very much in favor of the idea of Negroes moving into white neighborhoods. The mere idea will make you happy." Increases in positive affect appeared to increase the centrality of both components, while increases in negative affect appeared to decrease centrality. Even after the posthypnotic suggestion had been removed the centrality changes remained—although at lower levels—in a postexperimental session three days later.

If we were to consider only the basic variables of distinction, diffusion, and consensus, the DISC elements, and the system properties of differentiation and directional organization, it would be possible to specify 138 two-variable hypotheses relating a variable of one component with a variable of another. Obviously we have a long way to go before the formal structure of prejudice can be explicated.

The few other studies that have examined the structure of prejudice have been concerned with the relation of stereotype assignment and personal distance. These studies generally index stereotype assignments by the number of unfavorable stereotypes the respondent accepts. In turn, personal distance is typically assessed by the rank order the respondent assigns to the selected target groups, and the association of the two components is ascertained by rank correlation procedures.

All of these studies have shown a positive correlation between the components ranging from a low of .37 in a Brazilian study (Bastide and Van Den Berghe, 1957) to a high of .84 with a sample of Hindus and Moslems (Ansari, 1956).

The other studies include Morse and Allport (1952); Pettigrew (1959); Taft (1959); Sinha and Upadhyay (1960); and Williams (1964). Palmore (1962), in a very unusual study, demonstrated that the number of ethnophaulisms appearing in a dictionary of American slang correlated .95

(*tau*) with current rankings of the social distance of American ethnic groups.

The study of the structure of prejudice requires much more programmatic and microscopic research than it has received as yet. Before that occurs, a reexamination of some of its assumptive framework is in order.

Four assumptions have been made: assumptions about the linearity of attitude structure; assumptions about the isomorphism of attitude structures across targets and across individuals; and an assumption about the psychological independence of attitude structure. Since most of these assumptions are empirically testable, there is no scientific warrant for their persistence. This chapter closes, therefore, with two testable propositions which stand in contradiction to these past assumptions. First, virtually all research on prejudice has assumed that the relation of the components and their elements is linear. However, no researchers have reported any formal test of linearity. Moreover, if the following assumptions, which are also challenged, also are incorrect, then it is quite probable that relations among components may be nonlinear, at least for some persons and for some attitude objects.

Second, past research has typically assumed that the target of an attitude had no impact on the structure of the individual's attitude itself. In other words, attitudes toward social objects were assumed to have the same structure, more or less, regardless of what the social object was. If it is possible to make any inferences about this from the Ewens and Ostrom studies, then it is likely that the affective component of attitudes toward Negroes is more determinative of the magnitudes of the elements of the other components, whereas for attitudes toward the church, the conative component is strongest. Thus structure may vary by target; and the reasons for this are suggested in the discussion of the next two assumptions.

Third, almost all researchers have assumed (by their methodology) that attitudes toward a given target have essentially the same structure across individuals. When researchers have correlated the scores derived from one component measure with the scores derived from another, they have assumed that it is appropriate to sum the scores across individuals. For some purposes, performing arithmetic or statistical operations on attitude scores may be meaningful, for example, as a means of characterizing the attitudes of a group. But attitudes are a property of individuals, and any assessment of attitude structure across individuals may be highly misleading. Aggregate analyses have resulted in reports of mainly low-to-moderate intercorrelations of the components of prejudice. Unless everyone in a given sample had the same structure, then this is the best that could be expected.

Let's consider some hypothetical individuals. Person I has a highly stable attitude with the strength of each component being relatively equal. Person II is in the process of change as a result of some highly emotional experiences. As a consequence, person II has a relatively strong affective loading but a low level of organization of his cognitive and conative loadings. Person III has a highly intellectualized view of the attitude object (i.e., high cognitive development) but lacks any contact or experience, and thus has relatively low conative and affective loadings. Any aggregation of scores will, of course, result in a distortion of the individual structures.

I would like to propose, then, that individuals vary in the degree to which an attitude component is dominant. One implication of this is that changes which develop in the dominant component will bring about greater increments of change in the other components than will change in the weaker components. A second implication is that individuals may vary in the degree to which their attitudes toward social objects all have the same dominant mode. Thus it is possible, for example, that some people are more oriented to a cognitive relation to ethnic others and other people are more affectively oriented.

The fourth assumption, implicit in most theories of attitudes, is that of the psychological independence of attitude structure. Although no attitude theorist would ignore the social origins of attitudes, it is generally assumed that the mechanisms that determine and stabilize an attitude are exclusively psychological. I suggest, in contrast, that the structure of an attitude is partly determined by the state of knowledge in society concerning the attitude object. If, in fact, the societal levels of distinctiveness, diffusion, and consensus vary by the component of the attitude, then this should be reflected in individual attitude structures.

Rejecting this final assumption leads to the proposal that the polarization of ethnic attitudes varies by target and by component. Thus for some ethnic groups there is a highly distinctive, well-diffused, and consensual affective state, whereas for others, high polarization may be cognitive or even not present.

NOTES

1. Although most social scientists do not object to the use of verbal reports in a person's description of his or her beliefs or intentions to behave, the mystique that surrounds the concept of emotion does lead many people to object to the use of verbal reports here. These objections, which appear to focus on the degree to which emotions or affects are conscious and/or reportable, are discussed critically in Davitz (1969, pp. 136–141).

2. The summary of Cooper's work presented here is a direct excerpt and paraphrase from J. B. Cooper (1959).

Chapter Five

SOCIALIZATION AND THE SUPPORTING MECHANISMS OF PREJUDICE

Much as infants have a genetic heritage, so they also have a social heritage. Social structure like genetic structure sets the limits on individual variation. The mechanism for the transmission of this social heritage is conventionally labeled "socialization." Early socialization experiences seem particularly crucial in establishing the limits on subsequent development. The precise effects of early socialization are not known; nor for that matter are the limits of individual and social behavior clearly delineated. It is clear, however, from the research of the past 25 years, that humans are more plastic at all stages of the life cycle than earlier developmental, organismic, and psychoanalytic psychologies would have led us to expect.

Ethnic attitudes are a part of the social heritage of the developing child. They are transmitted across generations as a component of the accumulated knowledge of society. No person can grow up in a society without learning the prevailing attitudes concerning the major ethnic groups. In fact, given the polarization of ethnic attitudes, we ought to consider the question of how some people escape being prejudiced.

CHILDREN AND THE PRINCIPLES OF PREJUDICE

In the literature of prejudice, stereotypes of children often appear highly personalized and capricious. This observation led me to the intellectual strategy of, generally, not including the findings of research with children in documenting the principles of prejudice. Moreover, my concern that substantive differences between adults and children might bias my observations turned out to be essentially unnecessary, partly because of the rapidity with which attitudes are acquired and partly because most research has been done with children over the age of five who are already in school settings.

Although slightly different techniques of research have been used in the children's studies, by and large they are variants of standard procedures. There is a somewhat greater reliance on the use of pictures and dolls, story-telling and semiprojective techniques, and there is usually less concern with the problems of measurement errors. The quality of the research here, however, is not much different from that in the adult studies.

The primary assignment of this chapter is to introduce a set of principles and corollaries of socialization and support that will complete the basis for a theory of prejudice. Table 1 presents a reference guide to the relevant research, much of which has been discussed in previous chapters. The conclusion of that table can be put quite simply: *The principles of the prejudice apply alike to adults and children.*

PRINCIPLES OF SOCIALIZATION

The Anchors and the Constancy of Early Experience

In general, highly prejudiced persons report that they have had early "bad" experiences with persons who are members of those ethnic groups that are targets of their prejudice. Such early experiences may, in fact, come to be the anchor by which subsequent information and experience is coded and evaluated. The importance of anchoring in attitude development has been long recognized (see Sherif and Sherif, 1967, for a cogent summary), but almost no research has been conducted on anchor effects in the development of prejudice. Even more important, there has been no longitudinal research. In its basic and applied form, the principle of cognitive anchors remains to be firmly established.

9.* *Principle of cognitive anchoring.* Initial experiences with a social object are crucial in establishing a strategy of coding and the direction for attitude development.

9a.* Initial intergroup experiences are crucial in establishing a strategy of coding and the direction in which ethnic attitudes may develop.

Ringer (1967) and Williams (1964) both provide evidence to indicate that favorable teen-age intergroup experiences are strongly associated with positive ethnic attitudes. Williams concludes his data analysis: "The

TABLE 1. REFERENCE GUIDE TO THE
PRINCIPLES OF PREJUDICE AS MANIFEST IN STUDIES
OF PERSONS 2 TO 16 YEARS OF AGE.

Principle of Distinction
Confirmations: Lambert and Klineberg, 1967; Meltzer, 1939a, 1939b, 1941;
Radke, Trager, and Davis, 1949; Zeligs, 1948, 1950a, 1950b, 1952, 1953, 1955.
Principle of Diffusion
Confirmations: Lambert and Klineberg, 1967; Radke, Trager, and Davis,
1949; Taylor, 1966; Zeligs, 1948, 1950a, 1950b, 1952, 1953, 1955.
Principle of Change
Confirmations: Meltzer, 1939a, 1941; Zeligs, 1948, 1950, 1952, 1955.
Principle of Consensus
Confirmations: Lambert and Klineberg, 1967.
Principle of Categorical Placement
Confirmations: Gregor and McPherson, 1966; Melamed, 1968; Radke, Tra-
ger, and Davis, 1949.
Principle of Categorical Dominance
Confirmations: Gregor and McPherson, 1966; Radke, Trager, and Davis,
1949.
Principle of Categorical Congruity
Confirmations: Insko and Robinson, 1967; Rokeach, Smith, and Evans, 1960;
Stein, 1966; Stein, Hardyck, and Smith, 1965.
Principle of Ethnic Group Congruity
Confirmations: Horowitz, 1936.
Corollary of Reciprocity
Confirmations: Radke, Trager, and Davis, 1949.
Corollary of Directional Displacement
Confirmations: Gregor and McPherson, 1966; Mayo and Kinzer, 1950;
Meltzer, 1939a, 1939b; 1941; Springer, 1950.
Principle of Marginal Perspective
Confirmations: Fishman, 1955; Gregor and McPherson, 1966; Grossack,
1963; Helgerson, 1943; Hraba and Grant, 1970; Koch, 1946; Koslin, Amarel,
and Ames, 1969; Porter, 1971; Russell and Robertson, 1947; Springer, 1950.
Disconfirmations: Bird, Monachesi, and Burdick, 1952.

more close (interethnic) friendships one had during one's youth, the more
such friendships would one have as an adult" (p. 184).

Two questions remain to be examined. First, we need to know what
types of intergroup experiences have what kinds of effects. Second, we
need to know how early an experience can have an anchoring effect. Finally, whatever the precise effects of anchor experiences may be, we
should remember that they are themselves anchored in a social context,
and that the outcome of subsequent experiences of the developing and

maturing person is not mechanically predetermined by these earlier childhood events.

For very young children, the principle of cognitive anchoring is probably inapplicable, particularly to the learning of ethnic attitudes. The work of Piaget (1947) has demonstrated that young children, below the age of six or seven, have not yet developed a conception of the invariance of physical properties. Lacking a sense of permanence, the child's conceptual world must be clearly different from that of an adult. Further, the absence of a conception of the invariance of physical objects must be equally true in its application to social objects. That is, we should expect that the identities that people have should be viewed by children as being just as impermanent as weight, mass, number, and so on.

10*.   *Principle of Categorical Constancy.* The categorization of social objects does not become stable until the person develops beliefs about the constancy of those objects.

10a.*   Attitude toward ethnic groups cannot become stabilized until the person develops beliefs about the permanence of ethnic identity.

Kohlberg (1966), in his provocative analysis of the development of gender identity, provides important confirmation. Most children learn to use gender categories (boy-girl, man-woman, etc.) quite early, about age three. At that time, the majority can categorize their own gender correctly, and within the next two to three years can correctly categorize others (using mainly observable cues, as would be predicted by the corollary of categorical placement). Just the same, Kohlberg points out, "the young child is not certain of the constancy of gender identity before the age of five-six." In his study, "children of four to eight were asked whether a pictured girl could be a boy if she wanted to, or if she played boy games, or if she wore a boy's haircut or clothes. Most four-year-olds said that she could be a boy if she wanted to, or if she wore the appropriate haircut or clothes. By age six-seven, most children were quite certain that a girl could not be a boy regardless of changes in appearance or behavior" (p. 95).

No formal test of this principle has been attempted in the area, but considerable case material strongly indicates its applicability. From the rich interview materials of Radke, Trager, and Davis (1949), for example, one can clearly observe the fragility of the meaning of skin color to first and second graders:

"He got dirt on his face and his mamma didn't wash him."
"Little boys when they get dirty get into a colored boy and when they get clean they get into a white boy."

"I got brown when I went to Atlantic City."
"When he gets dirty he turns into a colored boy."

Similarly, the children in Hartley, Rosenbaum, and Schwartz' (1948) study when asked "What does it take to be . . . ? What does it mean to be . . . ?" "Jewish," "Catholic," responded with descriptions of these identities as impermanent activities:

> The meaning of "Jewish" to non-Jewish children seems reasonably clear and reasonably unanimous. At every age level it consists primarily of doing something. To the four-year-old non-Jewish child it is "A different kind of talk"; to the nine-year-old, "You go to Shul or Hebrew school—study and read books."
> At every age level the modal definition of the term "Catholic" is as an activity. To the Catholic child and to the non-Catholic alike, being Catholic generally means some variation of, "To speak Catholic"; "To go to church"; or "Go to Catholic school" (p. 379).

Finally, when asked, "Are you Jewish and American?" one 5-year-old answered, "I'm Jewish when I'm awake. When I sleep I'm American" (p. 383).

The principles of cognitive anchoring and categorical constancy point to two dimensions unique to early socialization. Despite their cogency, there has been almost no supporting research. Nevertheless, we should keep them clearly in mind when evaluating research on young children.

The Learning of Ethnic Prejudice

Children under five years of age begin developing ethnic attitudes even before developing the ability to correctly identify those to whom they are directed. However, many 3-year-olds and almost all by age 6 can identify their *own* ethnic status. Ethnic awareness develops earliest among those children in social locations where ethnic definition is of higher social concern. For example, for white American children and English-Canadian children at age 6, sex identity appears most distinctive, but for the South African Bantu child of the same age race is of dominant concern (Lambert and Klineberg, 1967).

The developing child has a three-way problem. The first is learning the major social categories in a community and society. The second is learning the criteria by which people are classified as members or nonmembers of a category. And the third is learning the appropriate modes of attitudinal and behavioral response to classes of people.

If there is any orderliness about this process of categorical learning in young children it remains to be demonstrated. It does not appear that the "solutions" to any of these three problems are taught to children, or learned by them, in any systematic or orderly manner. Thus some ethnic labels are learned by some children before they are fully comprehended; other children learn various coding criteria first; still others interact with their playmates in ways reflecting dominant racist norms even though they cannot identify the ethnicity of others (e.g., McCandless and Hoyt, 1961; Morland, 1958; Renninger and Williams, 1966).

Two new principles summarize the determinants of the rate of socialization.

11. *Principle of polarization.* The greater the polarization of attitudes in a social setting, the earlier their acquisition by children (or new occupants of the setting).

11.1. *Corollary of target visibility.* The more visible an ethnic group is in a social setting, the earlier the acquisition of attitudes toward them.

The effects of polarization and target visibility direct us further to consider a new facet of the principle of categorical placement.

7.2 *Corollary of categorical placement.* In learning the criteria of ethnic classification, persons acquire first those criteria that are most directly observable.

The supporting research, although not extensive, is quite consistent. Lambert and Klineberg (1967) provide basic support for all three principles. In their cross-national studies they interviewed 3300 children—100 6-year-olds, 100 10-year-olds, and 100 14-year-olds—from each of 11 countries: United States, South Africa (Bantu), Brazil, English Canada, French Canada, France, Germany, Israel, Japan, Lebanon, and Turkey. Judging from their data, nationality had no significant effects on the selection of ethnic targets or on the manifest content of the attitudes. (Moreover, national and regional references were relatively unimportant in children's self-identity.)

The younger children (age 6) were focused in their ethnic attitudes on physical features, clothing, language, and distinctive social customs. By age 10, there is a shift to criteria that are far less observable—personality characteristics and ideological differences in religion and politics. There is, of course, an increased differentiation in the responses of older children that is a consequence of their increased language skills; but these findings appear to be independent of that confounding possibility.

Studies conducted in ethnically heterogeneous areas show that young children are more ethnically aware and more accurate in their perception of race-related physical characteristics than are children normally found in Middle American samples (Springer, 1950). Another example of the effects of social location appears in Epstein and Komorita (1965). In a study of upper-middle-class children, the researchers found less rejection of others by race (oriental) than by class (working class).

✓ Renninger and Williams (1966) undertook a study of the awareness of the connotative meaning of white as good and black as bad among 3-, 4-, and 5-year-old children. A secondary aim of their study was the determination of the sequence of learning color connotations and beliefs about race. Picture and puzzle techniques were used in individual testing of the children. The picture technique employed the following procedure:

S was given the following instructions: "What I have here are some pictures I'd like to show you and tell you stories about, and I'd like for you to help me by finishing every story the way you think it should end. I'll show you what I mean." S was then shown the series of 8 picture cards in the order horses, airplanes, dogs, telephones, kittens, wagons, teddy bears, tops. As E held each picture upright on the table midway between E and S, she told a story. A typical story for the black-white test cards was: "One of these horses is a very *good* horse. Whenever Johnny goes out to the farm to see him, the horse runs right up to the fence and lets Johnny pet his nose. Which horse do you think is the *good* horse?" For the filler (non-black-white) cards, a typical story was: "Johnny took his airplanes out in the yard to play with them, and he flew them way up in the sky. One of them flew so high that it got caught up in a tree. Which airplane do you think got caught?" When the 8 picture cards had been shown once through, S was told, "Now let's look at the pictures again with some different stories"; and S was then shown the pictures again in the same order. In all, then, S was exposed twice to each of the 4 test cards and thus had 8 opportunities to respond to the black and white figures.

Each of the stories for the black-white test cards stressed one of eight evaluative words as the basis for S's choice. The words *good, clean, happy,* and *nice* were chosen to represent the positive end of the evaluative dimension, while *bad, dirty, sad* and *naughty* were chosen to reflect the negative end (p. 775).

In the puzzle technique, the researcher "interviewed" the child while playing with puzzles depicting white and black persons. This procedure established the child's degree of racial awareness and his or her ability to use categories designating "race."

Renninger and Williams' data indicated strikingly that young white children learn the evaluative meanings of white as good and black as bad in their preschool years. While 59% of the 3-year-olds were unaware of *both* race and color concepts, only 16% of those aged 4 and 2% of the 5-year-olds were unaware of both. Awareness of color meanings appeared to precede an awareness of the categories of race (Negro, colored, white) for about one-fourth of the children. Thus the polarization—high consensus, distinctiveness, and diffusion—of these color-meanings are a part of the societal background in which American children are socialized. Melamed (1968) employed a different design in studying the learning of criteria of categorical placements. Using a set of cards featuring line drawings of a face varying skin color, hair type, lip shape, and nose shape, he found that skin color was the predominant coding characteristic for 6-, 8-, and 10-year-old white, middle-class boys and girls in a sample drawn from a high-status suburb in Johannesburg, South Africa. Melamed's technique indicated that the probability of response to skin color, when all cues were present, was four times greater than the probability of a response to hair or lip shape and 10 times greater than the likelihood of using nose shape as a code criterion. There were no differences in coding behavior by age. That is, by age 6 "white children have already learned the primary discrimination utilized in South African society" (p. 7).

In virtually all of the studies of children, the learning of criteria of racial classification occurs early. Morland (1958) provides a dramatic illustration in these data:

	Three-Year-Olds	Four-Year-Olds	Five-Year-Olds	Six-Year-Olds
Low ability to identify Negroes in pictures or in person correctly	65%	23%	8%	3%

Not only had 35% of his sample already mastered the placement problem by age 3, but by age 4, in a major growth pattern, the majority of children were able to make correct placements. Ammons (1950) has shown that one out of five 2-year-olds can even identify skin color and facial differences in dolls.

The patterns of attitude development require study, and few studies of the ethnic attitudes of children provide the kind of developmental data that we need. However, from the limited research two summary statements appear.

15.* *Principle of acquisition.* The components of attitudes develop at different rates.

15.1. *Corollary of acquisition.* Attitudes tend to become more differentiated and directionally consistent over time.

In one of the earliest developmental studies of prejudice, Horowitz (1936) hypothesized the existence of attitude growth curves. (Interestingly enough, no one followed up on his research.) Horowitz studied 470 white boys from kindergarten through the eighth grade in New York City. His growth curve hypothesis derived from the differing results he obtained from three measures of prejudice toward Negroes.

His first measure, the Ranks test, involved the boys' rankings of 12 full-face photographs: "Pick out the one you like best, next best, next best. . ." The second, the Show-Me test, used the same set of pictures. This time the subjects were asked a series of 12 questions all prefaced by "Show me all those that you. . . ." The personal distance options included "would play ball with," "want to be in your gang," "would go swimming with," "want to live next door to you." The third measure used, the Social Situations test, consisted of 30 photographs, 15 posed situations photographed once with four white boys and once with three white and one Negro boy. Each subject was shown a photograph and asked whether or not he would like "to join in with them and do what they're doing along with them." They could answer yes, no, or uncertain.

The Ranks test tapped affect, while the Show-Me and Social Situations tests dealt explicitly with personal distance. Probably because the Ranks and Show-Me tests used the same photographs, scores on both correlated more highly across grades than did the other tests.

The specific findings of this study indicate that the affective and conative components may have different rates of development. And from his data, Horowitz drew a set of smoothed curves—reproduced in Figure 1—which represented historically the initial statement of our principle of acquisition.

Further evidence supporting the principle that stereotypes, personal distance, and affective responses have different growth rates is sketchy and

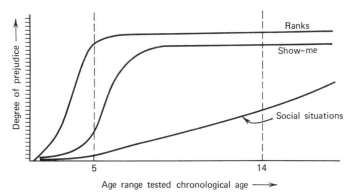

FIGURE 1.   Theoretical growth curves of attitude (after Horowitz, 1936).

virtually leaps a quarter of a century. For example, Tudor (1971), in comparing her research on social class attitudes in young children with earlier work, concludes essentially that the components of class attitudes display different determinants. Unfortunately, her evidence is only suggestive.

More concrete support is provided by Porter (1971), who presents data indicating the differential and rapid development of both stereotype acquisition and degrees of personal distance. Using dolls as a stimulus object, she asked approximately 185 white Boston area children which of two dolls is "lazy and stupid." Their choices, by age, were:

	Three Years	Four Years	Five Years
Chooses white doll	50%	33%	30%
Chooses Negro doll	50%	67%	70%

She also asked the children to choose the doll they would invite home to lunch. For the 107 children who selected the white doll, she asked if they would also invite the Negro:

	Three Years	Four Years	Five Years
Would not also ask Negro	13%	36%	42%

In both cases, the data indicate a rapid change in attitude development between the ages of three and four. And, although comparisons are difficult, the acceptance of the negative stereotype does appear to occur more rapidly than the behavioral rejection.

Even research documenting trends in the acquisition of a single component is rare. Radke and Sutherland (1949) uncovered an important trend in the development of directionally consistent stereotyping. They administered an open-ended questionnaire to the entire public school population of fifth through twelfth graders ($n = 275$) in a very small midwestern town. The questionnaire was handled by the classroom teacher with the following instructions:

Our school has been asked to help in a study of what school children (high-school students) think about various groups of American people. To do this, we are asked to answer some questions.

You will not be graded on these papers. You will not put your name on these papers. Your answers will not be read by the teachers. Your answers will be added to the answers of other children (students).

These are the questions about several groups of American people:
1. What do you think Americans are like?
   What makes you think so?
2. What do you think Negroes are like?
   What makes you think so?
3. What do you think Jews are like?
   What makes you think so?"

Write what you know and think about each question. Don't make up answers if you don't know.

Give your own ideas. You will have 25 minutes to answer the questions (pp. 450-451).

Considering the three targets, the relative frequency of negative stereotypes increases with age, according to the authors. The ratio of negative to positive was as follows:

Grades	American	Negro	Jew
5–6	1:31	1:39	1:1
7–8	1:15	1:5	1:1
9–10	1:8	1:3	1:0.6
11–12	1:10	1:2	1:0.6

Fishman (1955) also finds a change in the relative frequency of positive and negative stereotypes. In his study of Jewish school children ages 9 to 13, he reports that increases in age are associated with a decreasing number of negative stereotypes assigned to white Americans. This is the opposite of the trend reported by Radke and Sutherland, but it is consistent with the principle of marginal perspective.

We have seen, so far, that children learn ethnic attitudes at an incredibly early age; moreover, in past American research, the period between age 3 and age 4 has represented a time of rapid attitudinal development. It seems likely, however, that attitudes do not achieve stability until some time later. Unfortunately, very little research has been directed at the process of stabilization, and most studies begin with children already in school. Of the few reports, the results are all consistent. Zeligs (1938), in a longitudinal study of the personal distance responses of adolescents, and Koch (1946), in a cross-sectional study of second to tenth graders, both reported high conative stability. Meltzer (1941) reported data on the affective responses of 1000 fifth to eighth graders to 21 target groups with average rank correlations across grades of .91. Blake and Dennis (1943) reported high stability in stereotyping for fourth to eleventh graders. Lambert and Klineberg (1967), McNeil (1960), Radke, Trager, and Davis

(1949), and Wilson (1963) all provide further support for the increasing directional consistency of ethnic attitudes with age.

Occasionally researchers have asked adults to indicate when they first began to develop a negative attitude toward a specific ethnic target. In the two major studies where this questioning has occurred (Allport and Kramer, 1946; Rosenblith, 1949), the median response has ranged from 12 to 16 years of age, depending on the study and the target. In the absence of longitudinal information, these data are hard to interpret. One guess is that this age of recall probably reflects the period when a person's attitude became relatively stabilized.

THE PARENTAL FAMILY

The predominant effect of the parental family on the acquisition of ethnic prejudice—or for that matter most early learned attitudes—is extraordinarily well established. This section begins with a general statement of the principle of socialization, then considers the evidence, and concludes by detailing the ways in which the parental family (or the primary agents of socialization) operates as the major source for the transmission of ethnic prejudice.

14. *Principle of socialization.* People develop attitudes similar to those of their primary agents of socialization.

The research literature of social psychology shows moderate to high correlations of attitudes between husband and wife, between parents and children, and among brothers and sisters. In one of the first major studies Murphy, Murphy, and Newcomb (1937) reported parent-child correlations for 548 families in three attitude areas: war, church, and communism. All of their correlations ranged between .43 and .69, and their separate computations by sex of child and sex of parent indicated no substantial effects due to same sex and cross-sex pairings.

Two findings of particular significance are unique to this study. First, the researchers found that a child's attitudes were significantly related to those of his or her siblings. Although this is to be expected, its demonstration serves to point out how the family provides not only a locus for early attitude development but a supporting social network for attitude maintenance.

The second finding is based on their simultaneous control for parent-child age differences and for the parents' occupational level. Although there are some interesting variations in magnitude, the parent-child correlations in attitudes toward war, church, and communism still remained positive and at times strikingly high (e.g., church attitudes for relatively lower-status persons over 24 years of age correlate .86 with their parents' attitudes).

The strength of the parent-child correlations appeared to decrease with occupational status. Lower-status parent-child pairs had higher correlations than did upper-status pairs. Since the data presented by the researchers is sparse, it is hard to know what factors intervened. Presumably, the life circumstances of upper-status children and young adults (particularly when the research was done) provided a greater exposure to attitudinal diversity and a greater potential for the testing of the validity of one's attitudes.

In the research that followed this early study, the basic correlations in attitudes between parents and children (particularly ethnic and political attitudes) have become well established. Further, in almost all cases, parent-parent similarity is greater than parent-child similarity, and siblings display higher correlations with each other than with their parents. And controlled research has indicated that intrafamilial correlations are not the consequences of similarities in age or social location. Finally, the attitude research has indicated that, with respect to most attitudes, no particular parent-child pair displays significantly more resemblance than any other —thus ruling out hypotheses of same-sex and cross-sex conceptions of development (although this is probably not true for self or sex role attitudes).

Supporting evidence for the principle of socialization and these derivative findings can be found in Allport and Kramer (1946); Anisfeld, Munoz, and Lambert (1963); Bird, Monachesi, and Burdick (1952); Campbell, Gurin, and Miller (1954); Dodge and Uyeki (1962); Epstein and Komorita (1966a); Frenkel-Brunswik and Havel (1953); Frenkel-Brunswik and Sanford (1945); Goodman (1964); Hess and Torney (1967); Horowitz and Horowitz (1938); Hyman (1959); Jennings and Niemi (1968); Lane and Sears (1964); Levin (1961); Middleton and Putney (1963); Mosher and Scodel (1960); Radke and Trager (1950); Radke-Yarrow, Trager, and Miller (1952); Remmers and Weltman (1947); Rosenblith (1949); Sears (1969); Troll, Neugarten, and Kraines (1969); Weltman and Remmers (1946); and Wrightsman (1964).

Experiences guided by the primary agents of socialization—since they typically came first—may therefore comprise the basic anchoring experiences for the individual. In the case of parents, we know that they don't always agree, and the correlational evidence certainly indicates that full consensus between parents on ethnic attitudes is not common. Furthermore, ethnic attitudes may not be highly central for either or both parents and so they may exert little influence in this area on the developing child. Thus we should expect that parents, or other primary agents, should be most influential when they are in consensus and when their ethnic attitudes are central to them. These two hypotheses, which have been confirmed, are a part of sets of others that will be dealt with in the final section of the chapter, which is concerned with the effects of reference others.

At present, the parental family is the primary medium of social heredity. The family virtually monopolizes the control of children for many years, and relinquishes direct control only gradually over a period that may extend through early adulthood. There is nothing particularly obscure or esoteric about the patterns of childhood socialization; indeed its very commonplaceness probably has kept us from exploring its patterning. Consider, then, the following outline of how parents convey their ethnic attitudes. (Some of the details will be filled in later; others remain to be studied systematically.)

1. *Parents explicitly communicate their ethnic attitudes to their children in much the same way they instruct the child in all other modes of proper behavior.*

2. *Parents directly control many aspects of intergroup education and most of the opportunities that young children can have for intergroup contacts and experiences.*

3. *Parents engage in child-rearing practices which directly shape the patterns of self-attitudes and attitudes toward people in general that children may develop.*

4. *Parents establish a life style through which ethclass-specific selections of activities and friends come to be learned and accepted by their children.*

In retrospective studies in which adults are asked to report on their childhood experiences, the majority of persons—both those high and low in prejudice—indicate that they had taken over their parents' ethnic attitudes (Allport and Kramer, 1946; Rosenblith, 1949). Although only a relatively small number of people indicate that they reacted against their parents' ethnic attitudes, persons low in prejudice are four to five times more likely to say that than are those who are highly prejudiced. Triandis and Triandis (1962) add data indicating that persons scoring high on a measure of social distance reported that their fathers influenced them more than their mothers, whereas those scoring low reported the reverse.

When children are asked how they came to know about ethnic others, their replies validate the adult reports and add a new dimension. In the Lambert and Klineberg study (1967), 6-year-olds report their learning of ethnic differences to come primarily from their parents and secondarily from movies and television. From 10 years on, the reported sources change; older children do not report receiving their information about ethnic groups from other persons, and this includes their parents. Rather, the major reported sources have now become shifted to impersonal ones: TV, movies, books, magazines, school course work and textbooks— although teachers are seldom mentioned. The transition from personal to impersonal sources appears to be general across the 11 national and cultural groups studied.

Epstein and Komorita (1966a, 1966b), in two studies, examined the relation between children's social distance scores and their perceptions of their parents' scores. In their first study they had fifth-grade Negro children, 120 boys and girls, complete social distance scales for themselves and, three weeks later, complete the same scales they thought their parents would. The correlation between children's and perceived parental social distance was .73. In their second study, using the same measures on a sample of 180 boys and girls in the third to fifth grades of a predominantly lower-middle-class Catholic elementary school in Detroit, the authors found a correlation of .48. Although both correlations indicate the perception of attitudinal correspondence, the difference in the correlations across the studies is sizable and is not explained by the authors.

Surely not all persons reporting that their parents hold the same attitudes or that their parents were influential in producing their attitudes are correct. If assessing the effects of the family on producing ethnic attitudes depended exclusively on these reports, then measuring the errors involved in them would be crucial. However, parental effects can be determined independently of a person's perception of these effects, and the question of the correctness or incorrectness of a person's perception simply becomes another variable to be examined. Thus, observing the frequency and the degree to which children inaccurately perceive their parents' attitudes, we can ask what the nature of the familial relationship is that produces such divergence. More important, we can ask what aspects of that relationship itself determine the child's developing attitudes. This is what we explore next.

CHILD-REARING PRACTICES

In 1954, Gordon Allport attempted cautiously to summarize the existing research:

> It seems very likely that rejective, neglectful, and inconsistent styles of training tend to lead to the development of prejudice (p. 299).

. . . Children who are too harshly treated, severely punished, or continually criticized are more likely to develop personalities wherein group prejudice plays a prominent part (p. 300).

Allport's summary, based primarily on his own observations and on case study materials, holds today with some important qualifications.

Three studies of the relation of maternal child-rearing attitudes to prejudice development are typical of the past research and quite illustrative of the substance of Allport's summary. In one of the first studies in this area, Harris, Gough, and Martin (1950) compared the child-rearing attitudes and reports of mothers of 240 Minneapolis school children (fourth to sixth graders) who had scored highest and lowest on a carefully constructed omnibus measure of anti-Negro attitudes. Some of the items of maternal self-reports that differentiated the criterion groups at a statistically significant level are reproduced below. (The answers cited in parentheses are those selected by the mothers of highly prejudiced children.)

A child of school age should be made to take care of his own room, make his own bed, and the like. (False.)
Obedience is the most important thing a child can learn. (True.)
It is wicked for children to disobey their parents. (True.)
A child ought to be whipped at once for any sassy remark. (True.)
My child gets his own way. (Usually.)
I prefer a quiet child to a "chatterbox." (Very much.)

Dickens and Hobart (1959) contacted by mail the mothers of college freshmen and sophomores who had scored at the extremes on a social distance scale. The 84 questions of their mail questionnaire dealt with three topics: beliefs about possessiveness in parent-child relations, parental dominance, and parental ignoring. Mothers were asked to "think back to the way you felt when your child was still of preschool age." They were, of course, being asked to recall their beliefs of 12 to 15 years earlier.

The *dominance* scores indicated the mother's tendency to put the child in a subordinate role and to demand complete conformity under penalty of severe punishment. Mother's scores correlated (biserial r) .48 with the child's social distance score. Items that discriminated the mothers of prejudiced children were, for example, "Strict discipline is necessary to develop fine, strong character in children"; "A child should be taught that his parents know best."

The second questionnaire topic dealt with *possessiveness*, the tendency to "baby" the child and to value highly the child's dependence. There was no significant correlation between maternal possessiveness and childrens' social distance.

The third dimension, *ignoring*, referred to the mother's tendency to disregard the child as a member of the family. The correlation here was .51. The mothers of the prejudiced children were more likely to agree, for example, that "quiet children were much nicer than little chatterboxes" or to reject the idea that the needs of the children were "the most important consideration in planning home activities."

In the third study, Weatherley (1963) examined the correlation between the scores of 39 college women in two measures of anti-Semitism and their mothers' responses to a mail questionnaire dealing with the way they reacted to their daughter's aggression in childhood. The results suggested that maternal punitiveness was associated with anti-Jewish prejudice.

It is quite likely that the same parent behavior may have different meanings to different children, to siblings, and even to the same child at different ages or levels of development. Further, child-rearing practices vary by social class, and it is reasonable to expect that parental behavior would have different effects on children's attitudes as a consequence of class. One study does, in fact, suggest this.

McCord, McCord, and Howard (1960) report a longitudinal study of 45 lower-class males studied first in 1937–1940 (ages 9–12) and then in 1948 (ages 20–23). Dividing their subjects into three levels of prejudice toward Negroes and Jews, they report that not one of their 11 family background variables distinguishes any of the groups. The variables they used were: the nature of parental unit (i.e., how intact); parental affection for each other; parental dominance; parents' attitude toward the boy; parents' family role; parents' deviance, aggression, crisis reactions, values; disciplinary techniques and the consistency of their application. On the basis of their findings the authors suggested that lower- and middle-class child-rearing practices may have quite different links to the development of prejudice. In particular, they proposed the hypothesis that ethnic prejudice in lower-class persons may have its primary anchors in adult experiences, whereas for middle-class persons, childhood experiences may be the primary anchors.

Epstein and Komorita (1966b) provide evidence that does weaken (but does not disconfirm) the hypothesis of class-specific parental determinants of prejudice. To a sample of 120 working-class fifth graders and their parents (in Detroit, Michigan), they administered a measure of social distance. Their findings that parents' and children's scores correlated at .62 clearly points to strong parental effects.

Triandis and Triandis (1962) provide still another perspective by randomizing class differences in order to examine cross-cultural effects. In a study of Greek and American students, they tested the hypothesis that child training practices which may be expected to produce insecure adults will be found more frequently in the life histories of individuals showing large social distances than among individuals showing small social distances. The hypothesis was confirmed. In both cultures, the more highly prejudiced reported inconsistent punishment and poorer explanations of parental norms than did those lower in prejudice. In addition, there were some differences between the high and the low social distance subjects that reached statistical significance in only one culture. Thus the highly prejudiced Greeks reported that they were overprotected but also said that they were punished physically more frequently than did low-scoring Greeks. The highly prejudiced Americans, in contrast, reported that their home atmospheres were cold and their parents indifferent or rejecting. This was the opposite of what was reported by the less prejudiced American subjects.

Perhaps one of the most vital qualifications to Allport's summary of child-rearing practices should be given to the relative importance of punitive parental behaviors as compared to the importance of parental indifference. Although a firm linkage has not yet been established between parental indifference and the prejudice of children indifference is strongly associated with a child's negative self-attitudes—and, as we shall see, negative self-attitudes are strongly linked with prejudice.

Rosenberg (1965) attempted to explore the effects of parent-child relations on the development and correlates of self-attitudes. Deliberately ignoring the standard child-rearing variables, Rosenberg asked this straightforward question: How interested is the parent in the child, and what is the relation between parental interest or indifference and the child's self-esteem? He selected for analysis three diverse areas of general and recurrent importance—the child's friends, grades in school, and participation in mealtime conversation. Combining the three into an index of parental interest, the researcher was able to determine its effects on self-esteem, which he measured by a 10-item scale in an extensive sample of high school seniors and juniors. For those whose parents evidenced some lack of interest ($n = 241$), he found that 44% had low self-esteem. In contrast, only 26% ($n = 945$) of those whose parents did not appear to be indifferent manifested low self-esteem. Controls for class, religion, city size, and even reactions to parental punishment did not affect the relationship. Rosenberg concluded:

These data thus suggest that extreme parental indifference is associated with lower self-esteem in the child, and, in fact, seems to be even more deleterious than punitive parental reactions. . . .

Of course, it is probably not simply interest *per se* which accounts for the observed relationships. Very likely such lack of interest in the child goes along with lack of love, a failure to treat the child with respect, a failure to give him encouragement, a tendency to consider the child something of a nuisance and to treat him with irritation, impatience, and anger. But whatever other kinds of parental behavior may be reflected in these indicators, they probably at least reflect the idea that the child is important to someone else, that others consider him of worth, of value, of concern. The feeling that one is important to a significant other is probably essential to the development of a feeling of self-worth (p. 146).

Child-rearing practices are not in themselves of special interest in the study of prejudice. They are important in two ways. The first is their effect on the development of the child's self-attitudes and her or his concomitant attitudes toward others, including the parents themselves. We examine this in the following section of this chapter. The second area of significance is the effect of child-rearing practices on the development of basic anxiety and the child's ability to cope in problem-solving situations. We examine this later.

SELF- AND OTHER-ATTITUDES

Ethnicity is a major characteristic by which people code themselves and other persons in society. Some people use ethnicity as a basis for organizing their attitudes toward almost all persons. Others hold attitudes toward only specific ethnic targets. The use of ethnic categories displays normative as well as individual variation. In some communities, and at some stages of intergroup relations, ethnicity varies in social importance.

In American society, ethnicity is one of the dominant categories of interpersonal coding. It should not be surprising to observe, then, that some people who display a negative attitude toward one ethnic group also hold negative attitudes toward other ethnic groups. Nor should it be surprising that, for some people, negative attitudes toward ethnic groups are associated with negative attitudes toward other social categories of people, for example, the aged or the deaf (e.g., Chesler, 1965; Cowen, Bobrove, Rockway, and Stevenson, 1967; and Kogan, 1961).

Social scientists have generally confused two issues surrounding "attitudes toward others" and the presumed "generality" of ethnic prejudice. First, other-attitudes are not the same as ethnic attitudes. Presumably a person may hold a negative attitude to one or more ethnic groups (in keeping with the norms of a given community) without holding negative attitudes toward people in general. In contrast, it seems unlikely that one may hold negative attitudes toward people without holding negative attitudes toward specific ethnic groups. The direction of this relationship has never been formally tested. In the only two studies in which ethnic attitudes and other-attitudes have been jointly considered, the design and results indicate nothing more than that the two are correlated (Sullivan and Adelson, 1954; Rosenberg, Suchman, and Goldsen, 1957).

The second area of confusion involves two interconnected forms of evidence that have been exhibited as "proof" of the generality of prejudice. One form involves the repeated findings of low-to-moderate correlations between measures of attitudes toward different ethnic groups. This finding can scarcely be doubted; it has been replicated so frequently that it no longer bears citation. What does bear repeating, however, is the fact that the magnitude of these correlations tends to be underplayed while the presence of a positive correlation tends to be overplayed.

The other kind of evidence—among the earliest and most cited— were the dramatic findings that people would respond to even *fictional* ethnic group labels with displays of moderate prejudice. The original discovery of this intriguing but overblown finding was reported first by Hartley (1946). In 1938, to samples of students from eight northeastern colleges, Hartley administered an 8-point social distance scale which included 32 ethnic targets and three fictional groups, Pirenean, Wallonian, and Danirean. The correlations (r) of the mean distance responses to these groups with the 32 real groups ranged, by sample, from .78 to .85.

Although there have been many replications of that finding, some very recent (e.g., Epstein and Komorita, 1966a), the willingness of people to respond to hypothetical groups has been grossly overstated by prejudice researchers. Hartley's findings, in fact, were not quite as powerful as those who followed him seemed to think. A close look at his data indicates that 45% of his subjects would not respond to his query about the fictitious groups. (This estimate derives from Hartley's Table 8, p. 31.)

About seven years after Hartley published his findings, Prothro and Melikian (1953) attempted a replication with students from Arab Near Eastern countries who were enrolled at the American University of Beirut (Lebanon). They found that 93% of their sample refused to answer for the hypothetical groups. Even more than that, where Hartley found a split-half correlation (r) across all of his social distance targets of .95, Prothro and Melikian reported a correlation of .03 for their ethnic targets. They concluded that the findings of generalized prejudice or ethnocentrism probably represented the "special features" of America and similar cultures.

Somewhat later, Ehrlich and Rinehart (1965) and Ehrlich (1964) demonstrated the manner in which the extent and intercorrelation of ethnic prejudices were determined by the design of the instruments used to measure prejudice. The first study showed how a standard stereotype checklist would cause more people to respond and respondents to produce more responses than an open-end measure of stereotypes. For example, when using a preliterate group unknown to most people (the Alorese), the checklist resulted in 21% more people responding and nine times more stereotypes being assigned. In the second study, Ehrlich demonstrated how the correlation (C) of Negro and Jewish attitudes could be reduced from .54 to .37 by alterations in the response format of the questionnaires. That is, a forced response format increased the magnitude of prejudice responses. Fink (1971) presented corrobative data for both real and fictional ethnic groups.

Thus both the universality and the precision of research demonstrating the generality of prejudice is open to serious question. It should be clear that for some individuals, in some social locations, ethnic prejudices may be correlated, whereas for other persons in other social locations they may be discrete. There is some direct evidence, for example, that anti-Jewish and anti-Negro attitudes may be fairly independent (Prothro, 1952; Hoffstaetter, 1952; Ehrlich, 1962b; see also Chapter 3 of this book). Furthermore, the fact that most of the intercorrelations of ethnic attitudes have been reported as low-to-moderate may itself be indicative of their relative independence—given, particularly, the degree of over-statement that may be added through instrument errors. Finally, we need to reiterate that the selection of discrete ethnic groups as targets of prejudice is the social consequence of the historical relations among ethnic groups in society. If negative ethnic attitudes covary, we might first look to history and only subsequently to cognitive structures.

One body of research through which we can free ourselves from the constraints of social history is that of the investigation of "other-attitudes," that is, of attitudes toward people in general. Prejudice researchers have seldom examined this body of literature, despite the fact that it is crucial in several statements of social psychological theories. Recognition of the correspondence between the way in which people categorize others and the way in which they categorize themselves has come slowly. Yet self- and other-attitudes are linked inextricably. Positive self-attitudes provide the base for the acceptance of others; negative self-attitudes, for the rejection of others. In its basic form, this linkage is stated in the principle of self-congruity.

13. *Principle of self-congruity.* The more favorable are a person's self-attitudes, the greater the number of acceptable targets and the more positive their attitudes toward them; the more negative the self-attitudes, the greater the number of unacceptable targets and the more negative are attitudes toward them.

Self-acceptance is a partial consequence of a child's acceptance by her or his parents. The response of the child appears to be reciprocal: the acceptance of accepting parents or the rejection of rejecting parents. No single study has, as yet, covered all of the relevant variables, but the cumulative force of the available research is impressive and supports our hypothesis of a reciprocal response.[1]

Zuckerman, Baer, and Monashkin (1956) examined the correlations between self-attitudes, attitudes toward others, and attitudes toward parents in a psychiatric patient and normal subject sample. Self- and other-attitudes correlated (r) in both samples approximately at .40. Attitudes toward mother and father (which were computed separately) showed only minor variations within and between samples. Parental attitudes correlated with other-attitudes, on the average, at .44. Self-attitudes and parental attitudes did vary by parent and by sample. For the patients, self-attitudes were not correlated with attitudes toward their mothers but were correlated ($r = .40$) with father attitudes. In the normal sample, both correlations were strong with self-attitudes: .61 with mothers and .46 with fathers. Suinn (1961) also found favorable self-attitudes to be positively correlated with attitudes toward one's father. He reported a correlation (r) of .32 between his measures taken in a sample of 82 male high school seniors.

Studies involving direct measures of ethnic prejudice and parental attitudes are rare. Adorno and his associates (1950) found in their depth interviews that ethnocentric persons were highly ambivalent toward their parents. Although they appeared to idealize them, they essentially depicted their parents as stern, moralistic, and rejecting. Mussen (1950), studying boys 8 to 14 years of age, reported that those high in prejudice displayed more hostility toward their parents than those who were low in prejudice.

Wylie (1961, pp. 124–126) provides a valuable checklist of research problems and an extensive bibliographic guide to the issue of the relation of self-attitudes and parent-child behavior.

Two studies in 1949 began the formal quantitative investigation of the relation of self-attitudes to attitudes toward others. Sheerer (1949), in a clinical study of 10 persons in counseling, had independent judges code the self- and other-attitudinal responses through all of the counseling interviews of each subject. The correlation of the judges' ratings on these two dimensions was .51. A unique finding of this research, although not well documented, was the researcher's report that as self-acceptance increased through counseling, so the acceptance of others also increased.

Stock (1949) studied the *affective* responses made by persons about themselves and about others. Her sample was 10 cases in counseling, and her units of analysis were the coded contents of the counseling interviews—each subject had four to nine interviews. The degree of affect expressed was coded by the author and partly by two independent judges. The correlation of self and other affective responses computed across all interviews and subjects was .66.

Both the Stock and Sheerer studies were methodologically primitive, but their work instigated the development of formal instruments and more rigorous tests of the basic self-other relationship.

Phillips (1951) constructed a 25-item scale of self-attitudes and a 25-item scale of attitudes toward others. Both instruments had the subjects respond on a 5-point scale of salience—from "rarely or almost never true of me" to "true for me all or most of the time." Examples of items measuring attitudes toward others are:

I find it hard to accept some minority group members as equals.
One soon learns to expect very little of other people.
Some people are always trying to get more than their share of the good things in life.
A small group of obnoxious people stir up most of the troubles which we read about in the papers.

Phillips administered his scales to four specimen groups of college and high school students. The correlations (r) between the self- and other-attitudes scale scores ranged from .51 to a high of .74. The following year, McIntyre (1952), using Phillips' scales on a selected sample of freshmen dorm residents, reported self-other scale correlations of .46.

Berger (1952) also constructed his own scales of attitudes toward self and toward others. Administering his scales to five diverse groups, including college students, a prison sample, and a sample of persons with speech pathologies, Berger obtained correlations (r) ranging from .36 to .69.

Omwake (1954) administered to a group of 113 introductory psychology students the scales developed by Phillips and by Berger, as well as those introduced by Bills, Vance, and McLean (1951). All of the nine self- and other-attitudes scale correlations between the two sets of instruments were positive, ranging in magnitude from .18 to .41.

Fey (1955) devised still another pair of scales to measure these two variables and, as in the earlier research, obtained a moderate and positive correlation between them (r = .43). To these two scales, the researcher added a third, a measure of the subject's "estimated acceptability to others." Persons with positive self-attitudes perceived themselves as highly acceptable to others. The correlation between self-attitudes and perceived attitudes of others toward the self was .71. Williams (1962) replicated this study reporting a much higher self-other attitudes correlation (.64), and a slightly lower correlation between self-attitudes and the perceived attitudes of others toward oneself (.62). Thus it appears that not only do persons with favorable self-conceptions have more favorable attitudes toward people, but they perceive that other people share their favorable self-attitudes. Another perspective for assessing the validity of the principle of self-congruity is provided by the research of Lundy, Katkovsky, Cromwell, and Shoemaker (1955). They administered to 54 students a multiple choice personality description questionnaire calling for a self-description, a description of one's ideal self, and one's best-liked and least-liked same-sex friend. Positive and negative self-attitude scores were computed on the basis of the correspondence of self and ideal self descriptions. Comparisons were made between these positive and negative descriptions and the person's descriptions of their sociometric targets. The authors concluded from their analysis:

> As hypothesized, descriptions of positive sociometric choices were more similar to the Ss' acceptable self descriptions than to their unacceptable self descriptions. Descriptions of negative sociometric choices tended to be more similar to the Ss' unacceptable self descriptions than to their acceptable self descriptions. In general, Ss were found to describe persons they like best as more similar to themselves than persons they like least. However, the extent of this similarity appears to be determined in part by the individual's acceptance or un-acceptance of himself. A significant positive relationship was also found between adjustment and similarity between self and positive sociometric choice.

A new consideration is added by the research of Suinn and Hill (1964). They administered to 92 college students two measures of anxiety (test anxiety and general anxiety) and the Phillips self-other questionnaire. As expected, the correlation between self-acceptance and the acceptance of others was positive ($r = .35$). Both measures of anxiety, however, were negatively related to the self- and other-acceptance scores. The effects of anxiety were particularly pronounced for self-acceptance—the correlation (r) with general anxiety was $-.66$ and with test anxiety was $-.58$. The correlations between acceptance of others and the anxiety measures were $-.21$ (general) and $-.28$ (test). It appeared that anxiety had a greater effect on the direction of self-attitudes than on the direction of other-attitudes. This relation between anxiety and negative self-attitudes has been observed in a variety of studies of children and adults (e.g., Bledsoe, 1964; Coopersmith, 1959; Hanlon, Hofstaetter, and O'Connor, 1954; Ohn-macht and Muro, 1967; Rosenberg, 1965).

While anxiety can be linked directly to ethnic attitudes (e.g., Morse and Allport, 1952), its probable importance here is that anxiety and negative self-attitudes are together strongly associated with social conformity (see Marlowe and Gergen, 1969) and with dogmatism, a major supporting mechanism of prejudice to be discussed later.

Further evidence in support of the principle of self-congruity can be found in Crandall and Bellugi (1954), Fiedler, Warrington, and Blaisdell (1952), Fey (1957), Kipnis (1961), Lee and Ehrlich (1971), Levanway (1955), Pedersen (1969), Reese (1961), Rosenberg (1965), and Wylie (1957). In addition, the extensive research on mate selection undoubtedly contains much that would be germane to the principle of self-congruity. Marriage tends to occur between persons who are similar in marital status, age, generation, nationality and nativity, religion, social class, occupational strata, and intelligence. Goode, Hopkins, and McClure (1971) provide an extensive summary and bibliographic guide to the literature.

Very little research has dealt directly with self-attitudes and ethnic attitudes; all that has is supportive of the principle of self-congruity. Only three studies have been conducted specifically with children. Gough, Harris, Martin, and Edwards (1950) and Tabachnick (1962) found that children scoring high on an omnibus measure of anti-Negro attitudes displayed greater negative attitudes than those scoring low.

Tabachnick (1962) tested the hypothesis that "prejudice will vary systematically with the degree of satisfaction with self in children" (p. 194). To test his hypothesis, he sampled the fifth grades in six elementary schools in suburban San Francisco—approximately 302 boys and girls. The students were administered the 18-item scale designed by Gough, Harris, Martin, and Edwards to tap attitudes toward Negroes. Ten assessments of self-attitudes were obtained. Each child was asked to check "yes" or "no" in response to the question, "Am I pretty well satisfied with myself in this?" The response was made to 10 statements in each of 10 categories of self-attitudes. The eight categories significantly correlating with anti-Negro attitudes and their correlations were:

Category	r
Satisfaction with mental abilities	−.14
Satisfaction with social relations	
Opposite sex	−.15
Same sex	−.21
Parents	−.12
Teachers	−.14
Satisfaction with personality	
Social virtues	−.27
Happy qualities	−.17
Satisfaction with school subjects	−.13

Neither the categories of "satisfaction with physical abilities" nor "satisfaction with work habits" yielded significant correlations. The composite score for all of the self-attitudes categories and the anti-Negro attitudes score correlated at −.22. It is clear from Tabachnick's data that children who had developed positive self-attitudes were less prejudiced than those whose attitudes were more negative.

Trent (1957) studied 202 Negro children in New York City public schools. The sample ranged in age from 9 to 18 years, with a median age of 13.4. The students were administered scales tapping their attitudes to both Negroes and whites. They were also given a sentence completion test from which an index of self-attitudes was constructed. As expected, all scores were positively associated. The most self-accepting students expressed significantly more positive attitudes to both Negroes and whites than did the least self-accepting.

In two of the cities they studied, Williams and his associates (1964) were able to compile data on the self- and ethnic attitudes of 515 Negro residents. Using a three-item index of prejudice, directed toward foreigners, Mexicans, and Jews, they found "Negroes who reject a variety of outgroups also tend to accept negative stereotypes and criticisms of Negroes" (p. 76).

Vinacke (1956), in one of those studies that are so ahead of their time that they have to be rediscovered, examined the internal structure of the self- and ethnic attitudes relationship. More precisely, he studied the connection between the direction of specific beliefs applied to oneself and the directionality of that same belief as assigned to ethnic targets. He found that self-descriptive beliefs are of stronger directionality than those assigned to ethnic targets. Characteristics that were assigned to ethnic targets but not thought to be true of oneself had the lowest directionality. However, when a characteristic was thought to be self-descriptive and also descriptive of an ethnic target, it had the highest directionality. Thus Vinacke's microscopic analysis indicated that if a characteristic is assigned to both self and others, it has the highest directionality and is followed in magnitude by beliefs assigned to the self only, and then by those assigned to other targets only.

Pearl (1954), in another provocative early study, examined 12 male, hospitalized neurotic patients. Prior to their assignment to therapy, they were administered the E-scale and an ad hoc measure of self-attitudes. The patients were retested at the conclusion of therapy which averaged three months. Self-attitudes scores displayed a correlation of .67 with E-scale scores on the initial test and a correlation of .64 for the final test. There was suggestive evidence to indicate that those who developed more positive self-attitudes became less ethnocentric.

Why should self-attitudes display such an invariant relation to the rejection of others?

First, insofar as self-attitudes are generated initially in the child's relation to her or his parents, there may be some generalization that occurs from this relationship. That is, the child may generalize from rejecting or indifferent parents to perceiving other persons as similar.

Second, the child may generalize from his or her self-attitudes to other people. In this instance, particularly in the absence of information about others, the person may use his or her own self-attitudes as the criteria for classifying others. (See the principles of categorical congruity and self-congruity.)

Third, the deprecation of others may have the potential of enhancing self-attitudes. Thus negative attitudes toward others may, in part, be a mechanism of personal defense.

Finally, we should note that the same child-rearing factors that produce negative self-attitudes also operate to increase anxiety and probably to retard intellectual development. In particular, we should note that negative self-attitudes may be part of a syndrome of cognitive characteristics that enhance the acquisition and maintenance of ethnic prejudice.

To conclude this section, it should be noted that the human acquisition of identity—of a relatively stable and coherent set of self-attitudes—occurs over a long period of time. Changes in physical capabilities and well-being as a concomitant of age contribute to making self-attitudes continually change. And as these changes in the life cycle parallel changes in social locations and social networks, so the relation of one's self to other objects in the environment changes.

THE SUPPORTING MECHANISMS OF PREJUDICE

The "supporting mechanisms" of an attitude could be all of the objects in an individual's environment that contribute to the maintenance of that attitude. Here "environment" is used in that broad sense in which social psychologists have often used it to include the psychological characteristics of the individual as well as the specific life situations in which she or he is located. Such a use also includes the characteristics of the community and the society in which the individual lives.

Obviously such a construction of "support" is so broad as to require that we study everything in order to comprehend the stability of prejudice. The crucial question is what aspects of the total environment contribute most to the support of prejudice? Unfortunately the answer to that question does not really exist. In fact, it seems that no social scientist has even asked that question—at least in that form. How then can we proceed?

Let me illustrate the problem. Many social psychologists believe that there is a personality characteristic that we can appropriately term "sociability." Moreover, the available evidence indicates that persons who manifest low levels of sociability tend to score higher on measures of prejudice (Williams, 1964) and to display a set of other personality characteristics which are themselves supportive of ethnic prejudice (Rubenowitz, 1963). Nevertheless, I do not believe that sociability is a factor of causal significance in either the acquisition or the maintenance of prejudice. This I believe to be true about most of the dimensions which are conventionally labeled "personality." Therefore those materials are not reviewed here. The research literature reveals a surprisingly large number of hypothesized variables of personality which have displayed some measure of association with an indicator of prejudice. Unfortunately, there has been no systematic review of that research.

Another dimension that has received considerable attention among students of prejudice has been contact. It is clear from the available research, which is extensive, that certain properties of the contact situation between members of different groups are important in determining the stability or change of an attitude. For American children, and even to a large degree for adults, the determinants of personal contact are primarily ecological. Spatial segregation in residence, school, and recreational areas are the major societal mechanisms controlling the interethnic contacts of people. The occurrence of contact is most likely in highly structured, socially regulated situations. Such situations tend to be functionally specific, with relatively explicit objectives, with a narrow scope of activities, and clearly defined roles. These situational dimensions minimize the likelihood of attitude change and restrict its generality when it occurs. Where situational objectives are relatively unstructured, status-role relations equalized or vague, and activities diffuse, behavior is personalized. Under such conditions, particularly if they are repetitive or constant, the likelihood of favorable attitude development and its transfer across situations is maximized.

The instance of intergroup contact signals two possibilities for the testing of the cognitive placements and categorical responses that an individual typically employs for ethnic others. The contact situation, then, may be conceptualized as one in which people have the opportunity to test their attitudes. And one of the major effects of intergroup contact, which is not apparent from the traditional literature, is that contact operates to increase the veridicality of intergroup imagery. Preiss and Ehrlich (1966, Chapter 7) present one of the more dramatic illustrations of this in the context of police-civilian contacts. Intergroup contacts also provide the possibility of the establishing of a new social network for the individuals involved. The dimensions we need to consider are those that characterize the membership group and reference group matrixes of people. This means that we consider such variables as the legitimacy, power, visibility, sanctions, and centrality of the social relationship and not those that contact theorists have typically considered. Fortunately an excellent review of the traditional literature has recently been published (Amir, 1969), so that the reader curious or dissatisfied with the novel approach here may consult Amir's review.

There are two major categories of supporting mechanisms that warrant intensive social psychological analysis. The first are those mechanisms relating to the cognitive aspects of prejudice. The kinds of beliefs one holds and how these beliefs are organized are presumably a consequence of the cognitive abilities and the mode of cognitive organization that characterizes people. The second set of mechanisms are those that deal with the structure of social relationships, particularly reference group support for ethnic attitudes and intergroup behavior.

The Mechanisms of Cognitive Support

The cognitive abilities of an individual mediate between what goes on "out there" in society and what gets incorporated into the individual's systems of belief and disbelief. That elementary principle should be incorporated into our formal system—although, as we shall see, it entails some rather nonelementary consequences.

7.3. *Corollary of categorical learning.* The learning of social categories, the criteria of placement; and tests for the accuracy of placement are contingent on cognitive ability.

Hess and Torney (1967), in their prodigious nationwide study of the political socialization of approximately 12,000 school children in grades two to eight, provide important materials on the effects of intelligence. In general, their data indicate conclusively that high intelligence accelerates the acquisition of political attitudes, and that the brighter children are "more completely socialized" in their political attitudes and behavior by the eighth grade than are the less intelligent children. They concluded: "In summary, children of high intelligence are more active, more likely to discuss political matters, more interested in current events; they have a greater sense of efficacy and a greater sense of the importance of voting and citizen participation. Intelligence is associated with greater involvement in political affairs" (pp. 223–224).

Suppose that in contrast to most Americans, children were socialized into a community in which there was high consensus on the futility of electoral politics, the illegitimacy of the present government, and the malevolence of current leadership. Wouldn't we expect most children to manifest those attitudes? Using five questions dealing with attitudes toward the President of the United States, Jaros, Hirsch, and Fleron (1968) compared the responses of fifth- to twelfth-grade school children in the Appalachian region of Eastern Kentucky with the data of Hess and Easton (1960) from Chicago area children. The Kentucky children, responding in an environment which is considerably more hostile to the federal government and party politics than the environment of the Chicago children, report significantly greater negative attitudes toward the President than the Chicago area children.

Although Jaros and his associates have no measure of intelligence, the national data of Hess and Torney lead us to expect that the more intelligent children would be more hostile to the President. Or do they?

Socialization into prejudice differs from political socialization in at least two ways. First, despite the polarization of negative ethnic attitudes in this society, attitudes of ethnic tolerance are also well developed. Second, children insofar as they have opportunities for intergroup contact, directly or vicariously, have an opportunity to test the validity of their developing cognitive strategies. In contrast, attitudes toward established political processes have no highly polarized opposition, nor do young children have much of an opportunity to test the adequacy of their conceptions of the political system.

With respect to the acquisition and maintenance of negative ethnic attitudes, the corollary of categorical learning, in its application, postulates an inverse relation between cognitive abilities and negative attitudes toward ethnic groups.

7.3a.   The acquisition of and retention of ethnic prejudice is inversely related to cognitive ability.

7.3a(1).   High levels of intellectual ability retard the acquisition of ethnic prejudice.

7.3a(2).   Ethnic prejudice is associated with lower scores on formal tests of intelligence, greater problem-solving rigidity, and a more closed cognitive structure.

7.3b.   Changes in the level of ethnic prejudice are associated with changes in cognitive abilities.

Before we proceed to examine the supporting evidence, a note of caution is in order. With a few exceptions most of the research involving the cognitive mechanisms of support have employed ad hoc or omnibus measures of prejudice. The California Ethnocentrism scale is a good example. In its most commonly used version, the 10-item Form 45, it includes five targets (Negroes, Jews, zootsuiters, foreign ideas and agitators, America) with one conative and nine cognitive items. As a gross indicator of prejudice, it is adequate, but as a basis for making formal statements about the structure of prejudice and its nexus with the cognitive mechanisms, it permits only very general statements.

Kutner (1958) provides confirming evidence for most of the specific applications of the corollary of categorical learning. In his original study, he investigated the cognitive correlates of the ethnic attitudes of 60 7-year-olds in an upper-middle-class Boston suburb. His measure of ethnic attitudes was a structured-projective questionnaire using six ethnic targets. To assess cognitive abilities, he devised measures of concept formation, deductive reasoning, and inductive reasoning. Comparing the students who were high and low on prejudice, he characterized the "mental functions" of the two groups as follows (p. 42):

Prejudiced Child	Unprejudiced Child
1. Rigidity	1. Flexibility
2. Overgeneralization	2. Realistic generalization
3. Categorizing and dichotomizing	3. Individualizing
4. Concretization	4. Abstraction
5. Simplification	5. Retention of complexity
6. Furcation	6. Retention of totality
7. Dogmatism (omniscience)	7. Lack of dogmatism
8. Intolerance of ambiguity	8. Tolerance of ambiguity

Nine years later, Kutner and Gordon (1964) restudied the same group of children, then in their middle teens. As before, less prejudiced subjects displayed greater ability on the three measures of cognitive abilities.

Looking at the subjects performance over the nine-year interval, the researchers observed that when a person increases in his or her level of prejudice, "there is corresponding evidence that cognitive functioning declines moderately. When ethnic prejudice disappears there is a rise in cognitive ability" (Kutner and Gordon, 1946, p. 74).

Rokeach (1951a, 1951b), in an early set of studies, also provides important evidence documenting differences in the intellectual strategies of persons of varying degrees of prejudice. During the spring and summer of 1949 144 freshmen students at Michigan State University were administered a 10-item measure of ethnocentrism (containing items on Jews, Negroes, and foreigners) and a brief conceptual task designed to uncover selected aspects of their problem-solving strategies. Subjects were given a mimeographed page on which there appeared in alphabetical order the following five religious and five political-economic concepts: Buddhism,

Capitalism, Catholicism, Christianity, Communism, Democracy, Fascism, Judaism, Protestantism, and Socialism. First, they were asked to define each concept. Second, after they were finished, they were asked to describe "in what way any or all of these concepts were interrelated."

When the definitions were classified as concrete or abstract, the researcher observed that those scoring on the lowest quartile in ethocentrism gave significantly fewer concrete definitions and tended to give significantly more abstract definitions than all other subjects. When the subjects were classified as having a "comprehensive," "isolated," or "narrow" mode of organizing the 10 concepts, the cognitive deficits of the prejudiced were even more apparent. Subjects scoring low on the ethnocentrism scale organized the 10 concepts relatively more comprehensively than all others. Those in the middle quartiles organized their concepts in a more isolated fashion, while those highest in ethnocentrism were the most narrow in their cognitive strategies.

Attempts to show that negative ethnic attitudes serve to distort fundamental logical processes have not been successful. The findings have been mixed, but almost none of the research has been characterized by sound procedure, let alone by adequate measures of ethnic attitudes (Henle and Michael, 1956; Morgan and Morton, 1944; Prentice, 1957; Thistlethwaite, 1950; Thouless, 1959).

In two of the more careful studies, with the later designed as a replication, Thistlethwaite (1950) and Prentice (1957) achieved opposite findings. Thistlethwaite demonstrated that negative ethnic attitudes were associated with a lesser ability to solve syllogisms involving the attitudinally relevant ethnic groups and Prentice demonstrated that only those with positive ethnic attitudes had greater difficulty in their solutions.

Very few investigations have entailed a formal measure of intelligence along with a measure of ethnic attitudes. Group intelligence testing is generally so time consuming that most investigators have to rely upon the availability of such data in school or other institutional records. Partly for that reason, there have been very few reports of the association of prejudice and intelligence test performance. Table 2 summarizes the confirming studies. As you can see, the magnitude of the correlations are all fairly low. Two studies not shown in the table yield disconfirming evidence. Bolton (1935) reported no significant correlations, using the Hinckley scale and the Thurstone Psychological Examination. Kutner (1958) also indicated that his high- and low-prejudiced children were not differentiated on the Pintner-Durost intelligence test. No doubt these low correlations and occasional disconfirmations supplied another reason for the neglect of inquiry here.

Nevertheless, intelligence is not a cause of prejudice but rather one mechanism that should retard its acquisition or accelerate its rejection. Be-

TABLE 2. STUDIES OF THE RELATION OF INTELLIGENCE
TEST SCORES AND PREJUDICE

Source	Measure of Intelligence	Measure of Prejudice	Sample	Correlation
Applezweig (1954)	Navy General Classification Test	California Ethnocentrism (E) scale (20 items, form not specified)	79 Naval candidates for submarine school administered the E scale three times	tau=−.25, −.40, −.32.
Gough (1951)	Otis (no further specification)	California Anti-Semitism scale (Adorno et al., 1950)	271 high school seniors	r=−.37
	Otis-Pintner (no further specification)	Purdue scale of attitudes toward Jews (Grice and Remmers, 1934)	231 high school seniors	r=−.34 r=−.30
Levinson (in Adorno et al., 1950)	Army General Classification Test	E scale, Form 45	178 men enrolled in Maritime school	r=−.20
	Otis, Higher Form A	E scale, Form 45	50 male veterans	r=−.22
	Wechsler-Bellvue	E scale, form not specified	77 male inmates of San Quentin prison	r=−.28

cause of this, the significance of this variable is not to be found in the size of its correlation with measures of prejudice, but in the way in which it operates in specific social contexts. One of the few examples of the effect of intelligence (and presumably other mechanisms of cognitive support) as an accelerator of attitudinal effects can be seen in a recent study by Singer (1967). Singer compared fifth-grade white students in an integrated suburban New York City school (which she labeled "high-exposure" students) with those in an all-white school (which she called "low-exposure" students). She assessed their level of prejudice through four procedures: an omnibus attitude scale; a 6-target stereotype checklist; a 12-target social distance checklist; and a measure of familiarity with Negro celebrities. Level of intelligence was assessed by two group tests: the Henman-Nelson in the low-exposure class, and the Kuhlman-Anderson in the

Source	Measure of Intelligence	Measure of Prejudice	Sample	Correlation
Minard (1931)	Otis, Self-Administering Tests of Mental Ability	71 items dealing with race attitudes	100 7th–12th graders in Iowa schools	$r = .34*$
Rokeach (1951a)	American Council of Education (ACE)	E scale, Form 45	144 college freshmen at Michigan State	$r = -.28$
Sims and Patrick (1936)	Otis, Self-Administering, Advanced, Form A	Hinckley (1932) Scale of Attitude toward the Negro	Three samples of college students at Ohio University and the University of Alabama	Average $r = .18*$
Zeligs and Hendrickson (1933)	Otis, Form A	A social distance scale featuring 39 targets and 7 behaviors	178 Sixth-grade children, approximate average age of 12 years	$r = .31$

* The direction of these correlations is the arbitrary consequence of scoring; the relationship is inverse.

high-exposure group. Singer summarized her findings:

> On the attitude scale, the high IQ, high exposure students were significantly more favorably disposed towards Negroes and towards foreign nationalities than the other three categories of students. Although no significant differences were found between high and low exposure subjects in terms of the social stereotypes they attributed to various groupings, the high IQ, high exposure students did attribute more positive and fewer negative stereotypes to Negroes and to foreign groups than the other categories. On the social distance measures, these students also indicated willingness for a greater proximity with Negroes, and had the narrowest range of distance for the twelve groups. These students also indicated greater familiarity with and positive feeling for Negro celebrities (Singer, 1967, p. 114).

Rigidity and Dogmatism

The correlations between measures of problem-solving rigidity and intelligence are generally small, while intelligence and closed-mindedness appear almost completely independent. Thus rigidity and dogmatism appear to contribute quite independently to an individual's level of cognitive ability. The precise distinction between dogmatism and rigidity has yet to be determined. It is presently believed that the two, although related, can be shown to contribute independently to the solution of problems (e.g., Kerlinger and Rokeach, 1966; Parrott, 1971; Rokeach, 1960; Rokeach and and Norrell, 1966). Conceptually, Rokeach and Norrell (1966) offer the following discussion:

> Rigidity refers to the resistance to change of single beliefs, or sets, or habits, or to the presence of specific compulsive or obsessive tendencies within the individual. Dogmatism refers, on the other hand, to the resistance to change of total systems of beliefs. Whereas rigidity is conceived to be a hypothetical property of a single belief, or habit, or set, or expectancy, which prevents it from changing in the face of objective requirements, dogmatism is conceived to be a property of a total system of beliefs, which prevents the whole system qua system from changing. For example, we may speak of a person as being a dogmatic advocate of psychoanalysis, Marxism, or Catholicism, but as being rigid in tying his shoelaces, brushing his teeth, or preparing for bed. A rat may be said to behave in a rigid (fixated) manner but cannot be said to behave dogmatically. Similarly, a mentally retarded, pedantic child may be said to be-have rigidly, but not dogmatically. To say that a person behaves dogmatically implies that he adheres to, espouses, and defends some system or subsystem of beliefs (in religion, politics, or science) such that we gain the impression that the referent of his behavior is a whole system of ideas rather than a single idea (p. 5).

Studies involving assessments of rigidity have used a number of scales and techniques to determine rigidity, while typically using the California Ethnocentrism (E) scale to measure prejudice. Clinical confirmation of the effects of rigidity on prejudice can be found in the work of Frenkel-Brunswik (1948, 1949; and most fully in her contributions in Adorno et al, 1950). Reichard (1948) presents supporting evidence using the Ror-schach, and Rokeach (1948) using the Water Jar Test and a map reading analog of that test. O'Connor (1952), employing a scale measuring "intol-erance of ambiguity," found it correlated .55 with E-scale scores.

The most serious confirming evidence is to be found in the studies using the Flexibility (Rigidity) scale of the California Psychological In-ventory (Gough, 1957). Gough reports correlations of rigidity scale scores with the E-scale of .26, while Rokeach and Fruchter (1956) report a correlation of .62. Moreover, in two factor analytic studies Rokeach re-ports that rigidity, dogmatism, and E-scale scores all load on the same fac-tor (Rokeach and Novak, 1956; Fruchter, Rokeach, and Novak, 1958).

Studies involving the assessment of dogmatism and its relation to prej-udice include not only the two-factor analyses cited earlier but two others by Pyron, using a modified and expanded E-scale (which the author calls the "Rejection of People Test"). In both studies (Pyron, 1966; Pyron and Lambert, 1967) dogmatism and prejudice load on a common factor. The zero-order correlations between scores were −.33 and −.51.

In seven separate samples Rokeach (1956) reports correlations (r) ranging from .30 to .53 between scores on various 10-item measures of ethnocentrism and several forms of his dogmatism scale. Rokeach and Fruchter (1956) report a correlation of .52; Roberts (1962), a correlation of .56; and Sheikh (1968), a correlation of .65.

Other measures of prejudice add to the substantial support for this principle. Terhune (1964), using an ad hoc Nationalism scale, found it correlated with dogmatism at .13 with an American and .48 with a foreign student sample. Attitudes in support of the Vietnam war correlated .23 and .25 with dogmatism scale scores in two independent studies (Karabenick and Wilson, 1969; Bailes and Guller, 1970). Peabody (1961) provides indirect evidence indicating correlations between dogmatism scale scores and scores on a 20-item anti-Semitism scale ranging between .34 and .48 for samples of English and American college students on the original and reversed versions of both scales.

Lee and Ehrlich (1971) provided an exceptionally rigorous test of the relation of dogmatism to attitudes toward others. Since seven items of the dogmatism scale refer to self-beliefs and two items refer to beliefs about others, the researchers removed those items in order to avoid building in any correlation. Using a 31-item scale of attitudes toward others which they constructed, they obtained a correlation of .51 between the two scales in a sample of 444 college students.

Two studies examined attitudes toward mental patients. McCloud and Kidd (1963) and Canter (1963) both present evidence indicating that negative attitudes toward patients were highly associated with closed-mindedness. McCloud and Kidd observed that open-minded nurses and technicians treated psychiatric patients in a more effective therapeutic manner than did closed-minded personnel. The closed-minded were more likely to treat the patient as a subordinate and dependent person, whereas the behavior of the open-minded was in the direction of mutual communication and independence training. Canter (1963), in a study of student psychiatric nurses, reported correlations between dogmatism, scores on a 37-item scale of attitudes toward mental patients, and a 17-item scale measuring the nurse's attitudes toward favorable interpersonal relationships with patients (IRP). Dogmatism significantly correlated −.45 with IRP and .42 with attitudes toward mental patients. With students and teaching practices as the attitude objects, Vacchiano, Schiffman, and Crowell (1966) found a −.41 correllation between positive attitudes toward students (teacher permissiveness) and dogmatism. Disconfirming evidence is

reported in Genskow and Maglione (1965), who found no significant relation between dogmatism and attitudes toward disabled persons.

Kirtley and Harkless (1969) administered a measure of personal distance
involving 80 targets which were classified into eight categories: artists,
scientists, left-oriented political groups and organizations, right-oriented
political groups and organizations, physically deviant groups, ethnic minorities, businessmen and professionals, and clubs and service organizations. Dogmatism scores correlated significantly with the rejection of artists (.33), scientists (.26), leftists (.44), physical deviants (.27), and ethnic
groups (.29). Their data, along with those cited earlier, are indicative of
one relevant cognitive function of closed-mindedness. That is, it provides
persons with the socially polarized categories for the coding of others.

This can be seen most dramatically in one of Rokeach's crucial studies.
In Chapter 3 Rokeach's (1960) six studies of the effect of perceived similarity on personal distance toward eight religious groups were discussed.
The basic finding, illustrating the principle of categorical congruity, was
that as religious groups were perceived as increasingly dissimilar, the level
of personal distance toward them increased. One additional facet of that
research was the independent analyses conducted on the effects of dogmatism. In almost every instance (47 of 48 comparisons), highly dogmatic
subjects displayed greater personal distance at each level of perceived dissimilarity. The effect of closed-mindedness, then, was to increase the ac-
celeration of the curves of rejection.

Education and Information

A considerable body of research has been directed at assessing the consequences of increasing the amount of favorable information about an
ethnic group that an individual is exposed to and receives. The most elementary form of testing this relationship has been to examine the correspondence between amount of formal schooling achieved and responses to
scales or surveys on ethnic attitudes. Most research has indicated that
only a negligible association exists between the two. This should not be
surprising, first because, as we have seen in Chapters 2 and 3, the media of
mass education have been a major source of unfavorable ethnic information and second because school achievement has been more often a consequence of the social class position of the family (particularly their level of
education) than the intellectual ability of the child. Two asides are necessary. From a methodological standpoint, I doubt that there is any
informed justification for using level of education as a variable in this
context. Presumably, what researchers want to test is the effect of the
ethnic (or related) content of the classroom exposure. Moreover, I suspect

that the repeated claims for the efficacy of formal education in changing attitudes derive from political claims about the "openness" of this society and/or psychological beliefs about the role of "rationality" in mediating intergroup conflict.

On a speculative level, I propose that there is one instance in which educational achievement may result in favorable attitude change. This would occur in those instances where individuals are educationally highly mobile, that is, where their levels of achieved education are grossly discrepant and greater than those achieved by their family. My guess is that such mobility lessens social integration and increases the likelihood of a marginal perspective (see Principle 22). Stember (1961), in his review of the relation between education and ethnic attitudes as reflected in 26 national surveys from 1948 to 1959, provides substantial support not only for this hypothesis but also for my assessment of the effects of education.

The more precise procedure for assessing the effects of "information" on "attitudes" (the quotes are there because this is the general way in which the two are discussed—as if they were different or independent variables) has been an experimental or quasi-experimental procedure. Unfortunately, almost none of this research has been guided by a sophisticated view of attitude theory. Most of it, in fact, occurred before and right after World War II when many social scientists working in this area operated from the general conviction that "rational discourse" was the solution to the pressing social problems and their work was geared to demonstrating that increasing someone's knowledge of an ethnic group necessarily led to favorable attitude changes.

We have already seen—without any formal labeling—the effects of introducing new information as a basis for attitude change. These effects are accounted for, in part, in the principles of elemental organization. Increases in information (i.e., increasing differentiation) will make a difference to the degree that the acquisition of new beliefs results in increasing the magnitude of their DISC elements—their direction, intensity, salience, and centrality. As the DISC elements increase in value, so an individual's system of beliefs and disbeliefs should become more directionally consistent. This is what Principle 14 says. More new beliefs, if received and incorporated into a persons belief/disbelief system, should lead to greater articulation (i.e., and increase in the magnitude of the DISC elements) and to greater directional consistency. This is, in fact, the substance of the subparts of Principle 20, which are repeated here in their specific applications.

The greater the number of stereotypes, affective responses, and behavioral intentions persons assign to a target group, the more these will be evaluative, intense, salient, and important to them.

The more evaluative, intense, salient, and important are the stereotypes, affective responses, and behavioral intentions to a person, the greater their directional consistency.

The greater the number of stereotypes, affective responses, and behavioral intentions that persons assign to a target, the greater their directional consistency.

The testing of these principles was approached by Nettler (1946), clearly ahead of his time, and by Merz and Pearlin (1957), but they remain untested in the domain of ethnic attitudes. Sears (1969, pp. 348–353), reviewing the literature on political "information flow and opinion change," provides an amazing set of confirming studies. At least on a cognitive—and possibly conative—level, it is clear that new beliefs, if received and incorporated into an individuals belief/disbelief system, can cause the imbalancing of an attitude. Theoretically, however, the point at issue here is that these new beliefs (or disbeliefs, for that matter) are not "supporting" mechanisms of the attitude but rather are part of the attitude itself.

It is my contention that attitudes are very easy to change. What is difficult is maintaining that change. Consider a theory of prejudice. Since we can treat such a theory as an object of an attitude (I certainly have a well-developed attitude about this theory), I can assert that I have probably changed the attitudes of most people who have read this far in the book. Having introduced a good deal of new beliefs and belief statements, and having provided you with a guide for acting on them (i.e., testable propositions), I have caused your attitude to become more differentiated, I have no doubt changed the magnitudes of your DISC responses, and I have possibly changed the organization of your attitude. If we had a measure of your attitude now and before you read this far, it would probably register a significant change. The necessary condition for change, at least the change intended, is whether or how well you understood what I have attempted to communicate. This presumably is a consequence of your cognitive ability, which includes how much information on this subject you had before you started the book. Secondly, whether or not the changes that have occurred remain stable—whether a month or a year from now you display the same attitude structure that you now have about a theory of prejudice will depend on the ways in which you have built up a new relationship with the components of this theory. Obviously this is not quite like building social relationships, but the analogy is valid. The stability of the change is contingent on whether you actually do something with this theory or not. But whether you do something or not will sooner or later depend on the nature of your reference other matrix and the relation of its members to you and to theory. In that manner even conceptual changes implicate new social relationships.

There are three ways in which intelligence and other cognitive abilities may be important in the acquisition and support of prejudice. First, higher intelligence may make people more resistant to the acquisition of social categories that have few positively adaptive behavioral consequences. Second, higher intelligence and/or a more open belief system may operate against the retention of the prevailing nonveridical generalizations that are often the bulwark of negative stereotypes. Third, it may be that the comprehension of similarities is a more complex intellectual task than the comprehension of differences. Thus young children may initially learn to categorize people on the basis of their perceived differences. And change would then require the rejection of a set of old beliefs and the learning of new ones. Lambert and Klineberg (1967) noted:

> There is a nearly universal tendency for 6-year-olds to think of the social world about them as populated more by people who are different from than similar to their own group. In fact, for ten of the eleven cultures examined, the 6-year-olds view foreign peoples as different from their own group reliably more frequently than do 10- or 14-year-olds. This general age trend corresponds to one aspect of the normal intellectual development of children. . . . that children learn to make differentiations among events in their environments before comprehending similarities (p. 184).

It may therefore be that similarities are basically more difficult for young children to grasp than differences, in the sense that contrasting or coordinate categories of thought are more easily used than are superordinate ones. Furthermore, it also may be that differences are stressed more often than similarities by those who socialize young children; that parents and teachers in their discussions with young children emphasize contrasts and differences of foreign peoples (p. 185).

The Frustration-Aggression Hypothesis

There is clearly no research support in psychology or social psychology for the various instinctivist conceptions of aggression in man, nor for that matter is there any support among ethologists and biologists of the existence of any form of a self-stimulating aggressive system in lower animals. Holloway (1968), reviewing the nonhuman animal evidence, asserts:

> Nonhuman animal studies show that all animals are capable of aggression. There seems, however, to be fair agreement that animal aggression is not constant but fairly rare and that the stimuli evoking aggressive responses are specific to the animal's habitat and involve discrete cues associated mostly with mating and territorial behavior. . . . There seem to be no animals who attack

purely for attack's sake, the attack being related to the quest for food. . . . or when challenged by predatory species or by members of their own or different species for territory or mates" (pp. 37–38).

To be sure, aggression is a universal psychic and social occurrence. And the point of Holloway's review is that aggression should be accepted as a learned response to interpersonal and social events and not as a biological given. For too many social scientists, however, aggression has been construed as an almost invariant response to frustration, and aggression has been equated with prejudice.

The catalytic statement of the frustration-aggression hypothesis appeared in 1939 in Dollard, Doob, Miller, Mowrer, and Sears' *Frustration and Aggression*. The authors began: "The occurrence of aggressive behavior always presupposes the existence of frustration," and they completed that assertion "the existence of frustration always leads to some form of aggression."

Berkowitz (1962), reviewing the history of this area of inquiry, said:

"Two years after the publication of the book, in a symposium on the frustration-aggression hypothesis, Miller admitted that the basic generalization "was unclear and misleading." There was an implication, he pointed out, strong enough to override later statements in the book to the contrary, that "frustration has no consequences other than aggression." He suggested that a better phrasing was, "Frustration produces instigations to a number of different types of responses one of which is an instigation to some form of aggression. . . ." Nevertheless, this rewording did not alter the basic supposition that even frustration increased the likelihood of overt hostility.

Berkowitz went on to propose that "every frustration increases the *instigation* to aggression" (p. 46). This instigation, which he termed "anger," increased the probability of aggression; but, he concluded, aggression was not the only response to anger.

The frustration-aggression hypothesis led to a variety of *scapegoating* and *specific displacement* theories which, for whatever reason—in part their simplicity—have become enormously popular with the American college-educated public. Needless to say the scapegoating theories are based on a misconstruction of the relationship between frustration and aggression.

Certain features have been common to all scapegoating theories: (1) the blockage of goal-directed activities causes aggressive responses, but (2) frustrated persons are unable to direct their hostility toward the actual source of blockage (these theories never tell you why this is so), so (3) they find a scapegoat in an innocent victim who can be attacked without worrying about retaliation.

From the standpoint of understanding prejudice, most tests of the frustration-aggression hypothesis and scapegoating derivatives have been inadequate because of their almost exclusive subhuman or human laboratory context of study. Even from a purely experimental standpoint, most human research has been inadequate in that study designs have almost never permitted subjects to choose responses other than aggression.

Students of prejudice should recognize the following:

1. Frustration does not always lead to aggression.
2. Aggression is not always the dominant response to frustration.
3. Aggression is not always displaced from its source.
4. When displaced, it does not necessarily implicate minorities or "safe" targets.
5. Nothing about the theory of frustration-aggression could lead you to predict what the target of aggression might be.

Prejudice and its concomitant behaviors are learned responses—learned and socially approved responses in specific social situations.

The theory of frustration-aggression was designed to exclude what its framers quaintly termed "instrumental aggression" but what we might correctly call attitude-consistent behavior. There is thus no way we can construe frustration as a supporting mechanism of prejudiced behavior.

THE REFERENCE-OTHER MATRIX [2]

Attitudes cannot be maintained without social support. And almost all people live within a network of other persons who share their life style and their basic values and attitudes. However commonplace these remarks may appear, and however well accepted they may be even within social science, the fact is that they are difficult statements to prove rigorously.

The body of theory that underlies these statements is known as "reference group theory," and a brief introduction is in order. First, a *reference other* is generally defined as any person, group, or category of others whom the individual feels is important to him or her and whose expectations for behavior would be given serious consideration. A person's behavior can be designated as having *reference other support* to the degree that the person perceives that his or her reference others expect, agree with, or condone that specific behavior.

Although this theory is not highly formalized, there are six elementary propositions that are critical for the study of prejudice.

1. For any given individual, there is a relatively small set of others whom he or she conceives as being generally important.

2.   People are motivated to behave in a manner consistent with the expectations of their reference others.

3.   The strength of this motivation varies with the structure of the reference other matrix (i.e., the specific social locations and perceived properties of reference others).

4.   Although some attitudes develop before the acquisition of social support and influence the selection of reference others and some attitudes are learned from reference others, all enduring attitudes are in balance with the expectations of reference others.

5.   Since the reference others of an individual will not necessarily be in full agreement and since attitudes vary in their potency, both attitudinal and reference other support can have an independent effect on behavior.

6.   A person's behavior will always have an effect on his or her reference other matrix and attitudes, and the relation of the two.

The elementary nature of these propositions obscures the complexity of the analyses involved. As an example, consider the relevant data of Williams and his associates (1964). Their findings indicated that reference other expectations were more predictive of affective responses toward Negroes than an individual's past contact with Negroes (pp. 34–35). However, in their analysis of intimate personal distance toward Jews, they suggested that the perceived expectations of one's reference others was equal in importance to past contact with Jews (p. 181). While their data point to strong reference other effects, it is clear that differences in attitude components and in target change the character of these effects.

Several studies have attempted to investigate the relations among reference other support, ethnic attitudes, and intergroup behavior in quasi-experimental designs. The pioneer study was conducted by DeFleur and Westie (1958), who invoked the idea of reference other support to explain what they viewed as an inconsistency between the attitudes and behavior of their subjects. They asked college student subjects (who had been part of another laboratory study) if they "would be willing to be photographed with a Negro person of the opposite sex." Regardless of the person's answer, the researcher then gave their subjects a "photograph release agreement" which listed seven "uses" to which the photograph would be put. Subjects could sign any or none of them, and the set of releases varied along a continuum of visibility, ranging from being "seen only by professional sociologists," through use as a teaching aid in classrooms, to use in a "nationwide publicity campaign advocating racial integration." As a result of the earlier study, in which they had obtained a measure of personal distance toward Negroes, they were able to examine the relation between signing the agreements and personal distance. Further, following their response to the release statements, subjects were asked "Was there any particular person or group of people . . . who came to mind when you decided to sign (or refused to sign) this document? That is, are there people whom you felt would approve or disapprove?"

Although the researchers found that the level of prejudice and the form of release that a subject was willing to sign were strongly associated, they also observed that approximately 30% of their sample displayed "discrepant" behavior. The researchers attributed this discrepancy to the effect of the person's reference others. They concluded, although without showing the necessary data, that the majority of subjects had made a decision in agreement with their reference others.

Fendrich (1967) administered an omnibus scale to measure anti-Negro attitudes and a reference other questionnaire to 189 college students. Subjects were asked if each of five reference others would be willing to act in nine different ways with Negroes (e.g., protest against housing segregation or eat with a mixed racial group). The five reference others, arbitrarily selected by the investigator, were closest friends of the same sex, closest friends of the opposite sex, parents, roommates (or spouse), and some older persons whom you respect. Subjects were then given a reference other support score by summing each "yes" response given for each of the nine behaviors the five reference others were perceived as willing to do.

After completing the attitude and reference other scales, the student subjects were then asked if they were willing to attend small group meetings with members of the campus NAACP (National Association for the Advancement of Colored People). In the week following the administration of the scales, an NAACP representative contacted them to see if they were still interested. Of the 189 students, 34 (18%) agreed to attend a meeting, and Fendrich conducted his statistical analysis by comparing those 34 against the 155 who were not willing to attend. (Although he and subsequent writers have referred to this as a measure of "overt behavior," not all of the 34 subjects did attend a meeting.)

The results reported by Fendrich consisted of the primary and partial associations between the three variables. Negro attitudes and reference other support manifested gamma associations with the intended-actual behavior measure of .71 and .72, respectively. The two were themselves associated at .62. Fendrich then calculated the pair associations, partialling out the effects of the third variable:

Attitudes and reference other support   = .55
(with intended-actual behavior controlled)
Reference other support and intended-actual behavior   = .55
(with attitudes controlled)

Attitudes and intended-actual behavior   = .52
(with reference other support controlled)

These findings indicated that each of the variables was independently related to the other two. Similar results were obtained by DeFriese and Ford (1969). In a modified cluster sample of 262 persons in six census tracts in an urban, segregated neighborhood, DeFriese and Ford attempted the investigation of reference group effects regarding an open occupancy housing policy. Their interview schedule consisted of three parts: a 14-item scale of attitudes toward Negroes; a two-part measure of reference other support; and the behavioral opportunity to sign one of two "documents":

Document A

I, the undersigned, do hereby make public the declaration that I have no objection to having Negro families of social and economic characteristics similar to my own live in my neighborhood, and I would, in fact, uphold such practices within the community.

Document B

I, the undersigned, do hereby make public the declaration that I do object to having Negro families live in my neighborhood, regardless of their social and economic characteristics, and I would not, in fact, uphold such practices within the community.

Before they acted, the survey respondents were told that the researchers reserved the right to use the signatures any way they chose "including making them public through the news media." Fifteen people signed A; 76 people signed B; and 171 people refused to sign either. As expected, those signing Document A had less prejudice than those signing B; and nonsigners were intermediate.

Respondents were presented with a list of five reference others and asked to indicate their perception each held with regard to open occupancy. They were then asked to give their personal estimate of the degree of consensus existing among their reference others. The respondents' reference others were then classified as being for or against open occupancy *if* three of the five groups presented in the questionnaire were perceived as having the same position. Considering then those whose reference others were for, against, or "mixed" and the respondent's act of signing A or B, the researchers obtained a correlation (tau-*b*) of .51. And when both the perceived position of the reference other and their perceived level of consensus are considered as predictors, the correlation rises slightly to .55. Finally, when attitude scores are added, the prediction increases to .70.

These analyses were conducted for only those who signed either document. When nonsigners are considered, the correlation shrivels to .18. There can be no question that other factors, untapped by the research procedure, are in operation.

These earlier studies were inadequate in a number of ways. DeFleur and Westie, for example, resorted to after-the-fact explanation. Fendrich and DeFriese and Ford, although far more rigorous, arbitrarily selected the reference others to whom subjects could respond, failed to consider how subjects perceived the expectations of their reference others, and provided subjects with only one behavioral option. Ewens and Ehrlich (1969) attempted to correct for these methodological defects and to expand the treatment of reference others in a highly complex study.

Ewens and Ehrlich began by administering a screening questionnaire to 150 students in two group sessions. The attempt was to find those students who had roughly comparable backgrounds. Accordingly, to be selected for the experiment, subjects had to be single, 18 to 22 years old, full-time students, have completed one full semester at the university, be white, United States citizens, living on campus or in the adjacent college town, have a town which they recognized as their hometown, have a hometown which was different from the college town, not be living with parents or relatives, and have completed the entire questionnaire. On the basis of these criteria, 67 of the students who took the original questionnaire were eliminated.

Instruments were constructed to measure the affective, cognitive, and behavioral dimensions of attitudes toward Negroes. Each of these dimensions was measured by an adjective checklist balanced for directionality and salience. (These were described in detail in Chapter 4.)

A multiple-item instrument was used to measure reference other support. Eleven items were constructed which asked respondents to name those in the college town, their hometowns, and elsewhere who were important to them. With regard to the college town, for instance, the following questions were asked: Who are your best friends here at the University of Iowa and in Iowa City? What groups or organizations here in Iowa City are the most important to you? What other persons or groups here in Iowa City or at the University are the most important to you? Similar questions were asked with regard to the remaining two reference sectors.

These three reference sectors—hometown others, college others, and elsewhere others—were isolated in a pilot analysis. More than 80% of the reference others elicited by college students in this pretest were either from the respondent's hometown or the college town and the characteristics of these two sets of others differed widely.

Reference other support in the ethnic relations area was determined by asking the students whose opinions, among those listed, they would *consider* if they were deciding whether or not to perform six different civil rights activities. These activities involved deciding whether or not to join a civil rights action group, to allow a public statement concerning their racial views to be broadcast, to join a peaceful protest march, to speak on civil rights with a mixed racial group at a local church or civic organization, to endorse a strong pro-Negro newspaper statement, or to devote an afternoon to interviewing for a survey of racial attitudes. These same six activities were presented again in the overt behavior situation described below. For each of the others who respondents thought they would consider with regard to any of these activities, they were asked it this other would approve, be indifferent toward, or disapprove of their participating in the given activity. An average level of approval was obtained for each of the three reference sectors and the matrix of the respondents as a whole for all of the six civil rights activities.

The properties of each reference other matrix were determined by a series of structured questions.

Duration. How long have you known RO?

Frequency of Contact. On the average, about how much time do you presently spend per week with RO?

Importance. How important is RO to you as a person?

Visibility. How likely is RO to actually know if you were to (engage in specified behavior)?

Centrality. How important do you feel it is to RO that you behave according to his expectation with regard to (specified behavior)?

Legitimacy (1). How much right does RO have to expect you to behave in a certain way with regard to (specified behavior)?

Legitimacy (2). How accountable are you to RO for the way you might behave with regard to (specified behavior)?

Power. How much control would you say that RO has over you with regard to (specified behavior)?

Eight weeks after administering the questionnaire containing the attitudes and reference other support instruments, respondents were contacted individually and asked to participate as subjects in an experimental session. The experiment was conducted in a room with a television camera and monitor, a videotape recorder, and an assortment of other recording equipment. The subject was asked to sit in a chair directly in front of the television camera. Instructions were given by the experimenter as follows:

I work for the Center for Research in Interpersonal Behavior here at the university. Our organization has been hired by the Students for Minority

Rights, which is a civil rights action group with headquarters in Chicago, to do research concerning white college student attitudes toward Negroes.

What we want you to do is to give a three or four minute talk about your attitudes toward Negroes and the future of Negro-white relations in the United States as you see it. We are not interested in your poise or your ability to give speeches, but we are interested in your opinions.

Subjects were then given five minutes to organize their talks, and the talks were recorded on videotape. After they had finished the talk, they were presented with three behavioral release forms. The first contained two release statements which, if signed, would allow the subject's recorded statement to be publicly broadcast by college and hometown radio or television stations. The second release form, in a similar manner, asked the subject to indicate whether or not he or she would be willing to join a local chapter of Students for Minority Rights if one got started on the college campus or in their hometown.

The third release form asked the subject whether he or she would want to engage in eight different activities to be sponsored by the civil rights group. These activities involved deciding whether to join a peaceful protest march, to speak on civil rights with a mixed racial group at a local church or civic organization, to endorse a strong pro-Negro newspaper statement, or to devote an afternoon to interviewing for a survey of racial attitudes. The subjects could indicate their willingness to engage in each of these activities in either their hometown or the college community.

On these last two releases, subjects were asked to give their name, telephone number, hometown address and college address so that they could be contacted by representatives of the civil rights group. The intent was to convince the subjects that they were actually committing themselves to a line of future conduct. The behavior measured in this research as the dependent variable, then, was the subject's commitment in writing to perform one or more of the 12 different civil rights activities. While this is not the same as performing those acts, it does go one step beyond verbal assent.

Let us now consider the findings of this complex research in their most general form.

For any given individual there was a relatively small set others who were perceived as being generally important to them. All reference others were not, however, perceived as being equally important.

Those selected as ethnic reference others in the hometown were perceived as more important, legitimate, and powerful, as well as being known longer. For the college sector, the visibility of behavior, its centrality to the reference others, were the most important determinants of behavior.

The influence of reference other support was greatest when the subject reported that he or she had considered their expectations. Just the same, the subject's behavior could be predicted beyond a chance level from their reference other matrix even though they reported that they had not consciously considered the influence of others in deciding how to behave. Perhaps response to the expectations of others has become such a habitual behavior that people are not always aware of their dependence on reference others. Or perhaps the expectations of others have come to be identified, over time, as self-attitudes such that people become aware of their reference others only when their expectancies for behavior are unclear or contradictory. In either case these are just intriguing speculations.

An average of 49% of the students studied agreed to sign each of the 12 behavioral release statements. The range was from 78% agreeing to release their recorded talk to a college radio or television station to 24% agreeing to participate in a peaceful protest march in their hometowns. In general, respondents were more willing to interview for a survey, talk over a radio or television station, and join a civil rights group and less willing to give a civic talk, endorse a strong newspaper statement, and march in protest. The students were more willing to commit themselves to acts in the college community than in their hometowns.

The differential influence of reference others was examined by considering their properties. It was predicted that the greater the duration, frequency of contact, importance, visibility, centrality, legitimacy, and power of the reference others in the college and hometown sectors of the respondents' matrices, the greater would be the relationship between the degree to which respondents would be willing to commit themselves to the behavioral activities and the degree to which they perceived support from their reference others for these activities. To test these hypotheses, tables were computed for each respondent for all civil rights activities and reference other properties for both the hometown and college sectors (4648 tables for each sector). In brief, what we found was that only the length of acquaintance with the reference other (duration) appeared unrelated to a person's behavior. While each of the properties of reference others varied across sectors and behaviors, they all appeared to important concomitants of intergroup behavior.

The correlations (r) between reference other support and behavior were significant for the total matrix for all behaviors except interviewing. For all activities across all sectors, the correlation was .41. For attitudes, the comparable correlation was .45.

The correlations between racial attitudes and overt behavior indicated that the total attitude scores of respondents were significantly associated to performance of all of the activities except the college broadcast statement and the newspaper statement. For the total number of activities, a slightly higher correlation was found in the college reference sector than the hometown sector.

To summarize the findings with regard to the zero-order correlations among these three variables: It was found that for the college broadcast statement and the newspaper statement, behavior was predicted primarily on the basis of reference other support. Interviewing for a survey, on the other hand, was an activity almost entirely dependent on the ethnic attitudes of the respondents. Other activities such as hometown broadcast, the civil rights group, the protest march, and the civic talk were contingent on both reference other support and racial attitudes.

In general, reference other support was a better predictor of hometown activities than were racial attitudes. The opposite trend was apparent, however, with regard to the college sector. For college activities, racial attitudes were generally a better predictor of behavior than was reference other support.

A graphic way to understand the relative influence of reference other support and ethnic attitudes on the 12 behaviors is presented in Figure 2. The distance along the vertical axis measures the size of the correlations between reference other support and behavior. The distance along the horizontal axis measures the attitudes-behavior correlations. The figure is further divided into four quadrants which indicate the relative influence of the two predictor variables. In quadrant A, for example, are found five activities whose performance was directly related to the expectations of reference others but not related to subjects' racial attitudes. Four of these activities (college and hometown broadcast statement and college and hometown newspaper statement) were probably the most visible of the 12 behaviors, for each involved the statement of subjects' ethnic views over the mass media. In direct contrast were the behaviors in quadrant D (college and hometown interviewing), which were influenced by the ethnic attitudes of the respondents but not dependent upon reference other support. As opposed to quadrant A, these seem to be activities that were not very visible to reference others. Activities contingent on both of the predictors are presented in quadrant B. None of the 12 activities fall into quadrant C, which would mean that they were associated with neither of the predictor variables.

The multiple correlations, using reference other support and ethnic attitudes as joint predictors of behavior, ranged for any given act from .29 to .48. As would be expected, activities in quadrant B were generally better predicted by use of these two independent variables. The total number of hometown activities which subjects agreed to perform were somewhat better predicted ($R = .43$) than the total number of college activities which they agreed to perform. ($R = .52$)

Quite obviously, the amount of research that will have to be done in

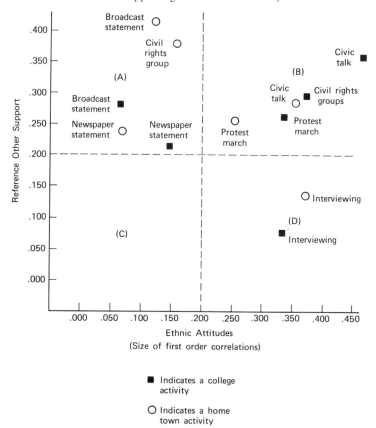

FIGURE 2.   Relative influence of reference other support and ethnic attitudes for each of the civil rights activities.

this area is a virtual program for social psychology. At this stage of inquiry, summary propositions that go beyond the six elementary propositions of reference other theory seem premature. But the importance of reference other support as a mechanism for the maintenance of prejudice seems unquestionable.

CONCLUSION

The primary causes of the transmission of ethnic attitudes from parent to child and the primary mechanisms for the maintenance of ethnic prejudice in society are not to be found in the psychology of people or in the social psychology of their interpersonal relationships. It is to be found in the peculiar historical conditions and present political economic structures out of which intergroup relations develop and are sustained.

Discussions of child-rearing, of parent-child relations, of cognitive mechanisms, and other matters of individual psychology often lead people to accept these early psychological events and their present manifestations as sufficient conditions of prejudice. Given the American cultural bias for psychological explanations, I feel impelled to repeat that this is wrong. These factors can only be construed as one set of necessary conditions. Only in conjunction with specific societal and situational conditions do these factors become operative as causes of ethnic prejudice.

I regard the development of a social psychology of prejudice as strategic. It is strategic for two reasons. First, through this book we can begin to direct our efforts toward a deliberate and scientifically sound program of attitude change. Second, I regard this as strategic because it leads directly to the development of a social psychology of love. The theory of prejudice should provide a model for a theory of love.

We conclude by reviewing the principles of prejudice, this time with the additions of this chapter and without direct reference to the components of stereotypes, personal distance, and affect.

The Societal Mechanisms

1. *Principle of distinction.* The attitudes directed toward the major ethnic groups in society are relatively distinct and exclusive.
2. *Principle of diffusion.* Knowledge of the attitudes directed toward the major ethnic groups in society is highly diffused.
    a. The greater the distinctiveness of ethnic attitudes, the greater their diffusion in society.
    b. The primary contexts for the diffusion of ethnic attitudes and for the legitimation of such knowledge are the family and the school.
    c. Prevailing ethnic attitudes are copied in the mass media of communication and the media of mass education.
3. *Principle of consensus.* There is high consensus on the attitudes directed toward the major ethnic groups in society.
    a. The greater the distinctiveness of ethnic attitudes, the greater the consensus concerning them.
    b. The greater the diffusion of ethnic attitudes, the greater the consensus concerning them.
4. *Principle of stability.* Ethnic attitudes are relatively stable historically within and across societies.
    a. The greater the distinctiveness, diffusion, and consensus in ethnic attitudes, the greater their stability.

5. *Principle of change.* Changes in ethnic attitudes follow changes in established ethnic group relations.
   a. Changes in the established relations between ethnic groups will decrease the stability of ethnic attitudes and modify their distinctiveness and their levels of diffusion and consensus.
6. *Principle of visibility.* Under conditions of stable group relations, the greater the visibility of an ethnic group, the greater the distinctiveness, diffusion, and consensus of ethnic attitudes.
   a. Under conditions of change, ethnic groups become temporarily more visible.

The Cognitive Mechanisms

7. *Principle of categorical placement.* Ascribing ethnic group membership to an individual is contingent on the joint effects of that person's characteristics, the criteria of ethnic classification, the person's eligibility for other social categories, and the context in which the person appears.
   a. If a person is assigned ethnic group membership, then the attitude toward that person will be contingent on the joint effects of the prevailing ethnic attitudes, the person's other characteristics, the person's eligibility for other social categories, and the situational context in which the person appears.
7.1. *Corollary of veridicality.* All persons assigned ethnic group membership must satisfy some social criteria of membership.
7.2. *Corollary of categorical placement.* In learning the criteria of ethnic classification, persons acquire first those criteria that are most directly observable.
7.3. *Corollary of categorical learning.* The acquisition and retention of ethnic prejudice is inversely related to cognitive ability:
   (1) High levels of intellectual ability retard the acquisition of ethnic prejudice.
   (2) Ethnic prejudice is associated with lower scores on formal tests of intelligence, greater problem-solving rigidity, and a more closed cognitive structure.
      a. Changes in the level of ethnic prejudice are associated with changes in cognitive abilities.
8. *Principle of categorical dominance.* If a person is assigned ethnic membership, then the initial attitudinal response will be more on the basis of ethnic membership than on the person's other characteristics.
8.1 *Corollary of categorical response.* The less knowledge available about an ethnic person, the greater the likelihood that response will be in accordance with the prevailing attitudes about that ethnic category.
9. *Principle of cognitive anchoring.* Initial intergroup experiences are crucial in establishing a strategy of coding and the direction in which ethnic attitudes may develop.
10. *Principle of categorical constancy.* Attitudes toward ethnic groups can-

not become stabilized until the person develops beliefs about the permanence of ethnic identity.

11. *Principle of polarization.* The greater the polarization of ethnic attitudes in a social setting, the earlier their acquisition by children (or new occupants of the setting).

11.1. *Corollary of target visibility.* The more visible an ethnic group is in a social setting, the earlier the acquisition of attitudes toward them.

12. *Principle of categorical congruity.* The greater the perceived similarity between an ethnic group and the membership group of the person classifying it, the greater the likelihood it will be assigned the characteristics of the person's own group.

12.1. *Corollary of ethnic congruity.* The greater the perceived similarity between an ethnic person and the actor, the lower the prejudice.

13. *Principle of self-congruity.* The more favorable are a person's self-attitudes, the greater the number of acceptable ethnic targets and the more positive the person's attitudes toward them; the more negative the self-attitudes, the greater the number of unacceptable targets and the more negative are attitudes toward them.

14. *Principle of socialization.* People develop attitudes similar to those of their primary agents of socialization.

Organizational Mechanisms of Attitudes

15. *Principle of acquisition.* The components of attitudes develop at different rates.

15.1. *Corollary of acquisition.* Attitudes tend to become more differentiated and directionally consistent over time.

16. *Principle of attitude structure.* The components of an attitude are established in ordinal relations.
   a. Cognitive, conative, and affective responses vary in their relative strength by attitude object and across persons.
   b. For any given person, the relative strength of the components varies by attitude object.

17. *Principle of attitude organization.* The components of an attitude are systemically related and tend toward directional consistency.

18. *Principle of elemental structure.* The elements of an attitude component are established in ordinal relations.
   a. *Direction and intensity.* The greater the favorability or unfavorability of assigned stereotypes, behavioral intentions, or affective responses, the more strongly they will be accepted or rejected.
   b. *Directionality and intensity.* As stereotypes, intentions, and affects become increasingly directional, they are accepted or rejected with greater intensity.
   c. *Direction and salience.* There is no necessary relation between the degree to which stereotypes, intentions, or affects are directed toward a target and whether they are favorable or unfavorable.
   d. *Directionality and salience.* The larger the proportion of target

group members encompassed by stereotypes, intentions, or affects, the more strongly favorable or unfavorable they will be.

e. *Direction and centrality*. The personal importance of stereotypes, intentions, or affects is independent of whether they are favorable or unfavorable.

f. *Directionality and centrality*. As stereotypes, intentions, or affects become more important, they become more favorable or unfavorable.

g. *Intensity and salience*. The larger the proportion of target group members encompassed by stereotypes, intentions, or affects, the more intensely these responses will be accepted or rejected.

h. *Intensity and centrality*. The more important are stereotypes, intentions, or affects, the more intensely they will be accepted or rejected.

i. *Centrality and salience*. The importance of stereotypes, intentions, or affects are independent of the proportion of the target group they apply to.

19. *Principle of differentiation*. The elements of attitude components vary in their differentiation.

20. *Principle of elemental organization*. The elements of attitudes are psychologically established in systemic relations and tend toward directional consistency.

a. The greater the differentiation of an attitude component, the greater its articulation (i.e., the more its elements are evaluative, intense, salient, and important).

b. The greater the articulation of an attitude component, the greater its directional consistency.

c. The greater the differentiation of an attitude component, the greater its directional consistency.

d. As consensus on ethnic attitudes increases in a society, individual variability in the structure of attitudes will decrease.

e. Increases in the magnitude of the direction, intensity, salience, and centrality responses of people to ethnic targets will result in increasing consensus on ethnic attitudes.

f. As the visibility of ethnic groups increases, the variability of direction, intensity, salience, and centrality responses across individuals should decrease.

The Marginality Mechanisms

21. *Principle of ethnic group congruity*. The attitudes held by ethnic persons toward ethnic targets other than their own are congruent with those consensually associated with those targets in society.

21.1. *Corollary of reciprocity*. Within the ethnic subsociety, the attitudes to dominant group targets are governed by the basic societal mechanisms (Principles 1-6).

21.2. *Corollary of directional displacement*. The attitudes held by ethnic persons about their own group tend to be similar but more favorable than those held by others about them.

22. *Principle of marginal perspective.* Marginal persons manifest more favorable attitudes toward ethnic targets than do the more socially integrated.

NOTES

1. The reciprocal character of the parent-child relation with respect to self-attitudes has its parallel in the response of minority group children to their confrontation with a rejecting society. The repeated interpretations that minority children have more negative self-attitudes, however, often confuses a rejection of status with a rejection of self, although the two are complexly related. The issue of minority self-hatred is only peripherally related to our discussion here, and the interested reader might consult the recent collection by Kurokawa (1970).

2. A number of studies have explored the relation between ethnic attitudes and the person's self-perception of how much ethnic information he or she had about the objects of his or her attitudes. While this research is interesting, and typically reveals that people tend to perceive themselves as being informed about the object of their attitudes, the problem of the self-perception of attitudes and their concomitants is not our subject.

3. Most of the material presented here is adapted from Ewens and Ehrlich (1969). Much of the conceptual structure had its origin in Preiss and Ehrlich (1966) and its refinement through my work with Ewens.

Epilogue

WHO ARE THE AGENTS OF SOCIAL CHANGE?

I have now been involved in the study of prejudice and ethnic group relations for almost 20 years. When I began lecturing on the subject, it was commonplace for members of the audience or class to ask me "What can I do?" And I would tell them, that is, I would rattle off a list of social reforms which seemed to me to take precedence among the many things that any good liberal advocate of change could work for. Times have changed. These days it is not common for members of an audience to ask me what they can do. I think that this is simply one indicator of the growing sense of political and social alienation in American society.

And today, when people do ask what is to be done I respond very differently. Although I certainly do not discourage them from working for social reform, reformist activities are no longer very high on my list of priorities. First, I tell them that people ought to work for reform since some reforms may make the lives of others more comfortable. Second, I tell them that by working for reform, I hope they will make their own lives more uncomfortable. That is, I believe that if they work effectively and properly for fundamental reform they will sooner or later be forced to recognize that whenever their reforms challenge the premises of the political economy of the society, they fail. Such recognition is one possible—if not necessary—process in the transforming of liberals to radicals. And my priority today is in building a movement for radical social change.

I also do something else these days when people ask me what they should do. I insult them. Now I try to do it gently, but what I do is to intimate that such a question is probably a "cop-out." By asking someone of authority what they should do, they are *once again* asking for external authority to provide direction and set limits on their behavior. The reliance on authority to validate social action is, after all, an integral part of the political socialization of persons in this society, in most societies. To advocate change in conformity to legitimate authority is almost (although not quite) self-contradictory. To begin with, persons who occupy positions of legitimate authority in society cannot advocate basic social change. Such advocacy disqualifies one from the continued occupancy of such a position. My authority, based on knowledge, will almost always lose in contest with persons whose authority derives from their political or social position. Moreover, there should be no question as to who has the power.

Many people, and particularly intellectuals, believe that knowledge is power. They are quite wrong. With all of my knowledge about the nature of prejudice and the state of intergroup relations in society, I have very little power. This is to say, quite simply, that I can do very little to control the outcome of community or national decisions concerning ethnic group relations.

Some persons will often counter my antiauthoritarian stance by pointing to the fact that many recruits to change-oriented social movements are (what we call in our specialized language) "authoritarian submissive." They are quite right; and my reply is that to change society through changes directed from the top—to change by people following orders —is not an acceptable model of social change for me in this society.

When people who are themselves working in programs to change intergroup relations ask me what they can do, I try to take their inquiry seriously. I begin, almost always, by annunciating the principle of change which is as close to a law as any generalization in the social sciences: *Changes in ethnic attitudes follow changes in established ethnic group relations.* The causal thrust of that principle is clear: Strategies of change must be directed primarily at the established structure of group relations.

Now most people resist this principle, as if scientific generalizations were subject to vote or to confirmation or disconfirmation by autobiographical anecdote. However, once the advocate of social reform agrees, the real issue becomes—What constitutes a genuine change in the structure of established group relations?

That is not a simple question; and I am not sure that there is a general answer to it. My preference is to inspect each proposal for change in terms of its presumed effect on the totality of group relationships. Let's take for an example the case of school desegregation. Whatever positive impact desegregation may have for the educational achievement of some students, we know that it will have relatively little impact on the composition of the labor force, the rate of unemployment, levels of poverty, and so on. We know, too, from census data that equality of educational achievement for black people does not bring equal occupational achievement. Even more, we know that black persons with both education and occupation equal to whites still earn less money. Although there are certainly more facets to the issue of desegregation (not the least being the quality of education and the opportunities for social mobility in what may no longer be an expanding occupational structure), it should be apparent that fundamental changes in group relations will not be extensively cultivated by this strategy.

Consider, as a counter example, the radical reform of separating income from work, that is, guaranteeing a satisfactory level of income to all persons in society. While the implications of that proposal go well beyond those of changing ethnic group relations, certainly a guaranteed income would bring about significant changes in the political and economic relationships among dominant and minority groups.

You may consider my counter example a bit unfair, and I will concede that, although I hope that you, in turn, will consider what it might have meant today if as much people power and social energy had gone into a campaign for a guaranteed adequate income as has gone into the fight for school desegregation.

Let's move now to a more balanced illustration. Many liberal activists have given priority to short-circuiting the media for the transmission of attitudes. We know unequivocally that prevailing ethnic attitudes are reiterated in the mass media of communication and in the media of mass education. And partly as a consequence, the knowledge of ethnic attitudes is highly diffused in society. Thus we have seen reforms aimed at removing the irrelevant expressions of negative ethnic attitudes in these media, the development of multiracial textbooks, the reintroduction of ethnic persons and ethnic histories in their proper context, changes in language use, and so on. These are vital steps, and such actions are well grounded in the social psychology of prejudice.

These activities do indeed comprise a genuine measure of liberal reform and, as such, I would not expect them to be very successful either on the level of attitude change or on the level of changing group relations. That they have not been very successful is a matter of contemporary fact.

Both liberal and radical activists would agree, more or less, on the kinds of reforms necessary in the mass media depiction of ethnic persons. Nevertheless, their priorities for change within this context are necessarily different. The primary radical strategy would be to work for citizen or community control over the facilities of broadcasting and publishing. Short of that, it would be to establish alternative media which are community controlled. Thus the radical objective would be to change the source of control over the media of communication.

Understanding the differences between a liberal and a radical perspective on change seems to me to be more crucial than my enumerating the ways in which almost all of the principles of prejudice may be adapted to either a liberal or a radical program.

As I see it, there are two clusters of attitudes that distinguish these perspectives. The first is a set of political attitudes.

To begin with, the liberal activist operates out of a conceit of order and history, that is, out of the belief that this is basically a good society and—even more—one which has progressed historically to increase the standard of living and level of justice accorded to all persons. *Meliorism* is a pivotal tenet of American liberalism. In its traditional usage, it referred to the belief that the world tends to get better, and that "man" can aid in its betterment. In its contemporary use, the principle of meliorism, as applied to the political order, views democracy as the medium for the betterment of society. The liberal democratic view, however, is pragmatic rather than utopian, and its time perspective is one that views today as better than yesterday, and tomorrow as being better still. The Constitution is the accepted and working guide for social legislation. Through its responsible application all persons will achieve representation and justice, sooner or later. Matters of social urgency are always tempered by this faith in tomorrow and by the constraints of the Constitutional processes.

From the radical standpoint, "progress" is rejected as a historical myth. Some crucial aspects of social life are clearly not changing or are becoming worse. For example, wealth and economic power in the United States are becoming more concentrated; water and city air space are becoming more polluted; natural resources are being depleted. Where changes are occurring it is too slow—as in the case of the 40 million Americans now living at or below a minimally adequate income.

Present Constitutional processes are seen as ineffective, first because legal-institutional procedures for correcting social injustices do not exist or are not operative for all persons. Second, they are inadequate because even where they do exist not all people have access to the political-economic resources to achieve social justice.

From the liberal perspective social justice is assured because the democratic political process is *pluralistic*. Pluralism in this context refers to the diffusion of power across political elites such that the outcomes of decision-making are not controlled by a single elite. Political outcomes are presumably the consequence of the competition of organized groups through electoral or other political processes.

Not all radicals would agree that even *in theory* pluralism insures social justice. But all radicals do agree that pluralism does not exist in American cities and certainly not in decision-making at the state and national levels of government. Political sociological research does in fact support this claim. Pluralism, then, is a tenet of liberal faith and not an empirically based description of political action. Further, the economic costs of political action, the growing expensiveness of political candidacy, and the legislated restrictions on third-party campaigns make it clear that the potential for pluralistic opposition in electoral politics is at best highly circumscribed.

Many radicals argue, as I do, that the idea of pluralism in this political economy is both obsolete and potentially antidemocratic. This arguement is based on six observations:

1. Community decisions only involve a small proportion of the population.

2. Pluralism *by itself* provides no guarantee that all social groups will be represented in the formation of social policy.

3. There is no institutionalized mechanism for the entry of new interest groups into the policy-making arena, and new entrants may have to resort to force.

4. People who are outside the major social groups are effectively denied representation.

5. Some interests are not adequately represented in the pluralist's arena, and in particular, the interests of the total community may not achieve representation in a political system designed for the competition of special interest groups.

6. Some interest groups are franchised by the government—a professional group like the American Medical Association is a good example —and the imbalance of power created by such coalitions virtually precludes meaningful opposition.

Finally, I think that liberals and radicals have come to disagree on the political principle of equality. To be sure, American egalitarianism has never been clearly explicated, and even de Tocqueville, an astute observer of the development of American democracy, thought that our concern with equality would result in our loss of freedom. I think that in present-day American liberalism, equality has developed a political definition and refers almost exclusively to equality of access to political and economic opportunity. (And I suspect that this has emerged primarily from the "equal protection" clause of the Fourteenth Amendment.) Given this political conception of equality, personal freedom is defined by the permissible behaviors that are consistent with the principles of civil liberty, constitutional meliorism, and pluralistic opposition. In this framework, I believe that personal freedom has come to take evaluative precedence over human equality. Although I know of no liberal who has argued that

we ought to increase inequality to expand our freedom, the present challenge to this liberal principle of equality has revived liberal fears that
their freedom is diminishing.

The point at issue is that, from a radical perspective, equality so defined
is morally and politically improper. In its social effects, equality of access
has resulted in the retention of prevailing inequalities. In this regard,
equality has become a political mechanism for maintaining stability and
an ideological justification for preserving the social order.

Equality, for the radical, is to be achieved through the redistribution of
wealth and power in society and to be maintained not in an arena of political pluralism but in a system of participatory democracy based on the de-
centralization of political-economic decision-making. Thus liberal objectives are presumably attainable within and through the existing political economic system. Radical objectives necessitate the alteration of the
political economic structure itself.

I have heard people argue that the differences between radicals and liberals are basically tactical—between working within or outside the system. This is clearly an incorrect reading of these distinctive systems of
political beliefs. To be sure, neither liberals nor radicals have presented an
entirely systematic view of the good society. But radicals in advocating
the redistribution of wealth and power and the reorganization of society
to minimize (if not eliminate) stratification on the basis of class, ethnicity,
sex, and even age are calling for something which is not attainable within
established political economic structures. Indeed, it is the centrality of
that very belief that distinguishes the two perspectives.

Just the same, some liberals share the radical's view of a good society.
And not all persons who lay claim to a radical identity are distinguishable
politically from liberal activists. There is, in fact, a second set of attitudes
that distinguishes their approach to social change.

Years ago (in my liberal activist days) I had a friendly but often "jok-
ing relationship" with a radical faculty colleague. One day he defined for
me a liberal as "someone who was always fighting other people's battles."
Ironically, my own shift to a radical stance came through my fighting his
battle when the University of Iowa fired him for his radical political activities.

At the time, his definition puzzled me. In retrospect, I can see that he
had come upon one of the central features of the distinction between liberals and radicals. For the liberal, politics is external. Political acts are a
public service performed in a set of social relationships that are conventionally defined as "political." To be a political liberal does not require
that one is liberal in other contexts—although a strain toward consistency is always present.

For the radical activist, politics is the way one lives and, as such, political actions are not viewed as those confined to any narrow set of social relationships. Politics in this sense is not external, that is, not something scheduled in time and place. Political behavior is a form of self-actualization. Thus while both radicals and liberals may derive a sense of moral worth from their activism, radicals also derive a sense of personal unity from their political behavior. And rather than view their acts as a public service, radicals tend to see their activities as a part of a collective movement—and a movement through which they achieve validation of their self-conception.

The strategy of my presentation has been to argue that a person's self-conception as a liberal or a radical activist derives from a set of political attitudes and the conjunction of those political attitudes with their self-attitudes.

How people adapt social science principles, such as the principles of prejudice, to programs of social change depends intimately on their self-conception as liberals or radicals. (This argument is itself an adaptation of the principle of categorical dominance.) We are socialized in American society not to view political attitudes as integral to self-attitudes, that is, our political attitudes tend to be not very well articulated or well developed. Thus my theory tells me that it is more important, right now, that people deliberatively consider their self-conceptions as a prelude to adapting these principles to social change.

It is my hope that such serious reflection leads to a radical reorientation. And I offer, as a final principle, the analysis of another observer of American racism: *If you are not part of the solution, you are part of the problem.*

REFERENCES

Abel, T. M. Attitudes and the GSR. *Journal of Experimental Psychology* 13: 47–60, 1930.

Abelson, R. P. et al. (eds.). *Theories of Cognitive Consistency: A Sourcebook*. Chicago: Rand-McNally, 1968.

Abelson, R. P. and D. E. Kanouse. Subjective Acceptance of Verbal Generalizations. In Feldman, S. (ed.), *Cognitive Consistency*. New York: Academic Press, 1966.

Ackerman, N. W. and M. Jahoda. *Anti-Semitism and Emotional Disorder: A Psychoanalytic Interpretation*. New York: Harper, 1950.

Adorno, T. W. et al. *The Authoritarian Personality*. New York: Harper, 1950.

Allport, G. W. *The Nature of Prejudice*. Cambridge, Mass.: Addison-Wesley, 1954.

Allport, G. W. and B. M. Kramer. Some Roots of Prejudice, *Journal of Psychology* 22:9–39, 1946.

Allport, G. W. and J. M. Ross. Personal Religious Orientation and Prejudice. *Journal of Personality and Social Psychology* 5: 432–444, 1967.

Altman, I. and W. W. Haythorn. Interpersonal Exchange in Isolation, *Sociometry* 28:411–426, 1965.

Ames, R. G., S. Y. Moriwaki, and A. K. Basu. Sex Differences in Social Distance: A Research Report, *Sociology and Social Research* 52: 280–288, 1968.

Ames, R. G. and A. F. Sakuma. Criteria for Evaluating Others: A Re-Examination of the Bogardus Social Distance Scale, *Sociology and Social Research* 54: 5–24, 1969.

Amir, Y. Contact Hypothesis in Ethnic Relations, *Psychological Bulletin* 71: 319–342, 1969.

Ammons, R. B. Reactions in a Projective Doll-Play Interview of White Males Two to Six Years of Age to Differences in Skin Color and Facial Features, *Journal of Genetic Psychology* 76: 323–341, 1950.

Anderson, A. R. and O. K. Moore. The Formal Analysis of Normative Concepts, *American Sociological Review* 22: 9–17, 1957.

Anderson, C. C. and A. D. J. Cote. Belief Dissonance as a Source of Disaffection between Ethnic Groups, *Journal of Personality and Social Psychology* 4: 447–453, 1966.

Anderson, N. H. Primacy Effects in Personality Impression Formation Using a Generalized Order Effect Paradigm, *Journal of Personality and Social Psychology* 2: 1–9, 1965.

Anderson, N. H. Integration Theory and Attitude Change, *Psychological Review* 78: 171–206, 1971.

Anderson, N. H. and A. A. Barrios. Primacy Effects in Personality Impression Formation, *Journal of Abnormal and Social Psychology* 63: 346–350, 1961.

Anisfeld, M., S. R. Munoz, and W. E. Lambert. The Structure and Dynamics of the Ethnic Attitudes of Jewish Adolescents, *Journal of Abnormal and Social Psychology* 66: 31–36, 1963.

Ansari, A. A Study of the Relation between Group Stereotypes and Social Distance, *Journal of Education and Psychology* 14: 28–35, 1956.

Applezweig, D. G. Some determinants of behavioral rigidity, *Journal of Abnormal and Social Psychology* 49: 224–228, 1954.

Arnold, M. B. Human Emotion and Action. In Mischel, T. (ed.), *Human Action*. New York: Academic Press, 1969.

Asch, S. E. Forming Impressions of Personality, *Journal of Abnormal and Social Psychology* 41: 258–290, 1946.

Asch, S. E., H. Block, and M. Hertzman. Studies in the Principles of Judgments and Attitudes. I. Two Basic Principles of Judgment, *Journal of Psychology* 5: 219–251, 1938.

Bailes, D. W. and I. B. Guller. Dogmatism and Attitudes Toward the Vietnam War, *Sociometry* 33: 140–146, 1970.

Barcus, F. E. and J. Levin. Role Distance in Negro and Majority Fiction, *Journalism Quarterly* 43: 709–714, 1966.

Barker, R. G. *Ecological Psychology: Concepts and Methods for Studying the Environment of Human Behavior*. Stanford, Calif.: Stanford University Press, 1968.

Barron, M. L. Ethnic Anomie. In Barron, M. L. (ed.), *Minorities in a Changing World*. New York: Knopf, 1967.

Bastide, R. and P. Van Den Berghe. Stereotypes, Norms and Interracial Behavior in Sao Paulo, Brazil, *American Sociological Review* 22: 689–694, 1957.

Bayton, J. A. The Racial Stereotypes of Negro College Students, *Journal of Abnormal and Social Psychology* 36: 97–102, 1941.

Bayton, J. A. and E. Byoune. Racio-National Stereotypes Held by Negroes, *Journal of Negro Education* 16: 49–56, 1947.

Bayton, J. A., L. B. McAlister, and K. Hamer. Race-class Stereotypes, *Journal of Negro Education* 25: 75–78, 1956.

Beilin, H. Impression Formation Under Varied Set of Stimulus-Trait Conditions, *Journal of Social Psychology* 60: 39–55, 1963.

Berelson, B. and P. J. Salter. Majority and Minority Americans: An Analysis of Magazine Fiction, *Public Opinion Quarterly* 10: 168–197, 1946; reprinted in Rosenberg, B. and D. M. White (eds.). *Mass Culture*. Glencoe, Ill.: Free Press, 1957.

Berg, I. A. The Deviation Hypothesis: A Broad Statement of Its Assumptions and Postulates. In Berg, Irwin A. (ed.), *Response Set in Personality Assessment*. Chicago: Aldine, 1967.

Berger, E. M. The Relation between Expressed Acceptance of Self and Expressed Acceptance of Others, *Journal of Abnormal and Social Psychology* 47: 778–782, 1952.

Berkowitz, L. *Aggression: A Social Psychological Analysis.* New York: McGraw-Hill, 1962.

Berry, B. *Almost White.* New York: Macmillan, 1963.

Biddle, B. J. and E. J. Thomas (eds.). *Role Theory: Concepts and Research.* New York: Wiley, 1966.

Bills, R. E., E. L. Vance, and O. S. McLean. An Index of Adjustment and Values, *Journal of Consulting Psychology 15:* 257–261, 1951.

Bird, C., E. D. Monachesi, and H. Burdick. Infiltration and the Attitude of White and Negro Parents and Children, *Journal of Abnormal and Social Psychology* 47:688–699, 1952.

Bjerstedt, A. "Ego Involved World-Mindedness," Nationality Images; and Methods of Research: A Methodological Note, *Journal of Conflict Resolution 4:* 185–192, 1960.

Blake, R. and W. Dennis. The Development of Stereotypes Concerning the Negro, *Journal of Abnormal and Social Psychology 38:* 525–531, 1943.

Blalock, H. M. *Toward a Theory of Minority-Group Relations.* New York: Wiley, 1967.

Bledsoe, J. C. Self Concepts of Children and Their Intelligence, Achievements, Interests, and Anxiety, *Journal of Individual Psychology 20:* 55–58, 1964.

Blom, G. E., R. R. Waite, and S. F. Zimet. Ethnic Integration and Urbanization of a First Grade Reading Textbook: A Research Study, *Psychology in the Schools 4:* 176–181, 1967.

Blumer, H. Race Prejudice as a Sense of Group Position. In Masuoka, J. and P. Valien (eds.), *Race Relations: Problems and Theory.* Chapel Hill: The University of North Carolina Press, 1961.

Bogardus, E. S. Measuring Social Distances, *Journal of Applied Sociology 9:* 299–308, 1925.

Bogardus, E. S. *Immigration and Race Attitudes.* Boston: Heath, 1928.

Bogardus, E. S. *Social Distance.* Los Angeles: The author, 1959.

Bogardus, E. S. Comparing Racial Distance in Ethiopia, South Africa, and the United States, *Sociology and Social Research 52:* 149–156, 1968.

Bolton, E. B. Effect of Knowledge upon Attitudes Toward the Negro, *Journal of Social Psychology 6:* 68–90, 1935.

Borgatta, E. F. and B. Crowther. *A Workbook for the Study of Social Interaction Processes.* Chicago: Rand-McNally, 1965.

Bray, D. W. The Prediction of Behavior from Two Attitudes Scales, *Journal of Abnormal and Social Psychology 45:* 64–84, 1950.

Brewer, M. B. Determinants of Social Distance among East African Tribal Groups, *Journal of Personality and Social Psychology 38:* 279–289, 1968.

Brink, W. and L. Harris. *The Negro Revolution in America.* New York: Simon and Schuster, 1964.

Brodbeck, A. J. and H. V. Perlmutter. Self-dislike as a Determinant of Marked In-group-outgroup Preferences, *Journal of Psychology 38:* 271–280, 1954.

Brookover, W. and J. Holland. An Inquiry into the Meaning of Minority Group Attitude Expressions, *American Sociological Review 17:* 196–202, 1952.

Brooks, L. M: Racial Distance as Affected by Education, *Sociology and Social Research 21:* 128–133, 1936.

Broom, L. and N. D. Glenn. Negro-White Differences in Reported Attitudes and Behavior, *Sociology and Social Research 50:* 187–200, 1966.

Brown, R. L. Social Distance and the Ethiopian Students, *Sociology and Social Research 52:* 101–116, 1967.

Brown, R. L. Social Distance: Jordanian and Israeli Students, 1968, *Sociology and Social Research 53:* 344–362, 1969.

Brown, R. *Social Psychology.* New York: Free Press, 1965.

Bruner, J. S. On Perceptual Readiness, *Psychological Review 64:* 123–152, 1957.

Bruner, J. S., D. Shapiro, and R. Tagiuri. The Meaning of Traits in Isolation and in Combination. In Tagiuri, R. and L. Petrullo, *Person Perception and Interpersonal Behavior.* Stanford, Calif.: Stanford University Press, 1958.

Buchanan, W. and H. Cantril. *How Nations See Each Other.* Urbana: University of Illinois Press, 1953.

Byrne, D. Interpersonal Attraction and Attitude Similarity, *Journal of Abnormal and Social Psychology 62:* 713–715, 1961.

Byrne, D., G. L. Clore, Jr., and P. Worchel. Effect of Economic Similarity-Dissimilarity on Interpersonal Attraction, *Journal of Personality and Social Psychology 4:* 220–224, 1966.

Byrne, D., W. Griffitt, and D. Stefenick. Attraction and Similarity of Personality Characteristics, *Journal of Personality and Social Psychology 5:* 82–90, 1967.

Byrne, D. and C. McGraw. Interpersonal Attraction toward Negroes, *Human Relations 17:* 201–213, 1964.

Byrne, D. and T. J. Wong. Racial Prejudice, Interpersonal Attraction, and Assumed Dissimilarity of Attitudes, *Journal of Abnormal and Social Psychology 65:* 246–253, 1962.

Cahalan, D. and F. Trager. Free Answer Stereotypes and Anti-Semitism, *Public Opinion Quarterly 13:* 93–104, 1949.

Campbell, A., G. Gurin, and W. Miller. *The Voter Decides.* Evanston, Ill.: Row, Peterson, 1954.

Campbell, D. T. Social Attitudes and Other Acquired Behavioral Dispositions. In Koch, S. (ed.), *Psychology: A Study of a Science.* Vol. 6, New York: McGraw-Hill, 1961.

Campbell, D. T. Stereotypes and the Perception of Group Differences, *American Psychologist 22:* 817–830, 1967.

Campbell, D. T. and B. McCandless. Ethnocentrism, Xenophobia and Personality, *Human Relations 4:* 185–192, 1951.

Campbell, E. Q. Scale and Intensity Analysis in the Study of Attitude Change, *Public Opinion Quarterly 26:* 227–235, 1962.

Canter, F. M. The Relationship between Authoritarian Attitudes, Attitudes toward Mental Patients and Effectiveness of Clinical Work, *Journal of Clinical Psychology 19:* 124–127, 1954.

Cantril, H. The Intensity of an Attitude, *Journal of Abnormal and Social Psychology 41:* 129–135, 1946.

Centers, R. An Effective Classroom Demonstration of Stereotypes, *Journal of Social Psychology 34:* 41–46, 1951.

Chant, S. N. and M. D. Salter. The Measurement of Attitude Toward War and the Galvanic Skin Response, *Journal of Educational Psychology 28:* 281–289, 1937.

Chase, W. P. Attitudes of North Carolina College Students (Women) Toward the Negro, *Journal of Social Psychology 12:* 367–378, 1940.

Chesler, M. A., Ethnocentrism and Attitudes toward the Physically Disabled, *Journal of Personality and Social Psychology 2:* 877–881, 1965.

Child, I. L. and L. W. Doob. Factors Determining National Stereotypes, *Journal of Social Psychology 17:* 203–219, 1943.

Clarke, R. B. and D. T. Campbell. A Demonstration of Bias in Estimates of Negro Ability, *Journal of Abnormal and Social Psychology 51:* 585–88, 1955.

Clarke, W. Portrait of the Mythical Gentile, *Commentary 7:* 546–549, 1949.

Cooper, J. B., Emotion in Prejudice, *Science 130:* 314–318, 1959.

Cooper, J. B. and J. L. McGaugh. *Integrative Principles of Social Psychology.* Cambridge, Mass.: Schenkman, 1963.

Cooper, J. B. and D. Pollock. The Identification of Prejudicial Attitudes by the Galvanic Skin Response, *Journal of Social Psychology 51:* 241–245, 1959.

Cooper, J. B. and H. E. Siegel. The Galvanic Skin Response as a Measure of Emotion in Prejudice, *Journal of Psychology 42:* 149–155, 1956.

Cooper, J. B. and D. N. Singer. The Role of Emotion in Prejudice, *Journal of Social Psychology 44:* 241–247, 1956.

Coopersmith, S. A Method for Determining Types of Self-Esteem, *Journal of Abnormal and Social Psychology 59:* 87–94, 1959.

Cothran, Tilman C. Negro Conceptions of White People, *American Journal of Sociology 56:* 458–467, 1951.

Cowen, E. L., P. H. Bobrove, A. M. Rockway, and J. Stevenson. Development and Evaluation of an Attitudes to Deafness Scale, *Journal of Personality and Social Psychology 6:* 183–192, 1967.

Cowgill, D. O. Social Distance in Thailand, *Sociology and Social Research 52:* 363–376, 1968.

Cox, K. K. Changes in Stereotyping of Negroes and Whites in Magazine Advertisements, *Public Opinion Quarterly 33:* 603–606, 1970.

Crandall, V. J. and U. Bellugi. Some Relationships of Interpersonal and Intrapersonal Conceptualizations to Personal-Social Adjustment, *Journal of Personality 23:* 224–232, 1954.

Davitz, J. R. *The Language of Emotion.* New York: Academic Press, 1969.

DeFleur, M. L. and F. R. Westie. Verbal Attitudes and Overt Acts: An Experiment on the Salience of Attitudes, *American Sociological Review 23:* 667–673, 1958.

DeFleur, M. L. and F. R. Westie. The Interpretation of Interracial Situations, *Social Forces 38:* 17–23, 1959.

DeFleur, M. L. and F. R. Westie. Attitude as a Scientific Concept, *Social Forces 42:* 17–31, 1963.

DeFriese, G. H. and W. S. Ford. Verbal Attitudes, Overt Acts, and the Influence of Social Constraint in Interracial Behavior, *Social Problems 16:* 493–505, 1969.

Derbyshire, R. L. and E. Brody. Social Distance and Identity Conflict in Negro College Students, *Sociology and Social Research 48:* 301–314, 1964.

Deutsch, M. The Directions of Behavior: A Field-Theoretical Approach to the Understanding of Inconsistencies, *Journal of Social Issues 5:* 43–51, 1949.

Deutscher, I. Words and Deeds: Social Science and Social Policy, *Social Problems 13:* 235–254, 1966.

Diab, L. N. National Stereotypes and the "Reference Group" Concept, *Journal of Social Psychology* 57: 339–351, 1962.

Dickens, S. L. and C. Hobart. Parental Dominance and Offspring Ethnocentrism, *Journal of Social Psychology* 49: 297–303, 1959.

Dickson, H. W. and E. McGinnies. Affectivity in the Arousal of Attitudes as Measured by Galvanic Skin Response, *American Journal of Psychology* 79: 584–587, 1966.

Dillehay, R. C., W. H. Bruvold, and J. P. Siegel. Attitude, Object Label and Stimulus Factors in Response to an Attitude Object, *Journal of Personality and Social Psychology* 11: 220–223, 1969.

Dodd, S. C. A Social Distance Test in the Near East, *American Journal of Sociology* 41: 194–204, 1935.

Dodge, R. W. and E. S. Uyeki. Political Affiliation and Imagery across Two Related Generations, *Midwest Journal of Political Science* 6: 266–276, 1962.

Dollard, J., L. Doob, N. Miller, O. Mowrer, and R. Sears. *Frustration and Aggression.* New Haven, Conn.: Yale University Press, 1939.

Dudycha, G. J. The Attitudes of College Students Toward War and the Germans Before and During the Second World War, *Journal of Social Psychology* 15: 317–324, 1942.

Duijker, H. C. J. and N. H. Frijda. *National Character and National Stereotypes.* Amsterdam, The Netherlands: North-Holland Publishing Co., 1961.

Edlefsen, J. B. Social Distance Attitudes of Negro College Students, *Phylon* 17: 79–83, 1956.

Ehrlich, C. The Male Sociologist's Burden: The Place of Women in Marriage and Family Texts, *Journal of Marriage and the Family* 33: 421–430, 1971.

Ehrlich, H. J. Stereotyping and Negro-Jewish Stereotypes, *Social Forces* 41: 171–176, 1962a.

Ehrlich, H. J. The Swastika Epidemic of 1959–1960: Anti-Semitism and Community Characteristics, *Social Problems* 9: 264–272, 1962b.

Ehrlich, H. J. Instrument Error and the Study of Prejudice, *Social Forces* 43: 197–206, 1964.

Ehrlich, H. J. Attitudes, Behavior, and the Intervening Variables, *American Sociologist* 4: 29–34, 1969.

Ehrlich, H. J. and D. B. Graeven. Reciprocal Self-Disclosure in a Dyad, *Journal of Experimental Social Psychology* 7: 398–400, 1971.

Ehrlich, H. J. and J. W. Rinehart. A Brief Report on the Methodology of Stereotype Research, *Social Forces* 43: 564–575, 1965.

Ehrlich, H. J. and J. W. Rinehart. Checklists *and* Open-Ended Questions: A Reply, *Social Forces* 44: 420–421, 1966.

Ehrlich, H. J. and N. Van Tubergen. Social Distance as Behavioral Intentions: A Replication, A Failure, and A New Proposal, *Psychological Reports* 24: 627–634, 1969.

Ehrlich, H. J. and N. Van Tubergen. Exploring the Structure and Salience of Stereotypes, *Journal of Social Psychology* 83: 113–127, 1971.

Elson, R. M. *Guardians of Tradition.* Lincoln: University of Nebraska Press, 1964.

Epstein, R. and S. S. Komorita. Parental Discipline, Stimulus Characteristics of Outgroups, and Social Distance in Children, *Journal of Personality and Social Psychology* 2: 416–420, 1965.

Epstein, R. and S. S. Komorita. Prejudice among Negro Children as Related to Parental Ethnocentrism and Punitiveness, *Journal of Personality and Social Psychology* 4: 643–647, 1966a.

Epstein, R. and S. S. Komorita. Childhood Prejudice as a Function of Parental Ethnocentrism, Punitiveness, and Outgroup Characteristics, *Journal of Personality and Social Psychology* 3: 259–264, 1966b.

Ewens, W. L. *Reference Other Support, Ethnic Attitudes, and Perceived Influence of Others in the Performance of Overt Acts*. Doctoral Dissertation, University of Iowa, Iowa City, 1969.

Ewens, W. L. and H. J. Ehrlich. Reference Other Support and Ethnic Attitudes as Predictors of Intergroup Behavior. Revised version of a paper presented to the joint meetings of the Midwest Sociological Society and Ohio Valley Sociological Society, Indianapolis, Ind., May, 1969.

Eysenck, H. J. and S. Crown. National Stereotypes: An Experimental and Methodological Study, *International Journal of Opinion and Attitude Research 2:* 26–39, 1948.

Fagan, J. and M. O'Neill. A Comparison of Social-Distance Scores among College Student Samples, *Journal of Social Psychology* 66: 281–290, 1965.

Feagin, J. R. Prejudice, Orthodoxy and the Social Situation, *Social Forces 44:* 46–56, 1965.

Fendrich, J. M. Perceived Reference Group Support: Racial Attitudes and Overt Behavior, *American Sociological Review* 32: 960–970, 1967.

Fernberger, S. W. Persistence of Stereotypes Concerning Sex Differences, *Journal of Abnormal and Social Psychology* 43: 97–101, 1948.

Fey, W. F. Acceptance by Others and its Relation to Acceptance of Self and Others: A Revaluation, *Journal of Abnormal and Social Psychology 50:* 274–276, 1955.

Fey, W. F. Correlates of Certain Subjective Attitudes towards Self and Others, *Journal of Clinical Psychology* 13: 44–49, 1957.

Fichter, J. H. *Parochial School: A Sociological Study*. South Bend, Ind.: University of Notre Dame Press, 1958.

Fiedler, F. E., W. G. Warrington, and F. J. Blaisdell. Unconscious Attitudes as Correlates of Sociometric Choice in a Social Group, *Journal of Abnormal Social Psychology* 47: 790–796, 1952.

Fink, H. C. Fictitious Groups and the Generality of Prejudice: An Artifact of Scales without Neutral Categories, *Psychological Reports 29:* 359–365, 1971.

Fishbein, M. A Consideration of Beliefs, Attitudes, and Their Relationships, In Steiner, I. D. and M. Fishbein (eds.), *Current Studies in Social Psychology*. New York: Holt, Rinehart and Winston, 1965.

Fishbein, M. The Relationships between Beliefs, Attitudes, and Behavior, In Feldman, S. (ed.), *Cognitive Consistency*. New York: Academic Press, 1966.

Fishbein, M. and B. H. Raven. The AB Scales: An Operational Definition of Belief and Attitude, *Human Relations* 15: 35–44, 1962.

Fishman, J. Negative Stereotypes Concerning Americans Among American-Born

Children Receiving Various Types of Minority Group Educations, *Genetic Psychology Monographs 51:* 107–182, 1955.

Fishman, J. Some Social and Psychological Determinants of Inter-Group Relations in Changing Neighborhoods: An Introduction to the Bridgeview Study, *Social Forces 40:* 42–51, 1961.

Flanagan, J. T. The German in American Fiction, In Ander, O. F. (ed.), *In the Trek of the Immigrants: Essays Presented to Carl Wittke.* Rock Island, Ill.: Augustana College Library, 1964.

Flora, C. F. The Passive Female: Her Comparative Image by Class and Culture in Women's Magazine Fiction, *Journal of Marriage and the Family 33:* 435–444, 1971.

Frenkel-Brunswik, E. A. Study of Prejudice in Children, *Human Relations 1:* 295–306, 1948.

Frenkel-Brunswik, E. Intolerance of Ambiguity as an Emotional and Perceptual Personality Variable, *Journal of Personality 18:* 108–143, 1949.

Frenkel-Brunswik, E. and J. Havel. Prejudice in the Interviews of Children: I. Attitudes toward Minority Groups, *Journal of Genetic Psychology 82:* 91–136, 1953.

Frenkel-Brunswik, E. and R. N. Sanford. Some Personality Factors in Anti-Semitism, *Journal of Psychology 20:* 271–291, 1945.

Frijda, N. H. Recognition of Emotion, in Berkowitz, L. (ed.), *Advances in Experimental Social Psychology.* Vol. 4, New York: Academic Press, 1969, pp. 167–223.

Fruchter, B., M. Rokeach, and E. G. Novak. A Factorial Study of Dogmatism, Opinionation, and Related Scales, *Psychological Reports 4:* 19–22, 1958.

Galanter, M. A. Dissent on Brother Daniel, *Commentary 36:*10–17, 1963.

Gardner, R. C. and D. M. Taylor. Ethnic Stereotypes: Meaningfulness in Ethnic-Group Labels, *Canadian Journal of Behavioural Science 1:* 182–192, 1969.

Genskow, J. K. and F. D. Maglione. Familiarity, Dogmatism, and Reported Student Attitudes toward the Disabled, *Journal of Social Psychology 67:* 329–341, 1965.

Gergen, K. J. The Significance of Skin Color in Human Relations, *Daedalus 96:* 390–407, 1967.

Gibbs, J. P. Norms: The Problem of Definition and Classification, *American Journal of Sociology 70:* 586–594, 1965.

Gilliland, A. R. and R. A. Blum. Favorable and Unfavorable Attitudes Toward Certain Enemy and Allied Countries, *Journal of Psychology 20:* 391–399, 1945.

Glock, C. Y. and R. Stark. *Christian Beliefs and Anti-Semitism.* New York: Harper and Row, 1966.

Goode, W. J., E. Hopkins, and H. M. McClure. *Social Systems and Family Patterns: A Propositional Inventory.* Indianapolis, Ind.: Bobbs-Merrill, 1971.

Goodman, M. E. *Race Awareness in Young Children* (rev. ed.). New York: Collier Books, 1964.

Goodnow, R. E. and R. Tagiuri. Religious Ethnocentrism and Its Recognition among Adolescent Boys, *Journal of Abnormal and Social Psychology 47:* 316–320, 1952.

Gordon, M. M. *Assimilation in American Life*. New York: Oxford University Press, 1964.

Gordon, M. and P. J. Shankweiler, Different Equals Less: Female Sexuality in Recent Marriage Manuals, *Journal of Marriage and the Family 33*: 459–466, 1971.

Gordon, R. Stereotypy of Imagery and Belief as an Ego Defence, *British Journal of Psychology, Monograph Supplement*, No. 34, 1962.

Gough, H. G. *California Psychological Inventory Manual*, Palo Alto, Calif.: Consulting Psychologists Press, 1957.

Gough, H. G. Studies of Social Intolerance: I. Some Psychological and Sociological Correlates of Anti-Semitism, *Journal of Social Psychology 33*: 237–246, 1951.

Gough, H. G., D. B. Harris, W. E. Martin, and M. Edwards. Children's Ethnic Attitudes: 1. Relationship to Certain Personality Factors, *Child Development 21*: 83–91, 1950.

Gould, J. and W. L. Kolb (eds.). *A Dictionary of the Social Sciences*. New York: Free Press, 1964.

Gray, J. S. and A. H. Thompson. The Ethnic Prejudices of White and Negro College Students, *Journal of Abnormal and Social Psychology 48*: 311–313, 1953.

Gregor, A. J. and D. A. McPherson. Racial Attitudes among White and Negro Children in a Deep-South Standard Metropolitan Area, *Journal of Social Psychology 68*: 95–106, 1966.

Grice, H. H. and H. H. Remmers. *A Scale for Measuring Attitudes toward Races and Nationalities*. Lafayette, Ind.: Purdue Research Foundation, Purdue University, 1934.

Gross, S. L. and J. E. Hardy (eds.). *Images of the Negro in American Literature*. Chicago: University of Chicago Press, 1966.

Grossack, M. N. Attitudes toward Desegregation of Southern White and Negro Children. In Grossack, M. N., *Mental Health and Segregation*. New York: Springer, 1963.

Gundlach, R. H. The Attributes of Enemy, Allied, and Domestic Nationality Groups as Seen by College Students of Different Regions, *Journal of Social Psychology 19*: 249–258, 1944.

Guskin, S. L. The Influence of Labelling upon the Perception of Subnormality in Mentally Defective Children, *American Journal of Mental Deficiency 67*: 402–406, 1962.

Gutman, R. Demographic Trends and the Decline of Anti-Semitism. In Stember, C. H. (ed.). *Jews in the Mind of America*. New York: Basic Books, 1966.

Haire, M. and W. F. Grunes. Perceptual Defenses: Processes Protecting an Organized Perception of Another Personality, *Human Relations 3*: 403–412, 1950.

Hall, E. T. A System of Notation of Proxemic Behavior, *American Anthropologist 65*: 1003–1026, 1963.

Hanlon, T. E., P. Hofstaetter, and J. O'Connor. Congruence of Self and Ideal Self in Relation to Personality Adjustment, *Journal of Consulting Psychology 18*: 215–218, 1954.

Harlan, H. H. Some Factors Affecting Attitude toward Jews, *American Sociological Review 8*: 816–827, 1942.

Harris, D. B., H. G. Gough, and W. E. Martin. Children's Ethnic Attitudes: II. Relationship to Parental Beliefs Concerning Child Training, *Child Development* *21:* 169–181, 1950.

Harris, J. J. Intergroup Relations in Social-Studies Textbooks, *Theory Into Practice* *2:* 128–135, 1963.

Hartley, E. L. *Problems in Prejudice*. New York: King's Crown Press, 1946.

Hartley, E. L. M. Rosenbaum, and S. Schwartz. Children's Use of Ethnic Frames of Reference: An Exploratory Study of Children's Conceptualizations of Multiple Ethnic Group Membership, *Journal of Psychology 26:* 367–386, 1948.

Heer, D. M. Negro-White Marriage in the United States, *Journal of Marriage and the Family 28:* 262–273, 1966.

Helgerson, E. The Relative Significance of Race, Sex, and Facial Expression in the Choice of Playmates by the Preschool Child, *Journal of Negro Education 12:* 617–622, 1943.

Henle, M. and M. Michael. The Influence of Attitudes in Syllogistic Reasoning, *Journal of Social Psychology 44:* 115–128, 1956.

Hess, R. D. and D. Easton. The Child's Changing Image of the President, *Public Opinion Quarterly 24:* 632–644, 1960.

Hess, R. D. and J. V. Torney. *The Development of Political Attitudes in Children*. Chicago: Aldine Publishing Co., 1967.

Hinckley, E. D. The Influence of Individual Opinion on Construction of an Attitude Scale, *Journal of Social Psychology 3:* 283–295, 1932.

Hofstaetter, P. R. A Factorial Study of Prejudice, *Journal of Personality 21:* 228–239, 1952.

Holloway, R. L. Human Aggression: The Need for a Species-Specific Framework, In Fried, M., M. Harris, and R. Murphy (eds.). *War: The Anthropology of Armed Conflict and Aggression*. Garden City, N.Y.: National History Press, 1968.

Horowitz, E. L. The Development of Attitude toward the Negro, *Archives of Psychology*, No. 194, 1936.

Horowitz, E. L. and R. E. Horowitz. Development of Social Attitudes in Children, *Sociometry 1:* 301–338, 1938.

Howe, I. The Stranger and the Victim; The Two Jewish Stereotypes of American Fiction, *Commentary 8:* 147–156, 1949.

Hraba, J. and G. Grant. Black is Beautiful: A Re-examination of Racial Preference and Identification, *Journal of Personality and Social Psychology 16:* 398–402, 1970.

Hyman, H. H. and associates. *Interviewing in Social Research*. Chicago: University of Chicago Press, 1954.

Hyman, H. *Political Socialization*. Glencoe, Ill.: Free Press, 1959.

Insko, C. A. and J. E. Robinson. Belief Similarity Versus Race as Determinants of Reactions to Negroes by Southern White Adolescents: A Further Test of Rokeach's Theory, *Journal of Personality and Social Psychology 7:* 216–221, 1967.

Irwin, M., T. Tripodi, and J. Bieri. Affective Stimulus Value and Cognitive Complexity, *Journal of Personality and Social Psychology 5:* 444–449, 1967.

Jahoda, G. Nationality Preferences and National Stereotypes in Ghana Before Independence, *Journal of Social Psychology 50:* 165–174, 1959.

Jaros, D., H. Hirsch, and F. J. Fleron. The Malevolent Leader: Political Socialization in an American Sub-Culture, *American Political Science Review* 62: 564–575, 1968.

Jennings, M. K. and R. G. Niemi. Family Structure and the Transmission of Political Values, *American Political Science Review* 62: 169–184, 1968.

Johnsen, K. P. A Progress Report on a Study of the Factors Associated with the Male's Tendency to Negatively Stereotype the Female, *Sociological Focus* 2: 21–35, 1969.

Johnson, G. B. The Stereotype of the American Negro, In Klineberg, O. (ed.). *Characteristics of the American Negro*. New York: Harper, 1944.

Jones, E. E. and H. B. Gerard. *Foundations of Social Psychology*. New York: Wiley, 1967.

Jones, M. A. *American Immigration*. Chicago: University of Chicago Press, 1960.

Jourard, S. M. *The Transparent Self*. Princeton, N.J.: Van Nostrand, 1964.

Just, L. R. A Study of Mennonite Social Distance Reactions, *Sociology and Social Research* 38: 222–226, 1954.

Karabenick, S. A. and W. R. Wilson. Dogmatism among War Hawks and Peace Doves, *Psychological Reports* 25: 419–422, 1969.

Katz, D. and K. W. Braly. Racial Stereotypes of 100 College Students, *Journal of Abnormal and Social Psychology* 28: 280–290, 1933.

Katz, D. and K. W. Braly. Racial Prejudice and Racial Stereotypes, *Journal of Abnormal and Social Psychology* 30: 175–193, 1935.

Kay, L. W. Frame of Reference in "Pro" and "Anti" Evaluation of Test Items, *Journal of Social Psychology* 25: 63–68, 1947.

Kelley, H. H. The Warm-Cold Variable in First Impressions of Persons, *Journal of Personality* 18: 431–439, 1950.

Kelly, J. G., J. E. Ferson, and W. H. Holtzman. The Measurement of Attitudes toward the Negro in the South, *Journal of Social Psychology* 48: 305–317, 1958.

Kerlinger, F. and M. Rokeach. The Factorial Nature of the F and D Scales, *Journal of Personality and Social Psychology* 4: 391–399, 1966.

Killian, L. M. The Adjustment of Southern White Migrants to Northern Urban Norms, *Social Forces* 32: 66–69, 1953.

Kipnis, D. M. Changes in Self Concepts in Relation to Perceptions of Others, *Journal of Personality and Social Psychology* 29: 449–465, 1961.

Kirtley, D. and R. Harkless. Some Personality and Attitudinal Correlates of Dogmatism, *Psychological Reports* 24: 851–854, 1969.

Klineberg, O. *Social Psychology*. New York: Holt, Rinehart and Winston, 1954.

Klineberg, O. Life is Fun in a Smiling, Fair-Skinned World, *Saturday Review*, 75–78, 87, February 16, 1963.

Koch, H. L. The Social Distance between Certain Racial, Nationality, and Skin Pigmentation Groups in Selected Populations of American School Children, *Journal of Genetic Psychology* 68: 63–95, 1946.

Kogan, N., Attitudes toward Old People in an Older Sample, *Journal of Abnormal and Social Psychology* 62: 616–622, 1961.

Kohlberg, L. A Cognitive-Developmental Analysis of Children's Sex-Role Concepts and Attitudes. In Maccoby, E. E. *The Development of Sex Differences*. Palo Alto, Calif.: Stanford University Press, 1966.

Komorita, S. S. Attitude Content, Intensity, and the Neutral Point on a Likert Scale, *Journal of Social Psychology 61:* 327–334, 1963.

Korn, H. A., and N. S. Giddan. Scoring Methods and Construct Validity of the Dogmatism Scale, *Educational and Psychological Measurement 24:* 867–874, 1964.

Koslin, S. C., M. Amarel, and N. Ames. A Distance Measure of Racial Attitudes in Primary Grade Children: An Exploratory Study, *Psychology in the Schools 6:* 382–384, 1969.

Kothandapani, V. Validation of Feeling, Belief, and Intention to Act as Three Components of Attitude and Their Contribution to Prediction of Contraceptive Behavior, *Journal of Personality and Social Psychology 19:* 321–323, 1971.

Krech, D., R. S. Crutchfield, and E. L. Ballachey. *Individual in Society*. New York: McGraw-Hill, 1962.

Kurokawa, M. *Minority Responses*. New York: Random House, 1970.

Kutner, B. Patterns of Mental Functioning Associated with Prejudice in Children, *Psychological Monographs 72,* No. 7 (whole no. 460), 1958.

Kutner, B. and N. B. Gordon. Cognitive Functioning and Prejudice: A Nine-Year Follow-up Study, *Sociometry 27:* 66–74, 1964.

Kutner, B., C. Wilkins, and P. Yarrow. Verbal Attitudes and Overt Behavior Involving Racial Prejudice, *Journal of Abnormal and Social Psychology 47:* 649–652, 1952.

Laffal, J. *Pathological and Normal Language*. New York: Atherton Press, 1965.

Lambert, W. E. and O. Klineberg. *Children's Views of Foreign Peoples*. New York: Appleton-Century-Crofts, 1967.

Landis, J., D. Datwyler, and D. S. Dorn. Race and Social Class as Determinants of Social Distance, *Sociology and Social Research 51:* 78–86, 1966.

Lane, R. E. and D. O. Sears. *Public Opinion*. Englewood Cliffs, N.J.: Prentice-Hall, 1964.

LaPiere, R. T. Attitudes vs. Actions, *Social Forces 13:* 230–237, 1934.

LaPiere, R. T. Type-rationalizations of Group Antipathy, *Social Forces 15:* 232–237, 1936.

Larrick, N. The All-White World of Children's Books, *Saturday Review,* 63–65, 84–85, September 11, 1965.

Lee, D. E. and H. J. Ehrlich. Beliefs about Self and Others: A Test of the Dogmatism Theory, *Psychological Reports 28:* 919–922, 1971.

Leeper, R. W. Some Needed Developments in the Motivational Theory of Emotions. In Levine, D. (ed.). *Nebraska Symposium on Motivation, 1965*. Lincoln: University of Nebraska Press, 1965.

Levanway, R. W. The Effect of Stress on Expressed Attitudes toward Self and Others, *Journal of Abnormal and Social Psychology 50:* 225–226, 1955.

Lever, H. Ethnic Preferences of White Residents in Johannesburg, *Sociology and Social Research 52:* 158–173, 1968.

Levin, M. L. Social Climates and Political Socialization, *Public Opinion Quarterly 25:* 596–606, 1961.

Lindzey, G. (ed.). *Handbook of Social Psychology*. Reading, Mass.: Addison-Wesley, 1954.

Linn, L. S. Verbal Attitudes and Overt Behavior: A Study of Racial Discrimination, *Social Forces 43:* 353–364, 1965.

Lohman, J. P. and D. C. Reitzes. Note on Race Relations in Mass Society, *American Journal of Sociology 58:* 240–246, 1952.

Long, B. H., R. C. Ziller, and E. E. Thompson. A Comparison of Prejudices: The Effects of Chronic Illness, Old Age, Education, and Race upon Friendship Ratings, *Journal of Social Psychology 70:* 101–109, 1966.

Luchins, A. S. Experimental Attempts to Minimize the Impact of First Impressions, In Hovland, C. (ed.). *The Order of Presentation in Persuasion*. New Haven: Yale University Press, 1957.

Lundy, R., W. Katkovsky, R. Cromwell, and D. Shoemaker. Self-acceptability and Descriptions of Sociometric Choices, *Journal of Abnormal and Social Psychology 51:* 260–262, 1955.

McCloud, K. and A. H. Kidd. Rokeach's Dogmatism Scale in the Selection of Psychiatric Nursing Personnel, *Psychological Reports 13:* 241–242, 1963.

McDaniel, P. A. and N. Babchuk. Negro Conceptions of White People in a Northeastern City, *Phylon 21:* 7–19, 1960.

McDavid, J. W. and H. Harari. Stereotyping of Names and Popularity in Grade-School Children, *Child Development 37:* 453–459, 1966.

McDill, E. L. A Comparison of Three Measures of Attitude Intensity, *Social Forces 38:* 95–99, 1959.

McDonagh, E. C. and E. S. Richards. *Ethnic Relations in the United States*. New York: Appleton-Century Crofts, 1953.

McManus, J. T. and L. Kronenberger. Motion Pictures, the Theater and Race Relations, *The Annals of the American Academy of Political and Social Science 244:*152–158, 1946.

MacCrone, I. D. *Race Attitudes in South Africa*. Capetown: Oxford University Press, 1937.

MacCrone, I. D. A Comparative Study of European and Non-European Differences in Race Preferences, *South African Journal of Science 35:* 412–416, 1938.

MacKinnon, W. J. and R. Centers. Social-Psychological Factors in Public Orientation Toward an Out-Group, *American Journal of Sociology 63:* 415–419, 1958.

Malof, M. and A. Lott. Ethnocentrism and the Acceptance of Negro Support in a Group Situation, *Journal of Abnormal and Social Psychology 65:* 254–258, 1962.

Maranell, G. M. An Examination of Some Religious and Political Attitude Correlates of Bigotry, *Social Forces 45:* 356–362, 1967.

Marcus, L. *The Treatment of Minorities in Secondary School Textbooks*. New York: Anti-Defamation League of B'nai B'rith, 1961.

Marden, C. E. and G. Meyer. *Minorities in American Society*. New York: American Book Company, 1962.

Marlow, D. and K. J. Gergen. Personality and Social Interaction. In Lindzey, G. and E. Aronson (eds.). *The Handbook of Social Psychology*, Vol. 3. Reading, Mass.: Addison-Wesley, 1969.

Martin, W. Seduced and Abandoned in the New World: The Image of Women in

American Fiction. In Gornick, V. and B. K. Moran (eds.), *Woman in Sexist Society*. New York: Basic Books, 1971.

Marx, G. T. *Protest and Prejudice*. New York: Harper and Row, 1967.

Mayer, J. E. *Jewish-Gentile Courtships*. New York: The Free Press, 1961.

Mayer, M. The Issue Is Miscegenation, *Progressive 23:* 8–18, 1959.

Mayo, G. D. and J. R. Kinzer. A Comparison of the "Racial" Attitudes of White and Negro High School Students in 1940 and 1948, *Journal of Psychology 29:* 397–405, 1950.

McCandless, B. R. and J. M. Hoyt. Sex, Ethnicity, and Play Preferences of School Children, *Journal of Abnormal and Social Psychology 62:* 683–685, 1961.

McCord, W., J. McCord, and A. Howard. Early Familial Experiences and Bigotry, *American Sociological Review 25:* 717–722, 1960.

McNeil, J. D. Changes in Ethnic Reaction Tendencies During High School, *Journal of Educational Research 53:* 199–200, 1960.

Meenes, M. A Comparison of Racial Stereotypes of 1935 and 1942, *Journal of Social Psychology 17:* 327–336, 1943.

Melamed, L. Race Awareness in South African Children, *Journal of Social Psychology 76:* 3–8, 1968.

Meltzer, H. Attitudes of American Children toward Peaceful and Warlike Nations in 1934 and 1938, *Journal of Psychology 7:* 369–384, 1939a.

Meltzer, H. Group Differences in Nationality and Race Preferences of Children, *Sociometry 2:* 86–105, 1939b.

Meltzer, H. Children's Thinking about Nations and Races, *Journal of Genetic Psychology 58:* 181–199, 1941a.

Meltzer, H. The Development of Children's Nationality Preferences, Concepts, and Attitudes, *Journal of Psychology 11:*343–358, 1941b.

Mensch, I. N. and J. Wishner. Asch on "Forming Impressions of Personality" Further Evidence, *Journal of Personality 16:*188–191, 1947.

Merz, L. E. and L. I. Pearlin. The Influence of Information on Three Dimensions of Prejudice toward Negroes, *Social Forces 35:* 344–351, 1957.

Middleton, R. and S. Putney. Student Rebellion Against Parental Political Beliefs, *Social Forces 41:* 377–383, 1963.

Mills, C. W. Situated Actions and Vocabularies of Motive, *American Sociological Review 5:* 904–913, 1940.

Minard, R. D. *Race Attitudes of Iowa Children*. Iowa City: University of Iowa Studies in Character, 1931. (Vol. 4, No. 2, Whole No. 217 n.s.)

Minard, R. D. Race Relationships in the Pocahontas Coal Field, *Journal of Social Issues 8:* 29–44, 1952.

Morgan, J. J. B. and J. T. Morton. The Distortion of Syllogistic Reasoning Produced by Personal Convictions, *Journal of Social Psychology 20:* 39–59, 1944.

Morland, J. K. Racial Recognition by Nursery School Children in Lynchburg, Virginia, *Social Forces 37:* 132–137, 1958.

Morse, N. C. and F. H. Allport. The Causation of Anti-Semitism: An Investigation of Seven Hypotheses, *Journal of Psychology 34:* 197–233, 1952.

Morsh, J. E. and M. E. Smith. Judgment of Prejudice Before, During, and After World War II, *Journal of Social Psychology 38:* 31–37, 1953.

Mosher, D. L. and A. A. Scodel. A Study of the Relationship between Ethnocentrism in Children and the Ethnocentrism and Authoritarian Rearing Practices of Their Mother, *Child Development 31:* 369–370, 1960.

Murphy, G. and R. Likert. *Public Opinion and the Individual.* New York: Harper, 1938.

Murphy, G. , L. B. Murphy, and T. M. Newcomb. *Experimental Social Psychology.* New York: Harper, 1937.

Mussen, P. H. Some Personality and Social Factors Related to Changes in Children's Attitudes toward Negroes, *Journal of Abnormal and Social Psychology 45:* 423–441, 1950.

Nettler, G. The Relation between Attitude and Information Concerning the Japanese in America, *American Sociological Review 11:* 177–191, 1946.

Nettler, G. and E. H. Golding. The Measurement of Attitudes toward the Japanese in America, *American Journal of Sociology 52:* 31–39, 1946.

Newcomb, T. M., R. H. Turner, and P. E. Converse. *Social Psychology.* New York: Holt, Rinehart, and Winston, 1965.

Novak, D. W. and M. J. Lerner. Rejection as a Consequence of Perceived Similarity, *Journal of Personality and Social Psychology 9:* 147–152, 1968.

Nowlis, V. Research with the Mood Adjective Check List, In Tompkins, S. S. and C. Izard (eds.). *Affect, Cognition, and Personality,* New York: Springer, 1965, pp. 352–389.

O'Connor, P. Ethnocentrism, "Intolerance of Ambiguity," and Abstract Reasoning Ability, *Journal of Abnormal and Social Psychology 47:* 526–530, 1952.

Ohnmacht, F. W. and J. J. Muro. Self-acceptance: Some Anxiety and Cognitive Style Relationships, *Journal of Psychology 67:* 235–239, 1967.

Olson, B. E. *Faith and Prejudice: Intergroup Problems in Protestant Curricula.* New Haven, Conn.: Yale University Press, 1963.

Omwake, K. T. The Relation between Acceptance of Self and Acceptance of Others Shown by Three Personality Inventories, *Journal of Consulting Psychology 18:* 443–446, 1954.

Osgood, C. and P. Tannenbaum. The Principle of Congruity in the Prediction of Attitude Change, *Psychological Review 62:* 42–55, 1955.

Ostrom, T. M. The Relationship Between the Affective, Behavioral, and Cognitive Components of Attitude, *Journal of Experimental Social Psychology 5:* 12–30, 1969.

Palmore, E. B. Ethnophaulisms and Ethnocentrism, *American Journal of Sociology 67:* 442–445, 1962.

Park, R. E. The Concept of Social Distance, *Journal of Applied Sociology 8:* 339–344, 1924.

Parrott, G. Dogmatism and Rigidity: A Factor Analysis, *Psychological Reports 29:* 135–140, 1971.

Pastore, N. A Note on Changing toward Liked and Disliked Persons, *Journal of Social Psychology 52:* 173–175, 1960.

Peabody, D. Attitude Content and Agreement Set in Scales of Authoritarianism, Dogmatism, Anti-Semitism, and Economic Conservatism, *Journal of Abnormal and Social Psychology 63:* 1–11, 1961.

Peabody, D. Two Components in Bipolar Scales: Direction and Extremeness, *Psychological Review 69:* 65–73, 1962.

Pearl, D. Ethnocentrism and the Self-Concept, *Journal of Social Psychology 40:* 137–147, 1954.

Pedersen, D. M. Evaluation of Self and Others and Some Personality Correlates, *Journal of Psychology 71:* 225–244, 1969.

Perlmutter, H. V. Relations between the Self-Image, the Image of the Foreigner, and the Desire to Live Abroad, *Journal of Psychology 38:* 131–137, 1954.

Perlmutter, H. V., Correlates of Two Types of Xenophilic Orientation, *Journal of Abnormal and Social Psychology 52:* 130–135, 1956.

Pettigrew, T. F. Regional Differences in Anti-Negro Prejudice, *Journal of Abnormal and Social Psychology 59:* 28–36, 1959.

Pettigrew, T. F. Social Distance Attitudes of South African Students, *Social Forces 38:* 246–253, 1960.

Pettigrew, T. F. *A Profile of the Negro American.* Princeton, N.J.: Van Nostrand, 1964.

Pettigrew, T. F. Parallel and Distinctive Changes in Anti-Semitic and Anti-Negro Attitudes. In Stember, C. H. et al. *Jews in the Mind of America.* New York: Basic Books, 1966.

Phillips, E. L. Attitudes toward Self and Others: A Brief Questionnaire Report, *Journal of Consulting Psychology 15:* 79–81, 1951.

Photiadis, J. D. and J. Biggar. Religiosity, Education, and Ethnic Distance, *American Journal of Sociology 67:* 666–672, 1962.

Piaget, J. *The Psychology of Intelligence.* London: Routledge, Kegan Paul, 1947.

Pierson, Donald. Race Prejudice as Revealed in the Study of Racial Situations, *International Social Science Bulletin 2:* 467–478, 1950.

Poirer, G. W. and A. J. Lott. Galvanic Skin Responses and Prejudice, *Journal of Personality and Social Psychology 5:* 253–359, 1967.

Poole, W. C., Jr. Social Distance and Personal Distance, *Journal of Applied Sociology 11:* 114–120, 1927.

Porter, J. D. R. *Black Child, White Child.* Cambridge, Mass.: Harvard University Press, 1971.

Preiss, J. J. and H. J. Ehrlich. *An Examination of Role Theory.* Lincoln: University of Nebraska Press, 1966.

Prentice, N. M. The Influence of Ethnic Attitudes on Reasoning about Ethnic Groups, *Journal of Abnormal and Social Psychology 55:* 270–272, 1957.

Proenza, L. and B. R. Strickland. A Study of Prejudice in Negro and White College Students, *Journal of Social Psychology 67:* 273–281, 1965.

Prothro, E. T. Ethnocentrism and Anti-Negro Attitudes in the Deep South, *Journal of Abnormal and Social Psychology 47:* 105–108, 1952.

Prothro, E. T. Cross Cultural Patterns of National Stereotypes, *Journal of Social Psychology 40:* 53–59, 1954.

Prothro, E. T. and J. A. Jensen. Comparison of Some Ethnic and Religious Attitudes of Negro and White College Students in the Deep South, *Social Forces 30:* 426–428, 1952.

Prothro, B. T. and J. D. Keehn. Stereotypes and Semantic Space, *Journal of Social Psychology* 45: 197–209, 1957.

Prothro, E. T. and L. H. Melikian. Social Distance and Social Change in the Near East, *Sociology and Social Research* 37: 3–11, 1952.

Prothro, E. T. and L. H. Melikian. The California Public Opinion Scale in an Authoritarian Culture, *Public Opinion Quarterly* 3: 353–362, 1953.

Prothro, E. T. and L. H. Melikian. Studies in Stereotypes: V. Familiarity and the Kernel of Truth Hypothesis, *Journal of Social Psychology* 41: 3–10, 1955.

Prothro, E. T. and O. K. Miles. A Comparison of Ethnic Attitudes of College Students and Middle-Class Adults from the Same State, *Journal of Social Psychology* 36: 53–58, 1952.

Prothro, E. T. and O. K. Miles. Social Distance in the Deep South as Measured by a Revised Bogardus Scale, *Journal of Social Psychology* 37: 171–174, 1953.

Pyron, B. A Factor-Analytic Study of Simplicity-Complexity of Social Ordering, *Perceptual and Motor Skills* 22: 259–272, 1966.

Pyron, B. and P. Lambert. The Generality of Simplicity-Complexity of Social Perception in a High School Population, *Journal of Psychology* 66: 265–273, 1967.

Radke, M. and J. Sutherland. Children's Concepts and Attitudes about Minority and Majority American Groups, *Journal of Educational Psychology* 40: 449–468, 1949.

Radke, M. and H. G. Trager. Children's Perception of the Social Roles of Negroes and Whites, *Journal of Psychology* 29: 3–33, 1950.

Radke, M., H. Trager, and H. Davis. Social Perceptions and Attitudes of Children, *Genetic Psychology Monographs* 40: 327–447, 1949.

Radke-Yarrow, M., H. Trager, and J. Miller. The Role of Parents in the Development of Children's Ethnic Attitudes, *Child Development* 23: 13–53, 1952.

Rankin, R. E. and D. T. Campbell. Galvanic Skin Response to Negro and White Experimenters, *Journal of Abnormal and Social Psychology* 51: 30–33, 1955.

Razran, G. Ethnic Dislike and Stereotypes: A Laboratory Study, *Journal of Abnormal and Social Psychology* 45: 7–27, 1950.

Reese, H. W. Relationships between Self-acceptance and Sociometric Choices, *Journal of Abnormal and Social Psychology* 62: 472–474, 1961.

Reichard, S. Rorschach Study of Prejudiced Personality, *American Journal of Orthopsychiatry* 18: 280–286, 1948.

Reigrotski, E. and N. Anderson. National Stereotypes and Foreign Contacts, *Public Opinion Quarterly* 23: 515–528, 1959.

Remmers, H. H. Attitudes toward Germans, Japanese, Jews and Nazis as Affected by the War, *School and Society* 57: 138–140, 1943.

Remmers, H. H. and N. Weltman. Attitude Inter-relationships of Youth, Their Parents, and Their Teachers, *Journal of Social Psychology* 26: 61–68, 1947.

Renninger, C. A. and J. E. Williams. Black-white Color Connotations and Racial Awareness in Preschool Children, *Perceptual and Motor Skills* 22: 771–785, 1966.

Richey, M. H., L. McClelland, and A. M. Shimkunas. Relative Influence of Positive and Negative Information in Impression Formation and Persistence, *Journal of Personality and Social Psychology* 6: 322–327, 1967.

Riddleberger, A. B. and A. B. Motz. Prejudice and Perception, *American Journal of Sociology 62:* 498–503, 1957.

Ringer, B. B. *The Edge of Friendliness: A Study of Jewish-Gentile Relations.* New York: Basic Books, 1967.

Roback, A. A. *A Dictionary of International Slurs.* Cambridge, Mass.: Sci-Art Press, 1944.

Robb, J. H. *Working-Class Anti-Semite: A Psychological Study in a London Borough.* London: Tavistock Publications, 1954.

Roberts, A. H. Intra-test Variability as a Measure of Generalized Response Set, *Psychological Reports 11:* 793–799, 1962.

Robinson, D. and S. Rohde. Two Experiments with an Anti-Semitism Poll, *Journal of Abnormal and Social Psychology 41:* 136–144, 1946.

Rokeach, M. Generalized Mental Rigidity as a Factor in Ethnocentrism, *Journal of Abnormal and Social Psychology 43:* 259–278, 1948.

Rokeach, M. Prejudice, Concreteness of Thinking, and Reification of Thinking, *Journal of Abnormal and Social Psychology 46:* 83–91, 1951a.

Rokeach, M. "Narrow-mindedness" and Personality, *Journal of Personality 20:* 234–251, 1951b.

Rokeach, M. Political and Religious Dogmatism: An Alternative to the Authoritarian Personality, *Psychological Monographs 70:* 1–43, 1956.

Rokeach, M. *The Open and Closed Mind.* New York: Basic Books, 1960.

Rokeach, M. The Organization and Modification of Beliefs, *Centennial Review 7:* 375–395, 1963.

Rokeach, M. Attitude Change and Behavioral Change, *Public Opinion Quarterly 30:* 529–550, 1967.

Rokeach, M. The Nature of Attitudes, In Rokeach, M. *Beliefs, Attitudes, and Values.* San Francisco: Jossey-Bass, 1968.

Rokeach, M. Race and Shared Belief as Factors in Social Choice, In Rokeach, M. *Beliefs, Attitudes, and Values.* San Francisco: Jossey-Bass, 1968.

Rokeach, M. and B. Fruchter. A Factorial Study of Dogmatism and Related Concepts, *Journal of Abnormal and Social Psychology 53:* 356–360, 1956.

Rokeach, M. and L. Mezei. Race and Shared Belief as Factors in Social Choice, *Science 151:* 167–172, 1966.

Rokeach, M. and G. Norrell. *Analysis, Synthesis, and Academic Performance.* Final Report of Cooperative Research Branch Project No. 879, East Lansing: Michigan State University, 1966.

Rokeach, M., P. W. Smith, and R. I. Evans. Two Kinds of Prejudice or One? In Rokeach, M. *The Open and Closed Mind.* New York: Basic Books, 1960, pp. 132–168.

Rose, A. *Sociology.* New York: Knopf, 1965.

Rosenberg, E. *From Shylock to Svengali: Jewish Stereotypes in English Fiction.* Stanford, Calif.: Stanford University Press, 1960.

Rosenberg, M., E. A. Suchman, and R. K. Goldsen. *Occupations and Values.* Glencoe, Ill.: The Free Press, 1957.

Rosenberg, M. *Society and the Adolescent Self-Image.* Princeton, N.J.: Princeton University Press, 1965.

Rosenberg, M. J. An Analysis of Affective-Cognitive Consistency. In Rosenberg, M. J., et al. *Attitude Organization and Change*. New Haven, Conn.: Yale University Press, 1960, pp. 15–64.

Rosenberg, M. J. Inconsistency Arousal and Reduction in Attitude Change, In Steiner, I. D. and M. Fishbein (eds.). *Current Studies in Social Psychology*. New York: Holt, Rinehart and Winston, 1965.

Rosenblith, J. F. A Replication of "Some Roots of Prejudice," *Journal of Abnormal and Social Psychology 44:* 470–489, 1949.

Rosenthal, R. *Experimenter Effects in Behavioral Research*. New York: Appleton-Century-Crofts, 1966.

Rubenowitz, S. *Emotional Flexibility-Rigidity as a Comprehensive Dimension of Mind*. Stockholm: Almqvist & Wiksell, 1963.

Rundquist, E. A. and R. F. Sletto. *Personality in the Depression*. Minneapolis: University of Minnesota Press, 1936.

Russell, D. H. and I. V. Robertson. Influencing Attitudes toward Minority Groups in a Junior High School, *School Review 55:* 205–213, 1947.

Saenger, G. H. and E. Gilbert. Customer Reactions to the Integration of Negro Sales Personnel, *Public Opinion Quarterly 4:* 57–76, 1950.

Saenger, G. and S. Flowerman. Stereotypes and Prejudiced Attitudes, *Human Relations 7:* 217–238, 1954.

Sappenfield, B. R. The Responses of Catholic, Protestant, and Jewish Students to the Menace Checklist, *Journal of Social Psychology 20:* 295–299, 1944.

Sarbin, T. R. Role Theoretical Interpretation of Psychological Change, In P. Worchel and D. Byrne (eds.). *Personality Change*. New York: Wiley, 1964.

Schacter, S. A Cognitive-Physiological View of Emotion. In O. Klineberg and R. Christie (eds.). *Perspectives in Social Psychology*. New York: Holt, Rinehart and Winston, 1965, pp. 75–103.

Saxton, S. Words which Measure Affect toward Negroes, 1968 (unpublished).

Schacter, S. Cognitive Effects on Bodily Functioning: Studies of Obesity and Eating, in Glass, D. C. (ed.). *Neurophysiology and Emotion*. New York: Rockefeller University Press, 1967, pp. 117–144.

Schoenfeld, N. An Experimental Study of Some Problems Relating to Stereotypes, *Archives of Psychology 38* (Whole No. 270), 1942.

Schwartz, M. A. *Trends in White Attitudes toward Negroes*. Chicago: National Opinion Research Center, 1967.

Schuman, H. and J. Harding. Prejudice and the Norm of Rationality, *Sociometry 27:* 353–371, 1964.

Scotch, N. A. The Vanishing Villians of Television, *Phylon 21:* 58–62, 1960.

Scott, W. A. Attitude Measurement, In Lindzey, G. and E. Aronson (eds.). *Handbook of Social Psychology*, Reading, Mass.: Addison-Wesley, 1968.

Seago, D. W. Stereotypes: Before Pearl Harbor and After, *Journal of Psychology 23:* 55–63, 1947.

Sears, D. O. Political Behavior, In Lindzey, G. and E. Aronson (eds.). *The Handbook of Social Psychology*, Vol. 5. Reading, Mass.: Addison-Wesley, 1969, pp. 315–458.

Secord, P. F. Stereotyping and Favorableness in the Perception of Negro Faces, *Journal of Abnormal and Social Psychology* 59: 309–314, 1959.

Secord, P. F. and C. W. Backman. *Social Psychology*. New York: McGraw-Hill, 1964.

Secord, P. F., W. Bevan, and B. Katz. The Negro Stereotype and Perceptual Accentuation, *Journal of Abnormal and Social Psychology* 53: 78–83, 1956.

Seeman, M. Adjustment to Minority Status and Intellectual Perspective, *Social Problems* 3: 142–153, 1956.

Shapiro, D. and A. Crider. Psychophysiological Approaches in Social Psychology. In Lindzey, G. and E. Aronson (eds.). *Handbook of Social Psychology*, V. 3, Reading, Mass.: Addison-Wesley, 1969, pp. 1–49.

Sheerer, E. T. An Analysis of the Relationship between Acceptance of and Respect for Self and Acceptance of the Respect for Others in Ten Counseling Cases, *Journal of Consulting Psychology* 13: 169–175, 1949.

Sheikh, A. A. Stereotype in Interpersonal Perception and Inter-correlation between Some Attitude Measures, *Journal of Social Psychology* 76: 175–179, 1968.

Sheppard, H. L. The Negro Merchant: A Study of Negro Anti-Semitism, *American Journal of Sociology* 53: 96–99, 1947.

Sherif, M. An Experimental Study of Stereotypes, *Journal of Abnormal and Social Psychology* 29: 371–375, 1935.

Sherif, M. and C. I. Hovland. *Social Judgment*. New Haven, Conn.: Yale University Press, 1961.

Sherif, M. and C. W. Sherif. *Groups in Harmony and Tension*. New York: Harper, 1953.

Sherif, M. and C. W. Sherif. *An Outline of Social Psychology*. New York: Harper, 1956.

Sherif, M. and C. W. Sherif. Attitude as the Individual's Own Categories: The Social Judgment-Involvement Approach to Attitude and Attitude Change, In Sherif, M. and C. W. Sherif (eds.). *Attitude, Ego-Involvement, and Change*. New York: Wiley, 1967.

Sherif, M. and C. W. Sherif. The Own Categories Procedure in Attitude Research, In M. Fishbein (ed.). *Readings in Attitude Theory and Measurement*. New York: Wiley, 1967.

Sherif, M. et al., *Intergroup Conflict and Cooperation: The Robber's Cave Experiment*. Norman, Okla. University Book Exchange, 1961.

Shim, N. and A. A. Dole. Components of Social Distance among College Students and Their Parents in Hawaii, *Journal of Social Psychology* 73: 111–124, 1967.

Shuey, A. M. Stereotyping tf Negroes and Whites: An Analysis of Magazine Pictures, *Public Opinion Quarterly* 17: 281–287, 1953.

Shuey, A. M., N. King, and B. Griffith. Stereotyping of Negroes and Whites: An Analysis of Magazine Pictures, *Public Opinion Quarterly* 17: 281–287, 1953.

Simmons, O. G. Mutual Images and Expectations of Anglo-Americans and Mexican-Americans, *Daedalus* 90: 286–299, 1961.

Simpson, G. E. and J. M. Yinger. *Racial and Cultural Minorities*. New York: Harper and Row, 1965.

Simpson, R. L. Negro-Jewish Prejudice: Authoritarianism and Some Social Variables as Correlates, *Social Problems* 7: 138–146, 1959.

Sims, V. M. and J. R. Patrick. Attitude toward the Negro of Northern and Southern College Students, *Journal of Social Psychology* 7: 192–204, 1936.

Singer, D. The Influence of Intelligence and an Interracial Classroom on Social Attitudes, In Dentler, R., B. Mackler, and M. E. Warshauer (eds.). *The Urban R's: Race Relations as the Problem in Urban Education.* New York: Praeger, 1967.

Sinha, A. K. P. and O. P. Upadhyaya. Eleven Ethnic Groups on a Social Distance Scale, *Journal of Social Psychology* 57: 49–54, 1962.

Sklare, M. and M. Vosk. *The Riverton Study. How Jews Look at Themselves and Their Neighbors.* New York: The American Jewish Committee, 1957.

Sloan, I. *The Negro in Modern American History Textbooks.* Chicago: American Federation of Teachers, AFL-CIO, 1966.

Smith, C. R., L. Williams, and R. H. Willis. Race, Sex, and Belief as Determinants of Friendship Acceptance, *Journal of Personality and Social Psychology* 5: 127–137, 1967.

Sommer, R. Small Group Ecology, *Psychological Bulletin* 67: 145–152, 1967.

Springer, D.V. Awareness of Racial Differences by Preschool Children in Hawaii, *Genetic Psychology Monographs* 41: 215–270, 1950.

Stagner, R. and C. E. Osgood. An Experimental Analysis of a Nationalistic Frame of Reference, *Journal of Social Psychology* 14: 389–401, 1941.

Stein, D. D. The Influence of Belief Systems on Interpersonal Preference: A Validation Study of Rokeach's Theory of Prejudice, *Psychological Monographs* (Whole No. 80), 29, 1966.

Stein, D. D., J. A. Hardyck, and M. B. Smith. Race and Belief: An Open and Shut Case, *Journal of Personality and Social Psychology* 1: 281–289, 1965.

Stember, C. H. *Education and Attitude Change.* New York: Institute of Human Relations Press, 1961.

Stember, C. H. (ed.). *Jews in the Mind of America.* New York: Basic Books, 1966.

Stock, D. An Investigation into the Interrelations between the Self-Concept and Feelings Directed toward Other Persons and Groups, *Journal of Consulting Psychology* 13: 176–180, 1949.

Stouffer, S. A. *Communism, Conformity, and Civil Liberties.* Garden City, N.Y.: Doubleday, 1955.

Stouffer, S. A., L. Guttman, E. A. Suchman, P. F. Lazarsfeld, S. A. Star, and J. A. Clausen. *Measurement and Prediction.* Princeton, N.J.: Princeton University Press, 1950.

Suinn, R. M. The Relationship between Self-acceptance and Acceptance of others: A Learning Theory Analysis, *Journal of Abnormal and Social Psychology* 63: 37–42, 1961.

Suinn, R. M. and H. Hill. Influence of Anxiety on the Relationship between Self-acceptance and Acceptance of Others, *Journal of Consulting Psychology* 28: 116–119, 1964.

Sullivan, P. L. and J. Adelson. Ethnocentrism and Misanthropy, *Journal of Abnormal and Social Psychology* 49: 246–250, 1954.

Summers, G. F. and A. D. Hammonds, Effect of Racial Characteristics of Investigator on Self-Enumerated Responses to a Negro Prejudice Scale, *Social Forces 44:* 515–518, 1966.

Tabachnick, B. R. Some Correlates of Prejudice toward Negroes in Elementary Age Children, *Journal of Genetic Psychology 100:* 193–203, 1962.

Taft, R. Is the Tolerant Personality Type the Opposite of the Intolerants?, *Journal of Social Psychology 47:* 397–405, 1958.

Taft, R. Ethnic Stereotypes, Attitudes, and Familiarity: Australia, *Journal of Social Psychology 49:* 177–186, 1959.

Tagiuri, R. Person Perception, In Lindzey, G. and E. Aronson (eds.). *Handbook of Social Psychology*, Vol. 3, Reading, Mass.: Addison-Wesley, 1969, pp. 395–449.

Tajfel, H., A. A. Sheikh, and R. C. Gardner. Content of Stereotypes and the Inference of Similarity between Members of Stereotyped Groups, *Acta Psychologica 22:* 191–201, 1964.

Taylor, R. G. Racial Stereotypes in Young Children, *Journal of Psychology 64:* 137–142, 1966.

Taylor, S. A. and D. R. Mettee. When Similarity Breeds Contempt, *Journal of Personality and Social Psychology 20:* 75–81, 1971.

Terhune, K. W. Nationalism among Foreign and American Students: An Exploratory Study, *Journal of Conflict Resolution 8:* 256–270, 1964.

Thistlethwaite, D. Attitude and Structure as Factors in the Distortion of Reasoning, *Journal of Abnormal and Social Psychology 45:* 442–458, 1950.

Thouless, R. H., Effect of Prejudice on Reasoning, *British Journal of Psychology 50:* 289–293, 1959.

Tittle, C. R. and R. J. Hill. Attitude Measurement and Prediction of Behavior: An Evaluation of Conditions and Measurement Techniques, *Sociometry 30:* 199–213, 1967.

Trent, R. D. The Relation between Expressed Self-Acceptance and Expressed Attitudes toward Negroes and Whites among Negro Children, *Journal of Genetic Psychology 91:* 25–31, 1957.

Triandis, H. C. Exploratory Factor Analyses of the Behavioral Component of Social Attitudes, *Journal of Abnormal and Social Psychology 68:* 420–430, 1964.

Triandis, H. C. Toward an Analysis of the Components of Interpersonal Attitudes, In Sherif, C. W. and M. Sherif (eds.). *Attitude, Ego-Involvement, and Change*. New York; Wiley, 1967.

Triandis, H. C. and E. E. Davis. Race and Belief as Determinants of Behavioral Intentions, *Journal of Personality and Social Psychology 2:* 715–725, 1965.

Triandis, H. C., E. E. Davis, and S. Takezawa. Some Determinants of Social Distance among American, German, and Japanese Students, *Journal of Personality and Social Psychology 2:* 540–546, 1965.

Triandis, H. C. and L. M. Triandis. Race, Social Class, Religion, and Nationality as Determinants of Social Distance, *Journal of Abnormal and Social Psychology 61:* 110–118, 1960.

Triandis, H. C. and L. M. Triandis, A Cross-Cultural Study of Social Distance, *Psychological Monographs 76:* 1–21, 1962.

Triandis, H. C. and L. M. Triandis. Some Studies of Social Distance, In Steiner, I. D. and M. Fishbein (eds.). *Current Studies in Social Psychology*, New York: Holt, Rinehart, and Winston, 1965.

Troll, L. E., B. L. Neugarten, and R. J. Kraines. Similarities in Values and Other Personality Characteristics in College Students and their Parents, *Merrill-Palmer Quarterly 15*:323–336, 1969.

Tudor, J. F. The Development of Class Awareness in Children, *Social Forces 49*: 470–476, 1971.

Turbeville, G. A Social Distance Study of Duluth, Minnesota, *Sociology and Social Research 34*: 415–423, 1950.

Turman, J. A. and W. H. Holtzman. Attitudes of White and Negro Teachers toward Non-Segregation in the Classroom, *Journal of Social Psychology 42*: 61–70, 1955.

Turner, R. and T. Tripodi. Cognitive Complexity as a Function of Type of Stimulus Objects Judged and Affective Stimulus Value, *Journal of Consulting and Clinical Psychology 32*: 182–185, 1968.

Vacchiano, R. B., D. C. Schiffman, and A. V. Crowell. Attitude Change as a Function of Intensive Training, Dogmatism and Authoritarianism, *Psychological Reports 19*: 359–362, 1966.

Valins, S. Emotionality and Information Concerning Internal Reactions, *Journal of Personality and Social Psychology 6*: 458–463, 1967.

Van den Berghe, Pierre L. Checklists *versus* Open-Ended Questions: A Comment on *A Brief Report on the Methodology of Stereotype Research*, *Social Forces 44*: 418–419, 1966.

Vander Zanden, J. W. *American Minority Relations*. New York: Ronald Press, 1966.

Vinacke, W. E. Explorations in the Dynamic Processes of Stereotyping, *Journal of Social Psychology 43*: 105–132, 1956.

Vinacke, W. E. Stereotyping among National-Racial Groups in Hawaii: A Study in Ethnocentrism, *Journal of Social Psychology 30*: 265–291, 1949.

Vidulich, R. N. and F. W. Krevanick. Racial Attitudes and Emotional Response to Visual Representations of the Negro, *Journal of Social Psychology 68*: 85–93, 1966.

Waite, R. R. Further Attempts to Integrate and Urbanize First Grade Reading Textbooks: A Research Study, *Journal of Negro Education 37*: 62–70, 1968.

Warr, P. B. and J. S. Smith. Combining Information about People: Comparisons between Six Models, *Journal of Personality and Social Psychology 16*: 55–65, 1970.

Weatherley, D. Maternal Response to Childhood Agression and Subsequent Anti-Semitism, *Journal of Abnormal and Social Psychology 66*: 183–185, 1963.

Weltman, N. and H. H. Remmers. Pupils', Parents', and Teachers' Attitudes— Similarities and Differences, *Purdue University Studies in Higher Education*, vol. 66, September, 1946.

Westie, F. R. Negro-White Status Differentials and Social Distance, *American Sociological Review 17*: 550–558, 1952.

Westie, F. R. A Technique for the Measurement of Race Attitudes, *American Sociological Review 18*: 73–78, 1953.

Westie, F. R. Race and Ethnic Relations, In Faris, R. E. L. (ed.). *Handbook of Modern Sociology*. Chicago: Rand-McNally, 1964.

Westie, F. R. and M. L. DeFleur. Autonomic Responses and their Relationship to Race Attitudes, *Journal of Abnormal and Social Psychology 58:* 340–347, 1959.

Westie, F. R. and D. Howard. Social Status Differentials and the Race Attitudes of Negroes, *American Sociological Review 19:* 584–591, 1954.

Westie, F. R. and M. L. Westie. The Social Distance Pyramid: Relationships between Caste and Class, *American Journal of Sociology 63:* 190–196, 1957.

Williams, J. E. Acceptance by Others and its Relationship to Acceptance of Self and Others: A Repeat of Fey's Study, *Journal of Abnormal and Social Psychology 65:* 438–442, 1962.

Williams, J. E. Connotations of Racial Concepts and Color Names, *Journal of Personality and Social Psychology 3:* 531–540, 1966.

Williams, J. E. and D. J. Carter. Connotations of Racial Concepts and Color Names in Germany, *Journal of Social Psychology 72:* 19–26, 1967.

Williams, R. M. et al. *Strangers Next Door*. Englewood Cliffs, N.J.: Prentice-Hall, 1964.

Willis, F. N., Jr. Initial Speaking Distance as a Function of the Speakers' Relationship, *Psychonomic Science 5:* 221–222, 1966.

Wilson, H. E. *Latin America in School and College Teaching Materials*. Washington: American Council on Education, 1944.

Wilson, H. E. *Treatment of Asia in American Textbooks*. New York: American Council on Education and American Institute of Pacific Relations, 1946.

Wilson, H. E. *Intergroup Relations in Teaching Materials, A Survey and Appraisal*. Washington, D. C.: American Council on Education, 1949.

Wilson, W. C. Development of Ethnic Attitudes in Adolescence, *Child Development 34:* 247–259, 1963.

Wishner, J. Reanalysis of "Impressions of Personality," *Psychological Review 67;* 96–112, 1960.

Woodmansee, J. J. The Pupil Response as a Measure of Social Attitudes, In Summers, G. F. (ed.). *Attitude Measurement*. Chicago: Rand-McNally, 1970.

Worthy, M., A. L. Gary, and G. M. Kahn. Self Disclosure as an Exchange Process, *Journal of Personality and Social Psychology 13:* 59–63, 1969.

Wright, G. H. *Norm and Action*. New York: Humanities Press, 1963.

Wrightsman, L. S. Parental Attitudes and Behaviors as Determinants of Children's Responses to the Threat of Nuclear War, *Vita Humana 7:* 178–185, 1964.

Wylie, R. C. Some Relationships between Defensiveness and Self-concept Discrepancies, *Journal of Personality 25:* 600–616, 1957.

Wylie, R. C. *The Self Concept*. Lincoln: University of Nebraska Press, 1961.

Young, K. and R. W. Mack. *Systematic Sociology*. New York: American Book Co., 1962.

Zeligs, R. Training Racial Attitudes through Adolescence, *Sociology and Social Research 23:* 45–54, 1938.

Zeligs, R. Children's Intergroup Concepts and Stereotypes, *Journal of Educational Sociology 21:* 113–126, 1947.

Zeligs, R. Children's Intergroup Attitudes, *Journal of Genetic Psychology* 72: 101–110, 1948.

Zeligs, R. Children's Concepts and Stereotypes of Dutch, French, Italian, Mexican, Russian, and Negro, *Journal of Educational Research 43:* 367–375, 1950.

Zeligs, R. Children's Concepts and Stereotypes of Polish, Irish, Finn, Hungarian, Bulgarian, Dane, Czechoslovakian, Hindu, and Filipino, *Journal of Genetic Psychology* 77:73–83, 1950b.

Zeligs, R. Children's Concepts and Stereotypes of Norwegian, Jew, Scotch, Swedish, and American Indian, *Journal of Educational Research 45:* 349–360, 1952.

Zeligs, R. Children's Concepts and Stereotypes of Turk, Portuguese, Roumanian, Arab, Chinese, French-Canadian, Mulatto, South American, Hawaiian, and Australian, *Journal of Genetic Psychology 83:* 171–178, 1953.

Zeligs, R. Children's Concepts and Stereotypes of American, Greek, English, Germans and Japanese, *Journal of Educational Sociology 28:* 360–363, 1955.

Zeligs, R. and G. Hendrickson. Racial Attitudes of Two Hundred Sixth-Grade Children, *Sociology and Social Research 18:* 26–36, 1933.

Ziller, R. C. and R. D. Behringer. Motivational and Perceptual Effects in Orientation toward a Newcomer, *Journal of Social Psychology 66:* 79–90, 1965.

Zuckerman, M., M. Baer, and I. Monashkin. Acceptance of Self, Parents, and People in Patients and Normals, *Journal of Clinical Psychology 12:* 327–332, 1956.

AUTHOR INDEX

SUBJECT INDEX

Affect, 7, 91–98, 103, 118–120, 131–132
   and emotion, 91–96
   introduced, 7
   language of, 96–98
   measure of, 103
Attitude, and behavior, 8–18
   cognitively articulated, 6
   defined, 4–5

Behavioral differential, 70
Behavioral intentions, introduced, 6–7.
   See also Personal distance; Social
   distance
Belief congruity, similarity, *see* Principle, of
   categorical congruity; Corollary, of
   ethnic congruity

Centrality, defined, 6; *see also* Principle, of
   elemental structure
Class, *see* Ethclass; Socioeconomic status
Corollary, of acquisition, 117–121, 163
   of categorical learning, 138–149, 162
   of categorical placement, 115–117, 162
   of categorical response, 41–43, 82–86,
   100, 162
   of directional displacement, 59, 88, 112,
   164
   of ethnic congruity, 82–86, 163

of reciprocity, 58–59, 88, 112, 164
of target visibility, 115–117, 163
of veridicality, 40, 162

Direction, defined, 5; *see also* Principle, of
   elemental structure
Dogmatism, 143–146

Ethclass, 40–41, 60n
Ethnophaulisms, 21–23, 106

Frustration and aggression theory, 149–151

Intensity, defined, 5; *see also* Principle, of
   elemental structure

Mass media, effects on prejudice, 32–33,
   72–73, 124, 168

Personal distance, 62, 67–69, 79, 81–82,
   87, 103, 118–120, 129
   introduced, 62
   scheme for classifying targets, 67–68
   and physical distance, 79
   and physical disability, 81–82
   see also Social distance
Pluralism, 169–170
Polarization, 101

207